Inside the Nation of Islam

Florida A&M University, Tallahassee
Florida Atlantic University, Boca Raton
Florida Gulf Coast University, Ft. Myers
Florida International University, Miami
Florida State University, Tallahassee
University of Central Florida, Orlando
University of Florida, Gainesville
University of North Florida, Jacksonville
University of South Florida, Tampa
University of West Florida, Pensacola

Inside the
Nation of Islam

A Historical and Personal Testimony
by a Black Muslim

Vibert L. White Jr.

University Press of Florida
Gainesville · Tallahassee · Tampa · Boca Raton
Pensacola · Orlando · Miami · Jacksonville · Ft. Myers

Library of Congress Cataloging-in-Publication Data
White, Vibert L., Jr.
Inside the Nation of Islam: a historical and personal testimony by a
Black Muslim / Vibert L. White, Jr.
p. cm.
Includes bibliographical references and index.
ISBN 0-8130-2082-4 (alk. paper)
1. Nation of Islam (Chicago, Ill.)—History. 2. Black Muslims—History.
3. Farrakhan, Louis. I. Title.
BP221.A1 W47 2001
297.8'7—dc21 2001027590

The University Press of Florida is the scholarly publishing agency for
the State University System of Florida, comprising Florida A&M University, Florida Atlantic University, Florida Gulf Coast University,
Florida International University, Florida State University, University
of Central Florida, University of Florida, University of North Florida,
University of South Florida, and University of West Florida.

University Press of Florida
15 Northwest 15th Street
Gainesville, FL 32611-2079
http://www.upf.com

To my wonderful wife, Alessandra

To my parents,
Vibert and Lorraine White
Thanks.

A father's love to Jira´, Kyle, Jarvis, Sherman

We will declare the truth and die for it.
Thanks to Allah for removing fear from us, and I pray

He puts it in them and may they fear and tremble every day.

The Honorable Elijah Muhammad,
Message to the Blackman in America

Contents

Foreword

Forty years ago a black reporter, Louis Lomax, arrived in the all-white Channel 13 newsroom in New York where I anchored the nightly half-hour newscast we called *News Beat.* It was the first half-hour newscast in New York television; the other channels were still doing basic head-line accounts of the news, fifteen minutes (including commercials), and Lomax called me to do a magazine takeout on our enterprising news operation.

In the course of our conversations that first day, Lomax filled me in about a group I'd not heard of before, the Black Muslims, headed by a man named Elijah Muhammad. Of course, I was hardly alone then in knowing nothing of the Black Muslims; white America (including, by and large, the white journalism establishment) shared my ignorance. But my curiosity was sufficiently piqued by Lomax's descriptions of this group's activities to ask if he'd like to help us do a series of reports about them. He replied that he would, and we did.

But it turned out I was not going to be able to do any of the reporting firsthand, for Elijah Muhammad and his Muslims wouldn't talk to white reporters. The reporter would have to be black, which meant that Lomax had himself a job at *News Beat* as the first black television correspondent in New York.

We produced five pieces on the Black Muslims (it turned out Lomax was a first-rate reporter and stayed on with us), and then we turned those five-minute pieces into an hour-long documentary called *The Hate That Hate Produced,* which was broadcast only on Channel 13 in New York in February of 1959.

For the hour following the documentary Lou and I had assembled a panel to evaluate what they'd seen. Our panel included Roy Wilkins (head of the NAACP), Jackie Robinson, Ann Hedgman (whom I used to describe as "the Eleanor Roosevelt of Harlem"), the Reverend Gardner Taylor of the Protestant Council of Churches, and Arnold Forster of the Anti-Defamation League of B'nai B'rith. The consensus was that we'd overstated the importance and the numbers of the Black Muslims, about whom they actually knew remarkably little. And Jack Gould, then the lead television critic for the *New York Times,* gave us the back of his hand. But the story was promptly picked up by various newspapers around the country, and even the *New York Times* eventually ran a long and detailed front-page story about the Black Muslims.

Our documentary gave white America its first look at Elijah Muhammad and Malcolm X and its first exposure to film of a Washington, D.C., rally of Black Muslims attended by thousands. At this rally whites heard Malcolm X read a script called "The Trial," in which a black court puts the white race on trial for assorted sins of which the "White devil" is eventually found "guilty as charged." That script had been written by an acolyte of Malcolm, Louis Farrakhan.

I recount this history to explain why Professor White asked me to write this foreword. He knows that Malcolm and I eventually became good friends, that Atallah Shabazz, Malcolm's eldest daughter, and I are friends as well, and that I've followed the ups and downs of the Nation of Islam during the past forty years with keen interest.

I first read this book in manuscript form in August 1998; it told me a great deal I hadn't known about the inner workings, the movers and shakers, the intrigues and the politics, the successes and the failings of an extraordinary cast of Nation of Islam characters.

Surely I cannot vouch for the accuracy of all of Professor White's account; I've not had the access afforded him down the years. But his work has the feel, the texture, the smell of authenticity. It is far and away the most personal and the most engrossing story I've read about Louis Farrakhan; and if the professor doesn't solve the riddle of just who Louis Farrakhan is (and perhaps the minister himself doesn't know that for sure), he has given us a fascinating history of the Nation, its various leaders, its accomplishments, its shortcomings, and—I'm afraid—a pessimistic look into its future.

Mike Wallace

Preface

I became acquainted with members of the Nation of Islam at a critical time in the development and history of the organization. In June 1975, four months after the death of Elijah Muhammad, the Messenger of Allah to devout Black Muslims, I met several members of the group. Shortly after, I began to study the teachings of Elijah Muhammad through books, records, articles, and old issues of the *Muhammad Speaks* newspaper. Within four years I was wearing suits and bow ties, selling bean pies, and preaching the values of Elijah Muhammad and the words of Minister Louis Farrakhan. In 1980 I graduated from Bethune-Cookman College, a small black institution in Florida, and began my graduate work at Purdue University in West Lafayette, Indiana. Purdue is less than a two-hour drive from Chicago, so I had the opportunity to begin a close and long-term relationship with the Nation as Brother Vibert L. X. After earning a master of arts degree in American history I journeyed to Chicago to work and live directly under the leadership of Louis Farrakhan.

In the Nation of Islam's National Center I taught history and martial arts, worked security, and studied in the special ministerial class to become a clergyman of Islam. During my tenure as a Nation of Islam member and minister, I became quite close to many powerful and influential leaders who openly discussed with me many of the internal matters of the Nation. Because of this position, I became aware of several troubling and contradictory issues within the organization. These problems presented a picture of political and economic corruption and of exploitation of the movement's finances and members. This book focuses on those issues and my experiences in the Nation from my beginning as a regular foot soldier in the Fruit of Islam (FOI), the Nation's military arm, to a position as minister and, later, as an internal analyst of activities under the leadership of Louis Farrakhan.

In 1982 I started to take extensive notes on the Nation, but I would not seriously consider writing a book until ten years later. The thought of authoring a monograph on the Nation was inviting, exciting, and frightening. Academic colleagues, close friends, and family members, as well as Muslim associates and enemies, warned me about writing an open and honest account of the Nation, suggesting that I could be putting my life in jeopardy. Some concerned Muslims even stated that I should get Minister Farrakhan's permission to write a book. Ignoring the concept of academic freedom, although living in a society that allows the Nation to express its views freely and without censorship, they maintained that a black person does not have the right to review Farrakhan and his organization. Others argued that even though the Nation has problems, the Black Muslims have demonstrated for more than forty-four years an undying devotion to the African American community. Therefore, inside information or anything illustrating the truth, perhaps exposing the problems of the Nation, should not be written or published. The opinions expressed by these individuals led ultimately to the title *Inside the Nation of Islam.*

After extensive deliberation and meditation I started writing in 1996. At this time I must acknowledge the kindness of Minister Louis Farrakhan, who opened doors of the Nation of Islam for analytical review. Also I must thank Abdul Akbar Muhammad, Benjamin Chavis Muhammad, and Khallid Muhammad for their candid and open dialogue about the movement. Without individuals like Akbar, Benjamin, and Khallid the manuscript would not have been written. But specifically, I must thank Khallid Muhammad for his painful honesty; Akbar Muhammad for his keen insight into the old and new structure of the Nation of Islam; Maryam Aziz for her candid views on the rights of women in the organization; Al Saladin, the real curator of the Nation, who constantly supplied me with historical information; Barney Muhammad, an outstanding investigator on the internal affairs and one who always knew what was happening in the organization; Malik Robert Gordon, former lieutenant of Khallid Muhammad; and Wali Muhammad, the former editor of the *Final Call,* who always challenged my analysis of the Farrakhan question.

I am grateful to my mentor, Dr. Warren Van Tine of Ohio State University, who encouraged me to "stay the course"; Dr. C. Eric Lincoln, who laid the historical model for all writings on the Nation of Islam; Dr. Darlene Clarke-Hine, who always had a kind word of support; Dr. Harold Woodman, the scholar who encouraged me to write on the Nation as a young graduate student; Dr. Helen Edmonds, who always believed in challenging the polemics of alleged race leaders; Dr. Val Carnegie, who constantly reminds me through his actions that brothers of the Caribbean always show character and strength against opposing forces; and Dr. Benny Kraut, whose consuming passion for Jewish heritage was both necessary for me and much appreciated. Also, I must recognize friend and attorney William Krajec for candid advice and support of the project and Debbie Landgreen for her patient and careful reading as copy editor and typist.

Foremost, I must thank my father, Vibert White Sr., and my mother, Lorraine White, who stood with me during my transition from a member of the African Methodist Episcopal (AME) Church through my evolution as a socialist, black nationalist Marxist, and Black Muslim until I finally returned to our family's religion of Santeria/Vodun. Alessandra, my wife, stood as strong pillar in my quest for truth. My gratitude extends to my sisters, Virginia, Judith, and Sonia, who always asked in either English or Spanish about the status of the manuscript. A thank you to my Baha'i brother Dr. Christopher Buck, Cicil Bogle, Lawrence Williamson, and Sadie Oliver, who continually encouraged me through kind words and prayers. And last, to my daughter, Jira´, who was born October 25, 1997, the morning of the Million Woman March.

Introduction

The Nation of Islam (NOI) is the oldest and most stable black nationalist organization in the United States. Throughout its history its radical theology of black supremacy and its strict adherence to black economic self-sufficiency have caused intellectuals and laypersons, private organizations and government agencies to study, critique, and write about the Black Muslims. Scores of monographs, hundreds of articles, several movies, and at least two plays depict some aspect of the Nation of Islam.

In 1963 Dr. C. Eric Lincoln wrote the first serious study of the organization. In *Black Muslims in America* Lincoln recorded the Muslims' social, political, and religious ideology. He described a group that developed as a result of America's racist treatment of its black community. Isolated and brutalized, blacks retreated into several social-religious organizations. Racial groups such as Noble Drew Ali's Moorish Science Temple Movement, Marcus Garvey's Universal Negro Improvement Association, and Father Divine's Peace Mission organization filled the void of underclass African Americans who had lost hope in America's promise for a pluralistic society. The Nation of Islam followed the lineage of these groups to become the most established and recognized black nationalist religious organization in the United States.

Professor Lincoln also documented the objectives of the Black Muslims prior to the mid-1960s. The leadership of Elijah Muhammad represented a benign hatred of American society. He preached that white Americans used their privileged position and economic wealth to exploit the uneducated black masses. Paradoxically, however, he argued that blacks must follow the examples of white culture to create a self-sufficient society that would generate respect, admiration, and fear. Muhammad's thoughts ran deep through his followers, especially within the top echelon of the Nation's hierarchy. Individuals such as Malcolm X, Wallace Muhammad, Lemuel Hassan, Jeremiah X, Silas Muhammad, and Louis Farrakhan followed Elijah Muhammad's ideas until the Nation became the largest and most successful black American Islamic organization.

Lincoln concluded *Black Muslims in America* with the reasoning that America produced the Nation of Islam. If racism, bigotry, and disfranchisement continued, the Nation would remain an outlet for the black underclass. Lincoln's observation prompted a storm of research on the Nation of Islam for the next thirty-five years. But until *Inside the Nation of Islam* no one has continued Lincoln's internal review of the organization. The majority of published manuscripts are biographies of Elijah Muhammad, Wallace Muhammad, Muhammad Ali, Malcolm X, and Louis Farrakhan or documentaries on the Nation of Islam as a religious entity for Islam or a religious cult.

The first half of *Inside the Nation of Islam* details the historical framework of the NOI in the United States, documenting the development of Islam prior to the formation of the organization. These chapters emphasize the importance of Elijah Muhammad and Malcolm X in organizing and stabilizing the Black Muslim movement. The second half of the book scrutinizes the Nation's operational structure, examining numerous activities about which knowledge is unavailable not only to the general public but also to the grassroots membership of the group. It details the history, direction, and organizational design of Louis Farrakhan's movement.

This book represents more than ten years of journal writing and hundreds of hours of interviewing individuals associated with the Nation. Research also included primary and secondary source materials. The views expressed are my own. Opinions that were given by interviewees have been omitted unless they greatly impact the overall theme of the story. I take full responsibility for any errors that may appear as a result of faulty analysis. Finally, *Inside the Nation of Islam* presents a generous amount of documentation for others who wish to pursue the light of truth. It is not intended to condemn or to endorse the Nation of Islam but to begin the process of reviewing leaders and organizations that claim to represent the interests of minority racial and ethnic groups in the United States.

Early American Islam

The Building Blocks for the Nation of Islam

The Nation of Islam was founded in the ghettos of Detroit, Michigan, in 1930 by Fard Muhammad, an immigrant from Saudi Arabia. Fard Muhammad, who was eventually referred to as Allah and Master Fard Muhammad, perceived a social, political, and economic vacuum in the lives of black Americans in Detroit. To fill this deficit, he introduced a new religious ideology into African American society—a Black Islamic concept.

The Lost Found Nation of Islam in the Wilderness of North America, known to millions as the Nation of Islam, was not the first Islamic or black nationalist movement to reach America, but it is the most successful. To understand the nationalist and the non-Christian black religious movements in the United States, it is necessary to review early African religion in the Western Hemisphere. During the era of the last three great empires of West Africa—Ghana, Mali, and Songhai—people practiced an assortment of religions. These people, comprising several ethnic groups such as Arabs, Berbers, Mandigos, Hausas, and Wolofs, practiced their religious ideas peacefully and openly without threat of harassment or imprisonment. Timbuktu, the greatest cosmopolitan city in ancient Africa, was known throughout Europe and Asia as a city that allowed free expression in science, scholarship, politics, and religion. The liberal religious atmosphere continued in West Africa until the arrival of the European explorers, who radically destabilized Songhai, the last of the great West African empires and ushered in the Atlantic slave trade in the sixteenth century.

The Atlantic slave trade transformed West Africa, Europe, and the Americas, creating a continental shift that caused several distinct and unique groups to trade cultures, ideologies, and human conditions. Before the slave trade and modern bondage, West African peoples were self-sufficient and self-determined. Fortunately, one of the few elements they were able to keep and develop was their basic concept of religion and spirituality. The transporting of Africans into Europe and the Americas spanned more than two hundred years and brought over sixty million people to an entirely different society. Africans who were forcibly removed from their homes comprised the Yoruba, Melinke, Kisi, Limba, Ebo, and many others. Although there were many types of African groups and many religions, these religions shared a crucial similarity: they were Islamic in nature. Thus, on their arrival in the Americas, the Africans combined their religions to create a New World religious philosophy as a bulwark for protection. One of the greatest tenets that survived the early years of human bondage was African Islam.

Islam came to Africa from Arabia after the death in A.D. 632 of its founder, the prophet Muhammad of the tribe of Shabazz. Its impact in northern and western Africa has been tremendous, its assimilation into African culture more successful than Christianity's. Unlike Christianity, which forced Africans to give up their way of life, Islam did not compel blacks to discard their culture as part of their conversion. By the end of the ninth century, Islam was well established in North Africa, West Africa, and the Saharan region of the continent,[1] although some scholars have argued that it was brought into the region by political conquest and control. These scholars also suggest that Islam spread as a result of trade and economic migration. By the end of the tenth century, blacks in Africa displaced Arabs as the leaders of this religion. Natives of West Africa especially followed the religious ideas of their parents who were not Muslims. Ethnic groups such as the Fon, Hausa, Wolof, and Ibo, to name a few, embraced the new religion but refused to give up their cultural religious customs. Instead, they combined their ethnic religions with the new Islamic dogma. This practice was not out of line with Muslim tradition. The ideas of the indigenous African population became part of an Islamic school of thought called Sufism. Islamic mysticism, or Sufism, grew out of the Muslim fraternities or tariqas during the second century after the founding of Islam. Tariqas developed after many orthodox worshipers argued that Islam had become reactionary and was not meeting the needs of the community. The belief is that tariqas were commissioned to guide Muslims back to the true teachings or Sunna of the prophet Muhammad.

Much Islamic intellectual history revolved around Muslim mysticism, especially the mysticism of Arab and non-Arab Muslims. Orthodox Islam has maintained a major hold in the Middle East, with the majority of Muslims following the concept of Sunnism; in non-Arab nations, especially on the African continent, Sufi doctrines are prevalent. One reason Sufism flourishes is because it is willing to absorb various local concepts into the structure of Islam. For example, Sufism evidences influences from Christian monastics, the Upanishads, and Berber tribalists.[2] Today there are a number of tariqas in West Africa, and Senegal is usually cited as the capital of African Islamic Sufism and tariqas. The major groups of the tariqas in Senegal are the Tijaniyya, the Qudriyya, and the Lynenes.[3] These groups have also developed a large following of African Americans. For example, the Tijaniyya Islamic group has established several mosques in the Southeast, Northeast, and Midwest United States. According to this Islamic group, their membership in the United States ranges between seven thousand and twenty-five thousand people.[4]

The traditions of Islamic groups in West Africa are shared by twentieth-century African Americans who created the first Islamic groups in the United States. Throughout much of the history of the United States the activities of Muslims have been either ignored or eradicated from academic discussion. For example, there are early signs of Islamic life in America during the slave trade of the sixteenth century. Many Africans who came from the continent were Muslims. An overwhelming number of them came from Senegambia. Because of the religion's emphasis on solidarity and its tendency to influence slaves to rebel, slaves were not allowed to practice Islam in the Americas. By 1830 the majority of African Americans had lost their practice and understanding of and belief in Islam. It was not until the early twentieth century that Islamic practices resurfaced among various African American groups.[5] However, recent evidence suggests that Muslims had established an agency during the late nineteenth century to influence the intelligent masses toward Islam. Mohammed Alexander Russell Webb's *Islam in America: A Brief Statement of Mohammedanism and an Outline of the American Islamic Propaganda* (1893) stated that a prominent and wealthy Muslim from Bombay by the name of Budruddin Abdulla Kur had established an organization to spread Islam among the uneducated American masses in

1873.[6] By 1891 every major city in the United States had branches of this group. Interestingly, the American Propaganda Islamic movement established its greatest influence in Chicago and Detroit—the first two Nations of Islam enclaves in the United States. Despite the reference to America in its name, American Islamic Propaganda, Inc., included Islamic leaders from Medina, Mecca, Jeddah, Bombay, Calcutta, Singapore, Egypt, and Turkey in its membership. By 1900 the organization had several hundred followers throughout the nation; however, foreign Muslims overwhelmingly controlled the group.[7]

In 1913 the first American Black Islamic society was formed in Newark, New Jersey. The new movement, called the Moorish Science Temple Movement, was created and led by Noble Drew Ali. Ali, whose Christian name was Timothy Drew, was reared and educated in South Carolina. However, like many southern blacks during the first quarter of the twentieth century, he left the land of the Old Confederacy to seek a better life in the northern states. Drew sought a society that would judge him by his character not by his skin color. He finally reached New Jersey, but Drew, like millions of his southern brothers and sisters, found the North as racist as the segregated communities he had left behind south of the Mason-Dixon Line. Drew often remarked that the only thing that welcomed the Negro to the North was the ghettos of Boston, New York, Philadelphia, and Chicago.[8] The conditions in these ghettos allowed a charismatic leader like Ali to appear as a savior among helpless and poor African Americans.

Drew, like millions of other southern blacks, grew up as a Christian in the Baptist Church. As a devout follower of the church, he believed that through the acceptance of Jesus Christ as the lord of the world, African Americans would find a divine bulwark that would protect them from white racism and hostility. Thus, on his arrival in Newark in 1907 he attempted to build a militant Christian group that would attack the ills of a segregated and racist America. Unfortunately, the Drew Baptist movement failed. With the growing influence of major black churches such as the African Methodist Episcopal Church and the Black Baptist Church and the growing list of Christian cult leaders like Daddy Grace and Father Divine, Drew found little room in the black community for his small, struggling religious group. Drew's Christian experiment ended almost as soon as it had begun. Nonetheless, Drew would continue his quest for a religious movement, discarding the notion of founding his new organization on Christianity and adopting instead the new concept of Islam.

The Moorish Science Temple Movement became the first Black Muslim group in the United States. Drew argued that blacks needed a new identity and a positive picture of their culture and history. He maintained that slavery, racism, and discrimination had caused blacks to view themselves as inferior to other cultures and peoples, especially white Americans. Therefore, a new or renewed belief system of race militancy and nationalism would inspire blacks to function as equals to white Americans. Drew borrowed superficial elements of traditional Islam for the creation of a Black Muslim system in the United States.

Noble Drew Ali told members of the Moorish Science Temple Movement that he had traveled extensively in North Africa, the Middle East, and India. According to the movement's record, Ali was taught by Islamic clerics who educated him on the fundamentals of Islam and Sufism. The theologians allegedly gave Ali the title of Egyptian adept or sheik, which gave the black leader the right to proclaim himself the Islamic leader of black Americans.[9] In Egypt he had the opportunity to visit the Sphinx and several of the great pyramids and universities. These tours illustrated that black people possessed a great culture and that they had originated judicial science, the hard sciences, math, and the fine arts. After his visit to Egypt he traveled to the Muslim holy cities of Mecca and Medina. In Mecca Sultan Abdul Aziz Ibn Saud received Drew and gave him the Arabic name Noble Drew Ali. According to Ali, this name granted him the right to teach Islam to the lost tribe of Israel in North, Central, and South America.[10]

Ali was apparently given permission from the Islamic masters to teach Americans the Sunna, the way of Islam and the prophet Muhammad. Instead Ali taught esoteric concepts, Christian dogma, masonry, and very little Islam. For example, Drew published his own version of the Holy Quran, the religious book of the Muslims; Ali's religious book was called the Koran. In his Koran Drew borrowed heavily from an Ohio white spiritualist named Levi Dowling, who authored *The Aquarian Gospel of Jesus the Christ*. Dowling's book was filled with mysticism and esoteric concepts.[11] Drew did not deliberately mislead his followers about Islamic ideology; rather, Drew was a victim of a worldwide Christian evangelical movement that found its way to India and Egypt—areas that hosted him during his search for the religion of the black man and woman. According to some historians, Drew probably found Dowling's teachings in Asia, not the United States.[12] Unfortunately, some doubt remains whether Drew actually made a trip to Asia to study religion at all. According to the State Department, there are no records granting a passport to Timothy Drew or Noble Drew Ali for international travel. It is more reasonable to argue that Drew was influenced by the American Islamic Propagation Society, which worked diligently to enlist blacks into their religious ranks. Historian C. Eric Lincoln maintained that they infiltrated such groups as Marcus Garvey's Universal Improvement Association in an attempt to preach Islam among black nationalist advocates.[13] The Propagation Society influenced only a marginal number of blacks to join its league. Most African Americans at this time were interested in the eradication of racism and not the growth of traditional Islam in the United States.

Noble Drew Ali, like many other blacks, represented a new type of Negro, one who was not afraid to challenge white traditions and laws that regulated the social, political, and economic movement of African Americans. However, whereas some blacks, like W. E. B. Du Bois, the great civil rights activist and scholar, favored political action through black participation in electoral politics, Drew sought religious and social escapism. According to the National Association for the Advancement of Colored People, between 1900 and 1930 more than one thousand African Americans were lynched by white terrorist mobs. The summer of 1919 witnessed twenty-six race riots.[14] Because of statistics like these, Drew believed that only through religion, culture, and race nationalism could a bulwark be developed to shield blacks from white hatred and bigotry. Thus, it is not surprising that by the summer of 1920 Drew was able to attract twenty-five thousand members to his religious congregation.

The Moorish Science Temple Organization sparked an intense interest among blacks, mostly in northern U.S. urban communities and particularly in Chicago and Detroit. Paradoxically, although Moors expanded their growth among blacks, their aggressive and often hostile attitude toward white society ultimately undermined their expansion. In Chicago male members who had taken on a bravado nationalist image started to confront whites in the downtown loop area of the city. Wearing long white gowns and red fezzes with the movement's emblem of the star and crescent, they abruptly stopped whites to inform them that they were devils and that Allah, through Prophet Noble Drew Ali, was going to destroy white America.[15] The members of the movement seemed to take great pride in telling whites about their evil system and society; understandably, however, the white community was less than enthusiastic to hear these words. At this time in Chicago racial tension was already at a peak. In the summer of 1919, often called the red summer because of the race riots mentioned above, Chicago experienced a race war that literally destroyed the city. On July 27, 1919, racial tension came to a climax when a young black boy who was swimming at the Lake Shore Beach accidentally crossed the imaginary line that segregated the races along the city's lakefront. As the teenager floated into the waters of white Chicagoans, a barrage of bottles, stones, and rocks thrown by whites caused him to drown. Blacks on the beach sought help from several white police officers, who responded to the concerned African Americans that the "nigger knew better than to swim in the White water."[16]

Meanwhile, whites in the Windy City had spread rumors that black gangs were attacking innocent white women, girls, senior citizens, and just about all Caucasians who could not protect themselves. Instead of black gangs assaulting whites, white hoodlums randomly mobbed any African American they could find and catch. A violent example was the brutal lynching of a pregnant black woman on Chicago's south side. The young victim was dragged from a streetcar, hanged from a light post, and disemboweled as a cheering crowd witnessed the removal of her unborn child. In spite of overwhelming numbers of whites attempting to create a holocaust among the city's black population, blacks fought back gallantly. Nevertheless, African Americans suffered a tremendous loss during the three-day bloodfest. Chicago saw 38 citizens killed and 537 wounded; hundreds of blacks were left homeless.[17] However, whereas African Americans experienced the brunt of the violence, whites suffered the psychological effect of fearing black citizens. African Americans who behaved in an assertive and aggressive manner toward whites represented an image of defiance, danger, and hatred. Noble Drew Ali's movement became a victim of this white fright and hostility.

In 1928 Moorish Scientists numbered twelve hundred members in Chicago. This was by far the largest chapter or temple in Ali's movement. The large membership caused alarm in the general white popula-tion, especially in extremist organizations such as the Ku Klux Klan, which had an estimated membership of twenty-five thousand in Chicago and northwestern Indiana. Terrorist groups like the Klan supported lo-cal, state, and federal programs intended to undermine Drew and his organization. Drew's Moorish Scientists had begun to experience the rage of the government in early 1927 through extralegal means such as intimidation, extortion, assault, and murder. The external attacks on the Moors quickly diminished their ability to govern their own internal matters. By the end of 1928 the Moors were riddled with tension among leaders and rank-and-file members. In fact, several leaders began to chal-lenge Drew for control of the organization. In cities such as New Orleans rival members took to violence. A major opponent of Drew was brutally murdered there, and although Ali was not in New Orleans at the time of the crime, he was unofficially linked to the murder. In December 1929 Chicago police questioned Ali about the New Orleans murder and about activities of the Moors in Chicago. Interestingly enough, while in the custody of the Chicago and Cook County authorities, Prophet Noble Drew Ali mysteriously disappeared. According to Moorish Science Tem-ple folklore, Chicago police joked that "the Prophet had been misplaced by his God."[18]

Before Drew's disappearance, however, on March 15, 1929, Sheik Claude Green, a rival of Noble Drew Ali for leadership of the Moorish Science Temple Movement, was brutally gunned down in Chicago. Drew Ali was immediately arrested as the prime suspect. The Muslim leader was shortly released on bond. Within a few weeks of his release he was allegedly murdered. Members of the organization speculate on two activities that may have led to Drew's disappearance.

Drew, according to several members, was a ladies' man who was ro-mantically tied to three women simultaneously, two teenagers (ages fourteen and sixteen) and a twenty-two-year-old woman. The theory is that one set of parents of the teenagers, both of whom allegedly gave birth to Drew's children, were outraged by the prophet's statutory rape of their daughter and had him murdered.

The other story is detailed by an elaborate plot of white police officers to destroy the Moorish Science Temple Movement. The plan was to break up the movement by killing Drew. After the death of the prophet several Moorish leaders fought for Drew's title as the "Prophet." In 1941 the first of several splinter organizations that claimed to be Drew's groups emerged in more than twenty-five major cities in the United States.[19]

The elimination of Prophet Noble Drew Ali effectively destroyed the Moorish Science Temple Movement. Drew's group, despite its sizable membership, was essentially a personality cult. Drew's theology, preaching, and charisma kept the group together, and no records indicate that Drew laid a framework or structure to determine how the group would be led if he were not physically with the organization. Because of this fatal error, the organization splintered into groups with leaders who argued that they were inspired by Drew to govern the group. Some of these leaders claimed to be reincarnations of Noble Drew Ali.

During the rise and fall of the Moorish Science Temple Movement, another racial political group developed: the Universal Negro Improvement Association (UNIA). The UNIA, founded and led by Jamaican-born Marcus Garvey, used racial solidarity and the bigotry of white racism, discrimination, and hostility to build a movement that focused on black nationalism, economic development, and social-religious tenets. Garvey, who started the UNIA in 1916, during the era of the New Negro and the Negro Renaissance, was able to capitalize on black frustration with American-style apartheid and discrimination.[20]

Marcus Garvey maintained that blacks must have their own organization to challenge white supremacy and must fight for economic growth and development. Garvey maintained that economic expansion should not be limited to the rise of black entrepreneurs. He championed the creation of an African global international base that would utilize the natural resources of Africa, from the mining of raw materials to the selling of refined items to the world market. To accomplish this Garvey stated that blacks must take control of Africa and turn it into a "United States of Africa." Holding true to this objective, the UNIA ultimately became the largest and most successful of the "Back to Africa" movements in the history of the United States.[21]

Although the UNIA focused primarily on racial solidarity and economic development, it was also concerned with the formation of a civil religion. Garvey attempted to devise a theology that would explain why African Americans, as well as Africans in the Diaspora, suffered under white racism and imperialism. He borrowed from the Old and New Testaments to create rituals and a theology that maintained that blacks are God's chosen people; Africa is the promised land; Africa is the biblical Garden of Eden; human rights are guaranteed by God the Father; and suffering is a necessary condition of martyrdom. Garvey's beliefs grew out of the oppression and shared experiences of Africans in the Diaspora.[22] The UNIA's theology, in fact, used the history of chattel slavery and Christianity to forge a concept of revolutionary theology; that is, religion must be used to change the social and civil conditions of a people. Therefore, the religious factor within the "Back to Africa" movement was a very significant part of its foundation.

In 1928 Marcus Garvey also became a victim of a governmental conspiracy to destroy his character and movement. With the assistance of several leading black advocates and organizations, the court found Garvey guilty of mail fraud, and he was deported by President Calvin Coolidge's administration. Garvey desperately attempted to rebuild the UNIA in Jamaica and later in London, but all efforts failed. In 1940 the great race leader, whose organization once claimed a membership of ten million people, died a sad and broken man. However, before the demise of the UNIA, thousands of African Americans embraced Garvey's thoughts on race, politics, and religion. One of the individuals who embraced Garvey's teachings was Elijah Poole, the future leader of the Nation of Islam.[23]

Noble Drew Ali and Marcus Garvey captured the imagination of the black underclass in the United States. Both the Moorish Science Temple and the Universal Negro Improvement Association illustrated a new consciousness among black Americans: a thought pattern characterized by confidence, independence, black theology, and a concept of self-help attitude. Although Drew and Garvey were active during the same period and often in the same cities, they did not view each other as political or religious rivals. In fact, they complemented each other. The Moors and Garvey's followers viewed each other as partners in the fight against segregation and discrimination in the United States. For example, Lemuel Hassan, one of the first ministers of the Nation of Islam, stated that many of his converts to the Nation of Islam held membership in both Ali's and Garvey's organizations.[24] However, by the beginning of the 1930s the Moorish Science Temple Movement and the Universal Negro Improvement Association had lost most of their influence with the mainstream African American community. Other organizations such as

Father Divine's Peace Mission Movement and the National Association for the Advancement of Colored People labored in the void left by Ali and Garvey in the northern urban ghettos and in the southern black rural poor communities.

For a brief period George Baker, later known as Father Divine, capitalized on the fall of Ali and Garvey. His organization, the Peace Mission Movement, begun in 1919 in Long Island, New York, promised blacks and whites a heaven on earth—if only they obeyed and followed the laws of Father Divine. Divine's movement was quite similar to both the Drew and Garvey organizations. Divine labored for independence for his followers through economic freedom from government agencies and escape from the negative forces of political, social, and economic bigotry. By 1930 Father Divine held a following of over twenty-five thousand people throughout the North and South.

In the 1930s, the era of the Great Depression, Father Divine's group flourished. At that time, as blacks experienced termination from the jobs they had earned during the Roaring Twenties, evictions from ghetto housing, and mental depression, Father Divine offered hope, shelter, and food. In his Peace Mission Buildings Father Divine provided affordable housing, cheap food, and meager employment for his followers and for the larger black community. For example, in Philadelphia at the beautiful Lorraine Hotel, owned and operated by the Peace Mission, a person could get a haircut, a full-course meal, and a clean room for one dollar. Divine's program appealed greatly to the black community; however, black nationalists who once followed Ali and Garvey grew tired of Divine's philosophy on race.

Ali and Garvey maintained that blacks must remain separate from white Americans, who represented evil and ill will against the true and righteous African Americans; therefore, it was impossible to live and socialize among them in peace and harmony. Father Divine argued that all people under the leadership of "the father" are brothers and sisters, "lambs in the Garden of Eden." Holding true to this thought, Father married a white Canadian named Edna Rose. Father's revolutionary character on race relationships made the Peace Mission Movement the most integrated social religious movement in the United States. In addition, Father Divine campaigned actively against racism, lynching, and segregation within the political system. Distinguishing his political position from that advocated by Ali and Garvey, Divine sought to combat the social problems fragmenting American society from an integration- ist standpoint. Last, many black nationalists left the group because of Father Divine's views on sexuality.

As the leader of the Peace Mission Movement, Father Divine did not encourage marriage among the "angels of God." He taught the believers that in heaven marriage and sex are unnecessary because the greatest love is the spiritual bond that exists between Father (God) and the angels (members). Therefore, carnal needs are obsolete in heaven. For former Ali and Garvey members this was strange because they had been taught to multiply the world with strong black bodies for the development of a unified black world. However, Father's position changed in later years, signified by his personal decision to marry. Marrying a white Canadian who was fifty years his junior, Father stated, "My union to Sweet Angel represents the budding relationship of integration between the Negro and White in America."[26]

Father Divine's movement remained quite active until his death in 1965. But by far the movement held its greatest appeal among blacks and whites from the 1930s to the mid-1950s. During this period another group would develop that would capture the imagination of the black underclass. This was to be the Nation of Islam in the Wilderness of North America.

Morton represented the spirit of the period in "The New Orleans Blues" and "The Jelly Roll Blues." The harsh sounds and rough lyrics of Morton's songs inspired scores of blacks to sing about the soul, life, and hardships of the black community. Joseph "King" Oliver, for example, could not refrain from mentioning the hardships of black life in the South and in Chicago. Louis Armstrong may have performed with a smile in New Orleans, but he often wrote lyrics that depicted a different side of black life in songs like "Black and Blue." His works illustrate the feelings of the youth of the Jazz Age toward segregation and discrimination. The African American soul found expression not only in blues and jazz but in Negro spirituals, which also lamented the troubles and yearnings of black Americans.

Whereas blues and jazz enlightened the masses of blacks who frequented venues such as juke joints, saloons, pool halls, and speakeasies, spirituals played to church audiences. Carl Diton, J. Rosamond Johnson, and Nathaniel Dett wrote and edited scores of spirituals that electrified the black-consciousness movement. Paul Robeson, one of the best-known singers, along with associates like Lawrence Brown, communicated the meaning of black strength and suffering to American audiences. Robeson, a unique individual, represented the problems of blacks not only in his songs but also in his life. The great baritone sang a sad tale of his life as a black American who was discarded by his nation because of his political and social convictions. Robeson challenged the laws of the United States to protect the rights of black Americans as guaranteed by the Constitution. As he challenged existing American laws, Robeson critiqued the rules of communism that the Soviet Union followed. However, when several federal politicians discovered that Robeson was intellectually interested in socialism in Eastern Europe, he was branded a "red" conspirator. Ultimately, the State Department revoked his passport for international travel and banned him from giving lectures and concerts, which were his livelihood, outside of his home state of New York. Despite these problems, Robeson illustrated the new black consciousness and pride of the African American during the 1920s.

As authors, composers, and singers forged a stage for the development of the black community, artists also worked diligently to showcase the culture and history of the African American. Brilliant artists such as Laura Wheeler Waring and Meta Warrick Fuller expressed the feelings of their race through paintings, photographs, and sculptures. In an interesting twist, black artists influenced several white painters to create artwork on white America's mistreatment of its black population.

Although the major players of the renaissance resided in Harlem, every major black community in the United States experienced an awakening. The African American communities of Philadelphia, Pittsburgh, Cincinnati, Cleveland, Chicago, and Detroit attracted and created scores of people who, like their brothers and sisters in Harlem, labored aggressively to showcase and debate the state of the race. One of the greatest seedbeds for the renaissance was Detroit, Michigan.

In the 1920s the city of Detroit attracted thousands of blacks from the southern states of Mississippi, Tennessee, Alabama, and Georgia. These newcomers escaping the rigors of southern exploitation and oppression traveled to Detroit with only hopes and dreams that this major industrialized metropolis would treat them more favorably than had the South. For a while the North did prove the glimmer of hope that they had expected. Like other cities during the Roaring Twenties, Detroit experienced an economic upturn. The automobile industry was doing well, small businesses were being created, and employment was steadily increasing. As for the black community, gradually employment opportunities trickled down to the poor enclaves. However, blacks became the last group to experience the economic windfall and the first to witness its decrease. This was the case for Elijah Poole.

Poole, later to be known as Elijah Muhammad, was born on October 7, 1897, in Bolds Springs, near Sandersville, Georgia. Born to a sharecropper and his wife, named Wali and Marie, Elijah spent his formative years in poverty. Like his twelve siblings Elijah thought that the world encompassed white control and black suffering. Nonetheless, as a young boy he attempted to use his Bible to rationalize the misery that blacks suffered. Elijah was introduced to Bible scripture at a young age. His father, Wali, was the Baptist minister for the small black community where the Pooles lived. According to Elijah, his father constantly taught the Bible; however, he never explained why blacks were brought into slavery, why they were lynched, or whether blacks would ever achieve equality with whites.[6] Young Elijah's question was intensified in a tragic way during the early 1910s.

Wali and Marie attempted desperately to shield their children from the hazards of race hatred and violence. The Pooles instructed the children to avoid whites as much as possible but when addressed by them to behave passively and conservatively. One of the instructions was for Elijah not to take shortcuts through wooded areas. However, on one autumn day when Elijah was alone he decided to hike through the woods to his parents' small farm. What Elijah experienced that day would haunt him for the remainder of his life.

The path that Elijah took to his parents' home appeared peaceful and enjoyable. However, as he walked he unexpectedly heard several heavy boot steps rumbling through the woods. Fearing that the sounds came from his approaching brothers and sisters, Elijah Poole hid, aware if his siblings discovered him in the woods his parents would severely punish him. However, what he hid from were four white men chasing a middle-aged black male. To Elijah's surprise, the man the whites were after was a deacon of his father's church. The man, unable to escape his white pursuers, fell from exhaustion after which the white gang kicked and stomped their captive. After getting their fill of beating the man, the gang tied a thick rope around his neck and hanged him from a tree. The deacon struggled for air, but after a few minutes Elijah heard the man's neck snap, and the body went limp. Elijah, with tears streaming down his face, was horrified and angry as the white men laughed, shared a bottle of wine, and left the scene as if nothing had occurred.

Although lynchings occurred frequently in the black community, they were not the only illegal mechanism whites used to oppress African Americans. Jim Crow, or segregated southern governments, practiced an assortment of activities to limit black political participation. Schemes such as ballot-box stuffing and white primaries that turned the local Democratic or Republican party into private white clubs, excluding black participation in voting, were used widely, in violation of the Fifteenth Amendment. In one particular Mississippi voting incident, a white registrar required a black man to read and interpret the U.S. Constitution in English, Spanish, and French. When, to the surprise of the registrar, the African American was able to complete the task, he was ordered to read the assignment in Arabic. The black admitted that he was not versed in the North African language; consequently, he was not allowed to vote.[7] By 1908 eight southern states—Alabama, Louisiana, Mississippi, North Carolina, Oklahoma, South Carolina, Virginia, and Georgia—had revised their constitutions to disfranchise African Americans.[8]

The lynching that young Elijah Poole witnessed in the woods that autumn day left him stunned, horrified, and angered. Shortly after the episode the Pooles moved one hundred miles west to Weona, Georgia, another small town in the Peach State. The Pooles managed to buy a small farm that afforded them the opportunity to raise their own crops and cattle. Elijah was forced to leave school after completing fifth grade because he was needed to help run the homestead. At the age of fourteen he sought employment outside the family farm. During the next two years Elijah held several odd jobs that left him bewildered and uninspired about his future. The lot of the teenager changed when he met Clara Evans in 1915. Remembering the young Elijah, Clara reminisced that he was always neat and orderly, and he was always on time. "That was very important since I frequently was late for appointments."[9] Elijah and Clara eloped on May 2, 1917. Shortly after their honeymoon they moved in with Elijah's brother Sam and his wife. Within a year the newlyweds left Sam's home to move into their own. However, Clara encouraged Elijah to find a better and larger home if they expected to have children. In 1921 the first of Elijah's nineteen children was born. Elijah, now with an extra mouth to feed, left Clara and his young son, Emmanuel, to search for better employment. He found employment in Macon, Georgia, first as a construction laborer and later as an employee for the Southern Railroad Company.[10]

The railroad industry has played a crucial role in the social and political history of the African American. In 1898, in *Plessy v. Ferguson,* the United States Supreme Court ruled that railroad companies can legally segregate by race as long as both ethnic groups are given equal treatment and accommodations. However, the practice and later tradition of Jim Crow resulted in white Americans being given privileged treatment over blacks. Therefore, *Plessy* in practice meant "separate and unequal," and not the "separate but equal" ordered by the Supreme Court.[11] Paradoxically, while the railroad industry ushered in legal racial segregation, it became one of the leading employers of black men. For example, the Chicago Pullman Company's employment of African American men gave workers the security of living a lifestyle of travel, excitement, and economic opportunity that very few blacks enjoyed. George Pullman, the owner of the company, hired so many blacks as porters, cooks, and waiters and influenced train stations to hire so many African Americans as redcaps that all black railroad workers were affectionately called "George's Boys."[12] For two years Elijah Poole supported his family by being one of "George's Boys." According to Elijah, his experience on the rail system was mainly positive; however, one negative experience prompted him to quit the Southern Railroad Company. "'All was fine until the White [man],' stated Elijah, 'tried to attack me. . . . I decided to leave Georgia for Detroit. I saw enough of the White man's brutality to last me 26,000 years.'"[13]

In 1923, when Elijah, Clara, and Emmanuel arrived in Detroit, they met their old companions—racism, discrimination, hunger, and despair. The areas where blacks lived comprised dilapidated housing, poor schools, petty criminals, and crooked whites who operated as landlords and small-business owners. However, in the midst of misery Elijah saw a sparkle of light in Marcus Garvey's Universal Negro Improvement Association. After his arrival in the North he joined Garvey's Back to Africa movement. The concept of black pride, self-help, and race separatism appealed to Elijah, and he became a devout follower of Garvey's ideology. Within two years the Georgian had risen to the rank of corporal in the Chicago/Detroit division of the UNIA. An ardent Garvey follower, he became depressed and discouraged when Garvey was found guilty of mail fraud and subsequently deported from the United States. To make matters worse, Elijah lost his job at the Ford Automobile Company when the stock market crashed in 1929. With the loss of Garvey and his employment, Elijah found the wine bottle.

Unfortunately, Elijah was not alone. Thousands of African Americans in Detroit and millions throughout the United States suffered the brunt of the stock market crash. Families in America's black ghettos survived these extremely lean times by living off chicken feet and vegetable leaves, using railroad coals to heat their homes, getting secondhand clothing from sympathetic whites, and going to relief missions for family necessities such as toilet paper, soap powder, and baking soda. In a desperate attempt to change the course of his life, Elijah began to meet other black men every morning at 5:00 in front of manufacturing companies such as Oldsmobile and Ford, hoping to get hired for a day's labor. However, in most cases frustrated men went home without employment, money, or a sense of self-worth. As the economy grew progressively worse, scores of African Americans looked for alternative programs to alter their current conditions. By the 1930s several black groups emerged to offer solutions to the unemployment, racism, and discrimination that plagued African Americans. Many of these organizations were rooted in the concepts of black nationalism and anti-American dogma.

One of the leading groups of the era was the Peace Movement of Ethiopia. This organization preached that blacks should give up their citizenship and move to the African homeland of Ethiopia. The organization was endorsed and supported by racist politicians such as Mississippi's Senator Theodore G. Bilbo, who introduced a federal bill that would repatriate blacks to Africa. Bilbo, an avowed segregationist, attempted to frighten whites about the potential political and social rise of African Americans. While black attorneys such as William Hastie, Charles Houston, and Thurgood Marshall labored diligently for the National Association for the Advancement of Colored People to eradicate the legal text of segregation, Bilbo and his followers worked to keep American apartheid in effect. In response to the NAACP's legal fight against segregation, Bilbo offered blacks an alternative to equality—go back to Africa at the expense of the United States government. Most black Americans saw the senator and his program as antiblack and anti-American.

Similar to Bilbo's thesis was the National Movement for the Establishment of the Forty-Ninth State. This group of black nationalists argued that because they did not receive the promised forty acres and a mule in the nineteenth century, they should now receive a separate state from the government. Although this movement never attracted more than a few hundred members, it was a consistent voice for black separatists during the 1930s.

Individuals such as Queen Mother Moore, a Harlem activist and separatist, supported the goals and aspirations of the Forty-Ninth State movement. Moore, who also fought for reparations, believed that the movement would eventually force the United States to pay blacks for their suffering during the slave period.

For individuals who longed for racial and religious harmony, there was George Baker's Father Divine Peace Mission Movement, which promised members an integrated life on earth and in heaven. Father Divine, known to his followers as "God," promised that through his guidance racial tension would be eliminated and total integration would be established in the United States. Father Divine led by example, marrying a white woman who became known as Mother Divine. However, although the Peace Mission Movement attracted twenty-five thousand members between 1930 and 1960, it did not have the appeal of the Nation of Islam, the group Elijah eventually joined.

In July of 1930 Elijah Poole joined a small and eccentric religious cult in the Paradise Valley section of Detroit. This community that housed crime, poverty, and an assortment of vices became Elijah's lily of the valley. In the undeveloped community he met Wallace Fard Muhammad, a mystic who taught a radical religion named Islam. Muhammad's religion taught that blacks are mutually good and that whites are devils.[14] Wallace Fard Muhammad, whom Elijah would ultimately refer to as Master Fard Muhammad and Allah (God), had an unusual way of spreading his religious message to black Detroit. According to Detroit legend and Elijah Muhammad, this light-skinned, Oriental-looking man sold household products, silk clothes, and even his labor as a janitor to spread the message. Fard Muhammad often entered the homes of African Americans by telling tales of great African and Asian societies. He told potential customers and followers that his silks were of royal stock—the kind their ancestors wore in Mecca. He also preached of the greatness of Africa as a place of art, culture, and science. To get inside the homes of Detroit blacks, he occasionally offered to clean their homes for free. According to Elijah Poole, this man "must be speaking truth because Negroes usually don't work for free unless it [was] slavery."[15]

Elijah Poole fell in love with the strange man's lectures, ideas, and concept of history. Within a few weeks of meeting Fard Muhammad, Elijah joined the Nation of Islam, the newest and ultimately the most powerful black nationalist group in the history of the United States. The group was incorporated under the leadership of Master Fard Muhammad as the Nation of Islam in the Wilderness of North America. Shortly after Elijah became one of Muhammad's first followers, the small cult began to hold meetings in public lodges.

Fard, as he was often called, not only cleaned people's homes in exchange for a captive audience, but he occasionally paid people twenty-five cents to come to Nation of Islam Sunday meetings to hear his lectures.[16] According to many of the first followers, this was the only way to get blacks to hear Fard's fiery and antiwhite rhetoric. To an oppressed people, hearing someone call them great, wonderful, and gods, while referring to white store owners, landlords, and racist police as swine, devils, and the great Satan, allowed them to redeem a little of the self-worth that white America had taken from them. As Fard became more popular, he insisted that black converts discard their Christian or slave names and replace them with holy names. Following this advice, Elijah allowed Fard to christen him with the Arabic name Muhammad.[17]

This was not Elijah's first experience with Islam. His father, familiar with Black Islam, had urged Elijah to attend lectures of the Moorish Science Temple Organization. The elder Poole respected the Moors' doctrines of racial solidarity and black economic development. Following the advice of his father, Elijah attended several Moorish Science Temple services. Abdul Muhammad, a Moorish minister of Detroit, impressed Elijah greatly with his knowledge of the Bible and the condition of African American society. Elijah ultimately became a frequent visitor to the Moor's temple. In some weeks he attended more than one service. Members of the Detroit temple viewed Elijah as a friend and potential follower of Noble Drew Ali. However, his views of the organization changed radically when he recognized internal conflict among the group's leaders. As the Moor's infrastructure crumbled, Fard's Nation of Islam grew. Ultimately, Elijah broke with the Moors to join the Nation.[18] In an interesting twist of fate Abdul Muhammad also joined Fard's Nation of Islam; however, unlike Elijah, who became a trusted disciple, Abdul Muhammad became a controversial minister who attempted to oust Fard from his role as leader of the young NOI.

Elijah's belief and trust in Fard came from two sources, the 1930s Depression and the Bible. The 1929 stock market crash illustrated the dependency of the black community on the larger white community. Contrary to the 1920s image of black entrepreneurs and capital flowing into Harlem, Chicago's south side, and north Philadelphia, those businesses relied on the stability of white corporations to survive. In the 1920s, when white store owners and members of the upper class needed to save money, they simply fired their black help. Between 1930 and 1940, 60 percent of black domestics were fired by their employers.

Throughout his life Elijah was an avid student of the Bible. As a child, and later as an adult, he impressed people with his knowledge and understanding of the gospel. His review of the Scriptures culminated with the theory of the millennium. Fard and Elijah both preached that at the end of time God will make himself known to his people and their enemies. Fard Muhammad argued that God was in the midst of hell (America) to deliver his people (black Americans) and to teach them how to destroy their enemy (white America).[19] According to Nation of Islam historian

Abdul Akbar Muhammad, Elijah immediately recognized Fard and his place in biblical prophesy. Elijah identified Fard as the Messiah of the Christians and Mahdi of the Islam. During Fard's and Elijah's first meeting, Elijah stated, "Yes, Brother [Fard Muhammad]. You are that one we have read about in the Bible; the one that would come in the last day under the name Jesus." Fard Muhammad responded: "Yes, I am the one that you have been looking for in the last two thousand years."[20] Shortly after Elijah joined the Nation of Islam, his wife, Clara, became an active member. Clara immediately changed her home to fit the needs of a Muslim family. She stopped cooking pork, forbade the drinking of alcohol in the home, and dressed herself in modest female attire to meet the standards of a good Muslim wife.

Although Elijah and Clara viewed Fard as the savior of the black race and the Messiah, many people saw the light-skinned man as a street hustler and petty criminal. Wallace Muhammad, the son of Elijah Muhammad, concluded that Fard had a questionable past and that he used basic principles to misdirect his father's ignorance of Islam. Wallace Muhammad argued that Fard was appealing to the underclass of Detroit, especially during the Depression. Black residents of Detroit's slums were disheartened by their economic status and by the escalation of racism. Feeling hopeless, they understandably fell victim to Fard's personal theology.[21]

Between 1930 and 1933 Fard Muhammad presented his theology in an educational series called "The Supreme Lessons." The program was given in the form of questions and answers that members had to memorize and recite to Master Fard Muhammad. The lessons focused primarily on basic math, English, and reading. However, there were bizarre metaphysical statements that manipulated uneducated blacks to criminal activities. One such lesson focused on the killing of four devils (whites) to acquire a free trip to the Holy City of Mecca. In 1938 Professor Erdmann Doane Beynon of the University of Michigan documented this potential problem in an article recounting an event that had occurred on November 21, 1932: Robert Harris, also known as Robert Karriem, erected a sacrificial altar in his house. He then persuaded his roommate, John J. Smith, to present himself as a human sacrifice to Allah. Karriem believed that Smith's death would transform the victim into a "Savior."[22] Smith agreed to Karriem's invitation and died of a sharp knife wound to the heart. Throughout the decade several members of the organization participated in human sacrifices. Accounts of these senseless killings are occasionally still heard.

One such case was the infamous "Zebra Killings" in San Francisco during late 1973 and early 1974. According to court documents, the four murderers argued that they had followed the lessons of the Lost Found Nation of Islam. The butchers, who had decapitated fifteen San Francisco residents and permanently injured twelve others, stated that the killings were acts of religious obedience; the deaths of the white victims did not result from personal or vengeful motives but from the actions of deeply religious and spiritual men.[23]

The Zebra Killings, dubbed so by San Francisco police because of the interracial connection, took place during a period of 179 days, when a group of four black men decided to wage war with white Americans. The small band stated that they were members of an elite force within the Black Muslims called the Death Angels. According to members of this force, the Death Angels were financed by the Nation of Islam and had a brotherhood of two thousand people throughout the nation.

The case was solved when Anthony C. Harris, a police informer, testified to a grand jury that for promotion Death Angel members took photographs of their victims and that members received special commendation for mutilation. In addition, he identified the leaders of the California unit of the Death Angels, who ultimately were sentenced to life in prison for the murders of Manuel Moore, J. C. Simon, Larry C. Green, and Jessie Lee Cooks. Harris also stated that ring leaders were members of San Francisco's Muslim Temple Number Twenty-Six and were employees with the Nation of Islam's black self-help company, a moving and storage enterprise. Grand jury testimony also exposed that the local minister of Islam hired attorneys for the convicted men. Mayor Olioto and several investigators contend that the Death Angel squad is connected to eighty unsolved murders that took place between 1973 and 1974.[24]

Another interesting murder case with alleged Black Muslim connections was the Hanafi incident of January 17, 1973. The Hanafi Muslim organization was led by Hamas Abdul Khaalis (aka Ernest T. 2X McGhee). Khaalis, a former national secretary in the Nation of Islam, left in 1958 after Malcolm X demoted him. He then created the Hanafi movement.

The sect remained obscure until the early 1970s, when basketball star Lew Alcindor joined the group and changed his name to Kareem Abdul-Jabbar. At this time Khaalis pushed the movement to an aggressive posture when he sent a three-page letter to Nation of Islam ministers denouncing Elijah Muhammad and Fard Muhammad as false prophets.

On January 17, 1973, several members of the Nation of Islam decided to respond to Khaalis's accusations. The Black Muslim hit squad headed for Khaalis's home in Washington, D.C. On January 18 the Muslims entered Khaalis's home intending to murder the rival Muslim leader. However, Khaalis was out of town. The Black Muslims, nonetheless, continued on the warpath. They assaulted Khaalis's twenty-five-year-old daughter, Almena, and murdered her twenty-three-year-old brother, David, ten-year-old brother, Rahman, Abdur Nur (a teenage member of the Hanafi sect), and several small children.

Evidence at the crime scene led to Philadelphia's Muhammad Mosque Number Twelve. Ultimately, investigation pointed to James X Price of Philadelphia, a suspect in another homicide. In June 1973 Price confessed to the crimes and turned state's witness. His statements led to the arrest of the other assassins.

Strangely, the day before Price was to testify he was found hanged in his cell. Coincidentally, Louis Farrakhan delivered a forceful radio sermon concerning the murders and the Hanafi. Apparently Price committed suicide after hearing Farrakhan's address. Minister Farrakhan stated:

> Let this be a warning to those of you who would be used as an instrument of a wicked government against our rise. Be careful, because when the government is tired of you they're going to dump you back into the laps of your people.
>
> And though Elijah Muhammad is a merciful man and will say, "Come in," and forgive you, yet in the ranks of the black people today there are younger men and women who have not forgiveness in them for traitors and stool pigeons.
>
> And they will execute you, as soon as your identity is known.[25]

Unlike the Zebra and Hanafi cases, no clear legal connection was ever made between the 1932 killings and the Nation of Islam; however, it was apparent that Master Fard Muhammad's teachings influenced Karriem.

It was also clear, according to police records in California, Michigan, and Illinois, that Fard Muhammad had a criminal record.[26]

In 1943 the Federal Bureau of Investigation remarked that "Allah . . . has [an] arrest record in the Identification Division."[27] In a more serious vein the FBI found that Fard had spent time in San Quentin Prison for selling narcotics and had been in prisons in several midwestern states for fraud and theft. The FBI was so sure that the man they knew as nos. 56062, 1797294, and 16448F in California and as no. 98076 in Michigan was Fard Muhammad that they publicized his description and elements of his character. The bureau released that Fard had a dark [European] complexion, a good build, and beautiful and even teeth. The reports also listed Fard as a good scam artist with a bad temper.[28] In 1918 Fard allegedly operated a restaurant in Los Angeles known as Walley's Lounge; the name used to incorporate the enterprise was Wallace D. Ford [Fard]. On November 17, 1918, Mr. Ford demanded a deposit of $2.00 from a customer named R. W. Gilabrand before serving him the steak dinner he had ordered. Gilabrand, according to witnesses, defied Ford's demands. Ford responded by pulling a gun from beneath the counter, chasing the customer out of the building, and beating him into a bloody mess. Interestingly, no charges were filed against Ford. Ford also showed talents for selling drugs, bootlegging, and consorting with women. In January 1926 Ford was arrested for selling illegal beer to an undercover policeman. In the same year he was charged with transporting with the intent to sell and distribute drugs, and in 1929 he was found to have a common-law wife rearing his illegitimate son. However, the worst item listed under Ford's long record is his ethnic identification. Whenever Ford was arrested and booked, he described himself as a *white* man born in New Zealand.[29] Nonetheless, devotees of Fard Muhammad, like the young Elijah Poole, ignored all negative allegations against Mr. Ford. To Elijah he was God.

Elijah Muhammad taught that Fard Muhammad chose to suffer the abuse of whites by allowing himself to be placed in the white jails. Fard, according to his disciple Elijah suffered "three and one-half years to show his love for his people who suffered over 300 years at the hands of a people who by nature are evil, wicked, and have no good in them."[30] Elijah also maintained that each time Fard Muhammad was arrested he called for Elijah so that he "may see and learn the price of truth for us (the so-called Negroes)."[31] Because of the truth that Fard was teaching, he was forced to leave Detroit on May 26, 1933. Elijah preached that the enemies of Allah, the devils and hypocrites, were out to kill Master Fard Muhammad. However, according to the FBI, Fard left Detroit because of a power struggle that brewed in the Temple of Islam.

In 1932 Fard was arrested and imprisoned for the sacrificial death of John J. Smith. He was released but forced to leave Detroit. In 1933 Fard resurfaced in Chicago, where again he was arrested and imprisoned for various charges. Elijah Muhammad, a devout follower, offered Fard refuge in his home in Chicago. In early 1934 Fard Muhammad disappeared for the last time.

The official line of the Nation is that he left for Mecca. However, several members of the early Nation argued that he was befriended by individuals such as his student Elijah Muhammad and a former minister named Augustus Muhammad. These individuals suggest that Elijah ousted his teacher to become the new leader. Older insiders also suggest that Augustus constantly challenged Fard's ideals, ultimately believing that he was a better leader than Fard Muhammad. Augustus, holding this view, created a rival Muslim organization in 1933 called Development of our Own.[32]

Elijah Muhammad argued in defense of Fard that the FBI's files on the Messiah were wrong. The description of the man called Fard did not fit the real image of his Savior. Elijah warned Muslims not to allow "the devils to trick you into believing their false propaganda which are [sic] spreading all over the world."[33] Adhering to the theology of the Nation of Islam, Elijah Muhammad maintained that whites and the government of the United States would utilize a variety of lies to destroy the work of Allah and his Nation.[34] At the 1981 Savior's Day Convention Louis Farrakhan used the same logic to attack the U.S. government. He stated that the government and the media branded the Nation of Islam a group of thugs and criminals. But the real thugs are officials of the federal government who adhere to violence to serve the needs of the bureaucracy, especially against their own people.[35] However, former leaders of the Nation of Islam such as Malcolm X and Imam Warith Deen Muhammad viciously argued that the Nation was rooted in violent behavior toward its membership. The two advocates branded the Nation as a criminal organization that practiced intimidation against its own membership in an attempt to demand internal obedience and subjugation.

Malcolm X, the national minister and spokesman for Elijah Muhammad and the Nation of Islam between 1957 and 1963, was suspended from his position on December 1, 1963, when he referred to the assassination of President John F. Kennedy as a case of "chickens coming home to roost."[36] He strongly implied that Kennedy's administration followed the path of the United States in spreading global violence and murdering world leaders who did not align themselves with the political doctrines of America.[37] After three months Malcolm began to question Elijah Muhammad's motivation for his banishment and isolation as a minister. He concluded that the Messenger was fearful of his rising popularity and the knowledge of Elijah's infidelity in fathering several children from teenage girls. His questions caused Malcolm to be targeted by many Muslim leaders as a hypocrite, a term that in the Nation is equated with death. In response Malcolm publicly announced that Muhammad and his men had attacked, beaten, and even killed members who were viewed as rebellious to the group. For instance, in 1962 Elijah Muhammad Jr. warned Muslims in Boston of recalcitrant members. He stated that "recalcitrant brothers [would] be killed" if they defied the Nation.[38] Also in 1964 Barnette X, the secretary of Boston's Muslim Temple, was beaten severely by members of the Fruit of Islam, the Nation's paramilitary, when he told Minister Farrakhan that he planned to leave the Nation and to tell what he knew of attempts on Malcolm's life. Months before the beating, Farrakhan castigated Barnette as a hypocrite and "bourgeois Negro."[39] Malcolm would eventually claim that the Nation was out to kill him and his family. On February 13, 1964, when his home was bombed, he quickly lashed out at the Muslims, saying, "My house was bombed by the Black Muslim movement on the orders of Elijah Muhammad."[40] As this was going on, Malcolm's former student, Louis X, currently known as Louis Farrakhan, delivered lectures that called for the death of his mentor. In authored articles in the newspaper *Muhammad Speaks*, Farrakhan stated that "Malcolm's head should be cut off . . . his tongue should be pulled out of his mouth and mailed to Mr. Muhammad."[41] On February 9, 1964, Malcolm X was brutally murdered by Thomas 15X Johnson, Norman 3X Butler, and Talmadge X Hayer, all members of the Nation of Islam.

Warith Deen Muhammad, son of Elijah Muhammad and friend of Malcolm X, maintained that the Nation was riddled with internal violence. In 1975, when the Honorable Elijah Muhammad died, Warith, the highest ranking Muslim in the patriarch's family, was crowned the new leader of the Nation of Islam. Supported by the leadership of the organization, including Louis Farrakhan, Supreme Minister Warith radically restructured the group. One of the first items of change was the infamous Fruit of Islam, the paramilitary unit of the Muslims. Warith maintained that during the previous fifteen years the FOI had displayed ruthless behavior to enforce the Nation's business and rules. The function of the religion of Islam, argued Warith, was to lift up fallen humanity and not to assault and destroy people.[42] In later years Louis Farrakhan, Warith's chief rival, would enact policies to curb the use of terror and violence in the new Nation of Islam. These changes would come after his meeting with the new Christ and Mahdi of the Nation of Islam.

3

Malcolm

Mentor, Rival, Enemy

The Nation of Islam produced three of the greatest twentieth-century African American nationalist religious leaders: Master Fard Muhammad, Elijah Muhammad, and Malcolm X. These race advocates laid the foundation for the Nation of Islam, a unique organization that combined social-religious programs that incorporated spirituality, conservative political ideologies, economic empowerment, and social uplift of the race. Their race activism caught the imagination of millions of black Americans who dedicated themselves to the ideology that formed the Black Muslims. Louis Farrakhan, a follower and disciple of all three men, aspired to be like them. From the first day that Farrakhan joined the Nation in 1957, he set out to emulate the mentors, and eventually he became the leader of the Nation of Islam. However, the person that provided the greatest stepping stone for Louis Farrakhan was his onetime friend Malcolm X.

Farrakhan's rise to the top began in Chicago in 1957. Louis Walcott, as Farrakhan was known in those days, was a stylish, colorful, and talented musician (a skilled violinist, guitarist, and singer) and actor. At a very young age he was performing in clubs, dance halls, and amateur-hour television shows. By 1957 he was headlining such award winning shows as the "Calypso Follies," which played New York City, Philadelphia, Detroit, and Chicago. Nicknamed the Charmer, but also called Calypso Gene, young Louis saw himself as a future superstar or, as he often remarked, another Harry Belafonte. According to some observers, if he had continued with his entertainment career he would have surpassed the West Indian performer.[1] However, Louis's career would come to an abrupt end in August 1957.

During an entertainment job in Chicago, Louis and Betsy, his wife of one year, were invited to attend a Black Muslim Savior's Day celebration by long-time friend, Rodney Smith. Smith had grown up in Boston with

Louis, who was a new convert to the Nation of Islam. Louis, not really knowing anything about the Black Muslims, was a little intimidated because he heard that the Muslims were extremely militant and strict. According to young Louis, their views on race relationships were intimidating, as were their views on drugs and alcohol. As an entertainer, he was surrounded and influenced by the drug culture. One of Louis's occasional habits was smoking marijuana. He once stated that carrying a marijuana joint on his body was not uncommon. In fact, this was one reason he was hesitant about attending Muslim meetings because "the Muslims frisked at the door."[2] Louis's concern about the search process was well founded. When he and Betsy reached the Savior's Day celebration, the guards discovered a marijuana cigarette in the brim of his hat.[3] Reluctantly, Louis threw away the joint. Once inside, he became impressed with the manner and language of the Muslims. Louis recalled, "They were clean, but strong. They spoke with strength."[4] But the real prize for Louis came when the patriarch of the movement, Elijah Muhammad, delivered the main address.

The Honorable Elijah Muhammad delivered a lecture that focused on the founder of the movement, Master Fard Muhammad, and the need for African Americans to "accept their own and be themselves."[5] The frail senior citizen explored several reasons why African Americans are considered inferior to whites, Asians, and Arabs. He argued that the real inferior beings are white people, the devil.[6] Louis, sitting in the balcony, enjoyed Muhammad's message but often was distracted by Muhammad's southern dialect and grammatical errors. At one point during the presentation, Louis remarked to his wife that Elijah "could not speak."[7] As Louis uttered those words, Elijah suddenly looked at Louis and said, "Brother, don't pay attention to how I speak. Pay attention to what I'm saying. I didn't get the chance to go to the White man's fine schools, because when I tried to go, the doors were closed. But if you take what I say and place it into the beautiful way of speaking you know, you can help me save our people."[8] When Louis heard the Messenger's words, he became frightened. He indeed thought the elder statesman had read his mind. However, unknown to him the Messenger had been briefed about Louis's attendance by Malcolm X.[9] At the conclusion of Muhammad's sermon, Betsy and Louis joined the Black Muslims. However, it was not until several months later, when Louis met the Boston Muslim minister Malcolm X, that he decided to devote his life and work to the Nation.

In the 1950s and early 1960s Malcolm X was the Nation's leading minister. After his release from the Charleston Massachusetts Correctional Center, where he served time for burglary, Malcolm Little went to Detroit to formally join Elijah Muhammad's Black Muslim organization. Under the care of his brother, Wilfred, who had joined the Nation years earlier, Malcolm attended Detroit's Muhammad Temple Number One, the first temple that Fard Muhammad had established to promote Islam among black Americans. The former convict was impressed by the dedication and passion that the Detroit Muslims held for the teachings of Fard and Elijah Muhammad.[10] According to Malcolm, the Muslims created an atmosphere of respect, beauty, and love, elements not often present in African American organizations. During his tenure in Detroit Malcolm labored as an assistant to Minister Lemuel Hassan, one of the leading pastors in the Nation. Hassan, who had joined the movement in the early 1940s, was ordered by Muhammad to personally train Malcolm. Within one year after his release from prison Malcolm had become Hassan's assistant minister. During his tenure as an assistant minister Malcolm openly proclaimed Hassan's greatness as an accomplished, organized minister. However, like Louis X Walcott, who joined the Nation during another period, Malcolm's real ambition was to become a significant power broker within the Nation. In fact, Malcolm told his friend and confidant Johnny Davis Jr., "I expect to become Elijah Muhammad's lead minister shortly."[11]

Minister Hassan sensed that the young assistant minister had greater ambitions; however, he was unwilling and unable to communicate his fears to Elijah Muhammad. Instead, he recommended that Malcolm be transferred to the East Coast to build the growing but struggling Nation of Islam. Elijah responded by sending Malcolm to Boston.

Back to the city where he had worked as a professional criminal, Malcolm immediately sought out former buddies to help him build a mosque for Muhammad in Boston. Within five months of his arrival in Bean Town, he had enough followers to open a small storefront temple. As an Islamic leader, Malcolm's personal routine was uncompromising. For example, his dietary regimen rigidly followed Elijah's laws; he ate only one meal a day, fasted several times during the month, and did not chew gum or eat snacks between meals. His views on entertainment, women, and general sporting activities had also changed from the days when he was a thief, pimp, and dope user. He refused to go to dances and parties, frowned on sporting events as activities only for the enjoyment of whites, and perceived women as liars who used their bodies to exploit men of leadership. His views were fixed and extreme. Nonetheless, he expected all Muslims, especially in Boston, to adhere to his views. Malcolm's uniqueness made him an exotic and strange figure among people in the black community. However, it was Malcolm's social, political, and religious language that caused the greatest stir.

Malcolm's position as the minister of the Boston temple was only a small segment of his activities. His overall duties were to travel throughout the Northeast as a Muslim organizer. At this time the Northeast and Atlantic regions of the Nation of Islam had fewer than a thousand members.[12] Thus, Malcolm spent the majority of his time traveling; however, on one of the few times he spent in Boston he met an up-and-coming young entertainer named Louis Walcott. Louis Walcott (Farrakhan), recalling his first meeting with Malcolm, said,

> It was outside a night club that I had been performing in. Someone said, "There's Malcolm X, let's meet him, come on Louis." I was a little nervous, they said that man really spoke bad about White folk, calling them devils and such. I personally did not really care for White people, but I did not speak like that Muslim man. So, I went over to meet him. All I could see was this tall man, who wore a brown suit, brown shoes, brown hat, and brown gloves. I shook his hands very gingerly, then I got the hell away from him.[13]

Shortly after this meeting Louis found his way to Malcolm's Boston temple.

Louis X enjoyed listening to and learning from the older and wiser Malcolm. In fact, he thought of Malcolm as an older brother. However, the former-con-turned-minister would not remain in Boston much longer. Elijah Muhammad, with no advance notice, transferred him to New York City, leaving Louis in Boston. Unknown to the young Louis at the time, the senior Muslim's move to New York City would open up a career path in the Nation that he could not refuse.

Under the tutelage of Malcolm, Louis X became a valuable and dedicated student. After Louis's first few months in the Nation, Malcolm recommended him to the Messenger for the position of minister. Elijah Muhammad rejected the recommendation, however, scolding Malcolm and telling him to examine Louis's work as a follower. He then appointed Louis captain over the Boston branch of the Fruit of Islam, the paramilitary unit of the organization. As captain he was responsible for training male members of the Nation. Primarily, Louis taught the men how to introduce Islam to the black community. After Louis's brief tenure Muhammad promoted him from captain to minister of the Boston mosque.

Louis X took over a mosque that was small and politically weak in the organization. Even though Malcolm X had been its minister, it lacked the strength it needed in a major city like Boston. Chicago's Mosque Number Two, where Muhammad lived, had 600 members; New York, just before Malcolm's ministry, numbered only 350 members; and Boston had fewer than 100 registered Muslims. Louis concluded that Boston's numbers were entirely too low, and in a few short months he changed the small numbers and image of the Muslims.

Louis X's promotion brought many changes. With savvy, creativity, and sheer intelligence, he ultimately restructured not only his Boston temple but the entire Nation of Islam. Minister Louis, coming out of the Episcopalian denomination, was unaccustomed to storefront churches with dingy interiors and small audiences. Therefore, his first assignment to the believers was to find a legitimate religious venue. The young leader realized that African Americans are not willing to join new religious groups to attend locations that look poor and dilapidated. If he was to succeed, the Muslims needed an attractive venue for their religious activities. After several weeks of searching, one of the members of the temple located an orthodox rabbinical seminary for sale in Roxbury, ultimately the black section of Boston. Louis, ever cunning, told the Jewish leader that he was a Christian minister who needed a larger church for his growing congregation. If Minister Louis had said that a structure was needed for Muslims, the Jewish congregation most likely would not have sold the edifice to his group.[14]

The Muslim mosque, located on Interval Avenue, quickly became one of the flagship temples in the Nation; however, more work had to be done. Next on Louis's list was recruiting members. Unlike Malcolm, who recruited new members by distributing handbills and speaking on street corners as a "soapbox" orator, Louis used a simpler and more direct approach. Louis went to his former priest, the Reverend Nathan Wright of St. Cyprian's Episcopal Church, and told him that he had followed Wright's lead into the clergy. Speaking about the importance of God and religion, he tactfully asked Wright for assistance in recruitment and material items. Wright, a civil rights advocate of the 1950s, gave

Louis fifty chairs and a list of twenty-five men he had been unable to reach through the gospel of Christianity. Wright later boasted to Farrakhan's biographer, Arthur Magida, that "I gave him the first 25 members of his temple."[15]

The twenty-five-man gift that the Reverend Mr. Wright gave to Minister Louis X blossomed into a membership of two hundred in less than a year.[16] Malcolm X, now the minister in New York City, remarked about the amazing growth of the Muslims in Boston.[17] The temple soon became a permanent fixture in black Boston with its weekly meetings on Sunday, Monday, Wednesday, Friday, and Saturday evenings. The lectures that Louis X delivered were far from militant, except for references to the white race as "wickedly great and children of the devil."[18] On most occasions Louis X spoke on the conservative ideas of thrift, honesty, race solidarity, discipline, monogamy, black history, and Third World political issues. Boston, the home of several renowned universities such as Harvard University, Boston University, and Boston College, to name a few, was a haven for recruitment of NOI members. Benefiting greatly from this intellectual community, Louis, more than any other minister, attracted a great number of educated African Americans. Blacks who attended the Boston mosque were not just the typical pimp, prostitute, and hustler but were high school–educated and college-trained African Americans interested in Islam.

As a young minister and a college dropout, Louis X became quite intimidated with the influx of university-educated people. On more than one occasion Minister Louis X delivered steaming lectures that characterized these individuals as "toms and dogs" for white people and suggested that they were agents of the FBI, CIA, or IRS. Years later Farrakhan remarked how young and foolish he had been to "run people out of the temple."[19] He admitted that he became so depressed by his blatant misuse of power and his lack of clear reasoning in reference to his more educated audience that he asked the Messenger to remove him from the position of minister. The Messenger responded by allowing the abused members to rejoin the Nation of Islam but never dismissed or reprimanded Louis X for his actions. Most offended believers returned. However, there were a few like Brother Henry, who stopped going to the temple completely. Henry, who was assaulted by Fruit of Islam members because they viewed him as a spy, stated that the ignorance that was displayed was "not about Islam but about niggers."[20] Even so, Henry later used his Harvard law degree to represent the Nation as a client on issues of international trade. Minister Farrakhan admitted years later that he had been wrong to allow Henry's assault; however, his behavior toward the professional class would surface again in the 1980s and 1990s.

Minister Louis X's work in the Boston area continued at an alarming rate. The minister had the fastest growing temple in the Nation. Like Malcolm, Louis X used style, charisma, and oratory to attract people to the organization. By the late 1950s he would add music and theatrics as recruiting strategies. The Charmer, as Louis was called as a performer, created a calypso-style ballet entitled "White Man's Heaven Is a Black Man's Hell."[21] During the same period Louis wrote and produced the militant plays *Orgena: A Negro Spelled Backwards*, and *The Trial*. *Orgena* satirizes black Americans as dope addicts and ignorant Christian preachers and the professional class as uneducated, flashily dressed Uncle Toms. *The Trial* tells a tale of white hostilities and brutality against the black race. Near the end of the play the teachings of Fard Muhammad and Elijah Muhammad restore dignity and strength to African Americans. Also at the end of the play the white race is found guilty of several crimes against the humanity of blacks and is sentenced to death by an all-black jury.[22]

As Louis extended his influence through his creative genius, he also continued to watch and to emulate Malcolm X. By the late 1950s Malcolm was the premier minister in the Nation and the national spokesperson for Muhammad. Although Louis was gaining popularity within the structure of the organization, Malcolm had achieved fame outside the Nation. In 1959 Mike Wallace and Louis Lomax created a television documentary on the organization titled "The Hate That Hate Produced." The program exhibited the Nation to the larger white American community for the first time. The white population saw a defiant, militant, and antiwhite religious organization of blacks who believed in total racial segregation. The Nation's doctrine to white Americans and many blacks was quite interesting and disturbing. Because of the high profile civil rights movement that called for social and political integration, as illustrated in *Brown v. Board of Education of Topeka, Kansas* (1954), which declared segregation unconstitutional, the Nation appeared out of touch with the mood of most African Americans.[23] The Nation of Islam in the 1950s represented only a small fraction of the black community who favored separation over integration. Louis Farrakhan's Nation of the

1980s and 1990s would also run contrary to black mainstream thought. Farrakhan's view that there was an elaborate conspiracy by Jews and the United States government to destroy black Americans incited a minority of bullish, college-aged black nationalists to adopt the rhetoric of the Muslim leader.

4

Personal Testimony

Thus far I have given an academic review of the history of the Nation of Islam. The first forty-four years of the movement laid the foundation for Louis Farrakhan's Black Muslim organization. In 1977 Farrakhan utilized the storied histories of Fard Muhammad, Elijah Muhammad, and Malcolm X to forge a tale that encouraged thousands of young African Americans, including myself, to join the Nation of Islam under his direction.

My first relationship with the Black Muslims started during my adolescent years. My admiration grew during my family's frequent trips to New York City from wherever we happened to be living—Bermuda, Central America, Delaware, or Pennsylvania.

My father, Vibert White, and mother, Lorraine, were missionaries in the African Methodist Episcopal Church. Vibert senior, a brilliant organizer, with his trusted wife, a woman of Haitian parentage and a registered nurse, traveled throughout the Caribbean, Central America, and North America organizing congregations and building churches. They often lived outside New York City, but they frequented the city to attend various church board meetings. During these trips my parents enjoyed visiting two areas in the Big Apple: Chinatown and Harlem. In Chinatown we ate in crowded, noisy eateries that served the best Asian food west of Hong Kong. In Harlem my father especially enjoyed going around 116th Street and Lenox Avenue, where the Muslims congregated.

On our drive uptown to Harlem my father told stories of his immigration to the United States from Costa Rica and of his introduction to Malcolm X and the Muslims, often remarking on the way Malcolm and a young Muslim lady he was seeing at the time attempted to recruit him to teach Islam in Central America. With typical black Central American bravado my father told the Muslims he was too independent to join their organization. He also said that the Muslim brothers watched him closely but that he did not care because he was young, brash, and a good boxer from the barrios of Limon, Costa Rica.

As my father relived these stories the drive toward Harlem became more tense as my mother searched her memories of the Muslims in the early 1950s when she lived in the Bronx, remarking how the brothers always looked good but that the women dressed like maids wearing potato sacks. She did admit, however, that the sisters cooked great meals at their local restaurant. By the time my mother was finished with her story, we were in Harlem on 116th Street. At this juncture both parents smiled as several Muslim brothers surrounded our vehicle bombarding us with questions and statements such as "*Muhammad Speaks* newspaper today? Please support the Honorable Elijah Muhammad! Come listen to Minister Louis Farrakhan, the National Representative of the Nation of Islam and the Honorable Elijah Muhammad."

As if they were shopping for an automobile, clothes, or even a house, my parents would choose which Muslim brother to buy the newspaper *Muhammad Speaks* from. As a young boy in the 1960s, I found this experience tremendously exciting. I especially enjoyed watching these handsome, strong, and well-dressed men darting in and out of traffic to sell their materials. The diligence that they displayed brought forth a sense of pride in myself as a member of the black race. Unfortunately, years later I would find that many of these same brothers who looked as if they enjoyed selling the Nation's papers were being forced to sell them, often having to buy the papers from their own wages if they failed to meet a certain sales quota.

Nevertheless, my early introduction to the Muslims was rewarding. The image that they presented impressed me greatly. Silently, I wanted to learn more about this Harlem group. However, it would not be until the mid-1970s that an opportunity would allow me a closer look at the Nation of Islam.

In 1974 my father was transferred from the AME church that he had pastored in Reading, Pennsylvania, to Bradenton, Florida, where he became the minister of the denomination's mission church in the neighboring village of Palmetto. Our move to the Deep South did not initially give me much time to think about the Muslims. I was more concerned with lifestyle transformations. Moving from the urban North to the rural South was a tremendous change. In Reading I left the traditional and familiar surroundings of a black West Indian culture that comprised

Puerto Ricans, Haitians, Jamaicans, Costa Ricans, and Panamanians. I also left the security of living in an urban setting that followed a sense of order. This included bus routes, playground basketball leagues, and neighborhood rivalries of various sorts. Now I was placed in the American bush, where blacks spoke broken English or "geechee" and loved eating fried eggplants, greens, and chitterlings.

In the midst of this foreign land I was enrolled into Bradenton's Southeast High School, an institution known for its strong academic programs and its excellent basketball, track, and football teams. But because the school was located on the far southeast side of town amid farms and orange orchards, it was affectionately called the "cattle field." At the school I did not associate with Muslims or read any of their materials but I excelled in academics and track. When I graduated, I was awarded a partial academic and track scholarship to Bethune-Cookman College (BCC) in Daytona Beach, Florida. It was at BCC that I embraced fully the doctrine of the Nation of Islam. However, before my arrival in Daytona Beach I had a brief and positive encounter with members of the Nation in the Tampa Bay area.

During my late teens and early twenties I had become a very strong competitor in semicontact and full-contact karate. Starting my training in Reading, Pennsylvania, under the watchful eyes of Master George Dillman, a white karateka who briefly trained heavyweight boxing champion Muhammad Ali for his famous fight against a Japanese heavyweight champion shoot fighter and wrestler, I learned the fundamentals of martial arts. I also studied with a young white teacher who led classes at the Reading Police Athletic League (PAL). Different from Dillman, who was in his late thirties, conservative, and a well-known personality, Sensei John, the instructor at PAL, was a long-haired peace activist who enjoyed physical combat. He always entertained visiting guests with a five-minute bout of hard sparring. Later I continued my training in southwestern Florida with Bradenton's most feared black karate fighter, Master Charles "Cowpoke" Spencer. Spencer practiced an open-styled nontraditional fighting system that combined karate, judo, boxing, jailhouse rock combat, and black ghetto fighting. Master Spencer was always considered a little crazy. On occasion he would take one of his best students into a bar, or some other sleazy joint, to fight the tavern's bully. It is only by the grace of God that his students were not killed by irate street fighters. Nonetheless, under Spencer I became a regionally ranked lightweight/middleweight fighter. In May 1976 I had the pleasure of meeting a black Muslim competitor at the National Invitational Karate Competition in St. Petersburg, Florida.

The tournament brought together America's best fighters and instructors. Individuals like Joe Corbett, Jay T. Will, Bill Wallace, Thomas LaPuppet, Moses Powell, Chuck Norris, and George Dillman attended. However, the most impressive personality that I met was a fighter by the name of Sam Savage. Mr. Savage, or "Sensei" (teacher), as his students called him, was a cool, smooth fighter in his early twenties. If there was a Muhammad Ali of the martial arts, it was Savage, not Bruce Lee. He had an uncanny ability to slip punches and kicks by fractions of inches. Sometimes it seemed he had a special radar. His quickness and timing were unprecedented. A natural fighter, he slid into opponents while cracking reverse punches and roundhouse kicks to the face before his opponent could muster a counterattack. But the greatest draw to Savage was that he was a Muslim under the leadership of Elijah Muhammad. Unfortunately, I did not have the opportunity at this stage to fight or talk to Mr. Savage. Both of us were beaten in controversial decisions in semifinal bouts. Savage was disqualified for excess force in a semicontact match. I lost on points to a less-talented but very popular fighter.

Weeks later I would begin to see Mr. Savage in several quarters in black St. Petersburg selling *Muhammad Speaks* newspapers, the *Balalian News*, (the renamed *Muhammad Speaks* newspaper), and his own patented hair pomade called "Brother John's." Like the brothers I saw years earlier in New York City, Brother Savage had a wonderful way of sliding through traffic to sell his materials. When he was not selling papers, Brother Savage was running and training. Although I never spoke with him, this young man represented the strong black male image of the Nation. He was strictly about business, making money, keeping in shape, and promulgating the religion of the Nation of Islam. Even though Savage and I were fighters of equal ability, he probably would have defeated me at this stage in a martial arts bout. The edge would have been his divine commitment to Allah, Elijah Muhammad, and the Nation of Islam. Every time Savage fought, he performed with a zeal as if to prove that black Muslims were superior in all aspects of life, including fighting. Later that summer I went to Bethune-Cookman College, never to hear or see Brother Sam X Savage again.

At Bethune-Cookman College I came in contact with several types of

Muslims. Most of the Islamic students came from the urban Northeast; only a token few came from the Middle East. The Muslims identified themselves as members of the Five Percenters, an offshoot of the Nation of Islam; the Moorish Science Temple Movement, followers of Noble Drew Ali; the Ansura Allah Community, a splinter group of the Moorish Science Movement; the Balalians, followers of Wallace Muhammad, the son of Elijah Muhammad; the Hannifa Islamic Movement; members of the orthodox branches of Islam, the Sunni, Shiite, and the Tijannies of West Africa; and, of course, members of the Nation of Islam. Although BCC branded itself a conservative United Methodist private college, it apparently housed enough Muslims to be called the "little Mecca of the South."

My first intimate connection with Islam came through three fellow students from the metropolitan New York area. The first gentleman was a diligent, polite, but militant black nationalist student named Daniel. Daniel was from Newark, New Jersey. This young man was good looking and an outstanding football player who had won a scholarship to play on BCC's football team. But after one year Daniel transferred to the University of Delaware. A history major (like me), Daniel had a penchant for ancient African history. Through reading the works of Anta Diop and Chancellor Williams, he dreamed of the return of the ancient greatness of the African race. Daniel believed that this could only come about through the teachings of Elijah Muhammad. Daniel never missed a Sunday mosque or temple meeting. Every Sunday morning at 7:30 he would go to the mosque for military or manhood training and stay for the afternoon service. During this time Daniel would pass out flyers, inviting individuals to attend the Muslim services and sell the movement's papers. I admired his conviction, but I could not understand why he had to sell a hundred newspapers a week. On several occasions I argued about his commitment to selling Muslim newspapers and bean pies instead of completing his academic assignments, book reviews, and term papers. Politely he always responded that "Allah is God and Muhammad is his messenger" and that "the Quran is the best book to study."

Another college Muslim was a tall, lanky, bald, dark-skinned basketball player we called Jersey. Whereas Daniel was a mild and devoted religious follower, Jersey was brash, arrogant, and a militant race advocate. In short, this young man represented every concern and fear that Christians had about Islamic devotees. Jersey turned every discussion

as a student leader. I was president of the Lerone Bennett Historical Society, vice president of Phi Beta Sigma, a member of the track team, a karate team player, and an honor roll student. Although I showed displeasure for Farrakhan, I was instructed to present him with a warm BCC welcome address and to sit next to him onstage.

The national representative of the Nation of Islam and Elijah Muhammad gave a brilliant and stirring address on the plight of the black community in the United States. The standing-room-only crowd was mesmerized by the Muslim orator for over two and one-half hours. However, there were a few people who were not impressed by his words—the college administration and myself, although for totally different reasons. President Bronson, the chief administrator of BCC, did not like the Black Islamic presentation, which he thought went against the traditional religious ideology of the school. In addition, he believed that Farrakhan's lecture could cause the school to lose potential donations from white corporations and philanthropic organizations. On the other hand, I had started to flirt with communist thought, literature, and organizations, so after the mosque closed I joined the Marxist-Leninist party of America. My political outlook, therefore, was not just on race but also on class and caste systems. With an ideology different from Farrakhan's, together with my concerns about the breakup of the movement, I was not impressed with his lecture. However, the question and answer period that engaged Farrakhan with the student body after the lecture became the spark that propelled me toward the Nation of Islam.

When the lecture was over, scores of students huddled around Farrakhan like flies around unprotected food. The minister fielded questions of every sort from inquisitive and unread students. Many questions such as "What is a Muslim? What do Muslims eat? Can a Muslim man have more than one wife?" could have been researched with a minimum of exertion at the campus library. Then it was my turn to ask a question, "Minister Farrakhan, what's the big issue with you and Wallace Muhammad?" My question, or statement, seemed to cut through Farrakhan and the crowd like a cold steel knife through an unsuspecting warm body. In an angry tone he replied with the following statement: "Yes, we have problems; but don't you or anyone else get involved with our issue. This is a damn Muslim affair—leave it alone!"[1]

The minister's response caught me by surprise. On campus I was viewed as the aggressive, astute, and radical political theorist. Normally, I was able to talk down or even intimidate certain speakers, but not Farrakhan. The minister's reaction was so strong and straightforward that he scared me. I felt like a wounded dog with my tail between my legs. Although I had been put in my place by Farrakhan, I now felt a certain amount of respect for him. If a man could speak to me in that manner, perhaps he was worth following. From this point on I made it my business to attend any Farrakhan lecture in Florida; for the next two years I did so. With several of my peers I followed the touring speaker to such cities as Miami, Jacksonville, Orlando, Tampa, Sarasota, and Atlanta.

Farrakhan's activities at BCC were quite successful. For the next two years students talked about the Muslim, read articles about him, and became concerned about civil and human rights issues. Unfortunately, Professor Cosby, who was responsible for the Farrakhan lecture, was released by the college. As a member of the Nation, the young, militant, and outspoken professor did not fit into the future plans of Bethune-Cookman College.

In my remaining years at the college I continued to read books authored by Elijah Muhammad and other Muslim authors, while also conforming my lifestyle to NOI dictates. For example, bow ties and dark suits became my standard dress, and referring to all blacks as brothers or sisters, referring to whites as devils, and addressing Muslims in the Arabic language of As-Salaam-Alaikum became my calling cards. However, it would not be until my graduate school years that I formally became a member of the Nation of Islam.

In 1980 I graduated from Bethune-Cookman College cum laude as a history major. Because of my outstanding undergraduate academic record and excellent scores on the graduate record examination, I was recruited by several prestigious graduate schools in the United States, including the University of Florida, Duke, Vanderbilt, Ohio State, and Purdue. Ultimately, I decided on Purdue University in West Lafayette, Indiana.

Bethune-Cookman College and Purdue University were as different as day and night. BCC was a small, black, religious school located in one of the major vacation areas in the world. Purdue, was a major research university with over thirty-eight thousand, primarily white, students, located in a small rural town in northwest Indiana. The size of the school, its academic reputation, and its classification as a Big Ten institution filled me with pride and fear. I constantly asked myself during the first few weeks in West Lafayette, "What am I doing here? Can I succeed academically at Purdue?"

Shortly after enrolling in history classes, I found that my work was competitive with my fellow classmates from Brown, Notre Dame, Harvard, and several other major universities in the United States. I remember remarking to another black graduate student in the American history program that either I was as smart as everyone else, or they were as dumb as me. But the real reason I did so well was because of two outstanding professors who nurtured me—Professor Harold Woodman and Professor Darlene Clarke-Hine.

At the time that I met Dr. Woodman I was under the influence of the Nation of Islam. I thought that the Nation and, in particular, Louis Farrakhan were the answer to all the world's problems, at least the ills of the black community. Woodman was a scholar of southern history and an expert on race relations, but more important, he was a civil rights activist and liberal who considered himself an urban Jewish intellectual. Professor Woodman, always kind and helpful, talked to me for hours about living in the same neighborhood as Elijah Muhammad. While puffing on a pipe, Woodman told wonderful tales of the virtues of the Muslims in 1960s Chicago—how they dressed so neatly and conservatively, the reasons his family occasionally purchased food products from the Nation, and the apparent outstanding work ethic of the Black Muslims. Sometimes Dr. Woodman gave me the feeling that if he were not Jewish, he would have joined the Chicago Muslims. But more significant, Woodman taught me how to separate intellectual inquiry from emotional feelings about the Nation of Islam. Woodman's advice served me well as I started my research on the Black Muslims.

In contrast, Professor Darlene Clarke-Hine was a smooth-talking, somewhat brash black woman from Chicago. Destroying the myth that female scholars are grotesquely fat, disjointed, and masculine, Darlene Clarke-Hine was shapely, with beautiful black hair and shining dark skin that matched her brilliant intellect. Her works on race relations, the U.S. Constitution, and black nurses illustrated a passion for honest ethnic scholarship and a concern for the struggling underclass. However, her greatest academic gift was her ability to understand and play university politics—the publishing, promotion, and tenure game. In the mid-1980s she was the fastest rising star among black intellectuals.

At Purdue Clarke-Hine guided my passion for the Nation with sensitivity and steered me toward precise academic research. She never allowed my research to be dictated by emotion or polemics. As I look back, this must have been a tough task for her. I was then a candidate for my master's degree and had become engrossed with the imagery of the Nation as the vanguard group for the black community. Clarke-Hine's struggle to have me develop a normal attitude toward the Nation intensified during an off-campus evening event. During the spring break Professor Clarke-Hine and her husband, a mathematics professor, held a party in their small but cozy apartment. In the midst of the dancing, drinking, eating, and general good time, I put one of Farrakhan's records on the stereo. The song that I expected people to dance to was the minister's hit single among the Muslims, "White Man's Heaven Is a Black Man's Hell." Professor Clarke-Hine, at her limit with my Black Islamic lifestyle, emotionally responded, "Not that Muslim stuff again. We're having a party!" A little embarrassed, I took the album off the machine. Years later I would react to several of my Muslim students in the same way.

Although Professors Woodman and Clarke-Hine directed my young academic career at Purdue, I still managed to become attached to the underclass, militant movement of the Nation of Islam. In February 1980 I journeyed to Chicago to attend the Nation's annual Savior's Day celebration. This meeting was a three-day event to commemorate the birthday of Master Fard Muhammad and Allah and the work of the Most Honorable Elijah Muhammad. This Savior's Day was special. It was the first celebration of its type since the death of Elijah Muhammad in 1975, and it was Farrakhan's public announcement of the "Rebirth of the Nation of Islam." He used the event at the Conrad Hilton Hotel in Chicago as the platform to tell the black community, "The Nation is back." In addition, in a four-hour lecture he presented a strange thesis implying that the White House, Senate, Congress, Jews, Israel, Arabs, Communists, Uncle Tom Blacks, and the Messenger's family all conspired to murder Elijah Muhammad. But according to Farrakhan, they missed their mark. Even though they injected the Messenger with a serum to cause congestive heart failure, Elijah Muhammad escaped death. Farrakhan said Elijah Muhammad had rejected death because he was indeed the risen Christ and that Elijah was as alive as anyone in the group. As a neophyte believer I jumped up immediately looking for Elijah to walk onto the stage. The lecture was convincing. I left with a renewed dedication to become an activist for Farrakhan's Nation of Islam.

From West Lafayette I journeyed to Indianapolis to join the Nation. After having heard the minister's inspiring words and having seen the five-thousand-member Nation at the convention, I was shocked to find that the Indianapolis Muslims worshiped in a small storefront structure. Nonetheless, I joined the tiny band of Muslims, who registered themselves as Muhammad's Mosque Number Seventy-Four.

Like most Muslim groups outside the main mosque in Chicago, the Indianapolis believers' storefront mosque was located in the heart of the black community. The followers were nonetheless proud of their small building. Years later I learned the reasons why members of Mosque Number Seventy-Four were so proud of their venue; most of the Muslims in the United States met and worshiped in believers' homes.

Finding the Indianapolis Muslims took persistence. First, I drove to the Midwest city with the hope of locating my brothers and sisters. I asked policemen, men in barbershops and bars, and occasionally people walking the streets if they knew the location of Muhammad's Temple of Islam. But to no avail. Everybody knew of the Muslims or Moslems, but no one knew where they met. Often individuals mistakenly directed me to Muslim mosques of other disciplines. For example, there was a large Sunni Muslim population in the city. Thus, I was sent to them. I knew immediately that they were not my Muslims—they had white skin and Arabic accents. Eventually, I had to call the Muslims in Chicago for an Indianapolis contact. They gave me the name and number of Brother J. D. X, the minister of the central city temple.

"Brother Minister J. D.," as he was known, possessed the quiet strength and confidence of the stereotypical Muslim minister. He was a gentleman, never loud, arrogant, or brutish. He always carried himself in a disciplined and mild-mannered way. His stature reminded me of the Honorable Elijah Muhammad, a small, thin man with a large head. Except for his very dark skin, Brother J. D. could have been mistaken as a relative of Muhammad.

When I called J. D. and told him of my trouble finding the mosque, he was embarrassed but reminded me that the Nation was still in its infancy and that many people still did not know that Farrakhan was re-building the organization. However, on my next visit to the city he in-structed his captain and lieutenant to escort me to the mosque.

The two brothers who worked under Minister J. D. X were Captain Joseph, later to become Yusef Muhammad, and Lieutenant David X. Captain Joseph was an old warrior of the Muslims. During the leadership of Elijah Muhammad he had labored as a local official in Chicago, Louis-ville, and Indianapolis. His leadership and diligent service were known throughout the Nation. According to rumor, he served in many "holy squads" that enforced the laws of the Nation on suspected members who were deemed hypocrites or enemies of Allah and Muhammad. Brother David, on the other hand, was a young believer who knew virtually noth-ing of the "old" Nation. He joined the Nation out of a need to be part of a group that was problack and assertive.

In addition to the male leadership, several women played major roles in the local organization. For example, Sister Virginia, Joseph's wife, trained the women in her Muslim Girl Training class and the General Civilization class. In both classes she educated females on their role in the Nation and at home. Women also served as the security guards; they searched all women entering Muslim meetings, guarded female officers, and even on occasion served as personal body guards of Minister Farra-khan. Younger ladies, between the ages of seventeen and twenty-five, served as members of the elite Vanguards. Like the FOI they enforced the laws of the Nation on female members.

As a student at Purdue I was spared the daily demands and harassment of the Indianapolis mosque. The officials did not like the idea of driving two hours to West Lafayette to check on me or to enforce the dietary or moral laws of the organization. In fact, the only time they did visit me was during a financial crisis within the mosque. On this occasion they called and ordered me to give $200 or $300 to the mosque. Most of the time money was used to increase the Number 2 Poor Treasury, whose funds went directly to the leader of the Nation, in this case Farrakhan. For such a crisis Joseph and David made the two-hour drive in an hour and one-half. Although I usually functioned as a distant FOI to Mosque Number Seventy-Four while at Purdue, there were times when my dis-tance did not protect me from the wrath of the Nation of Islam.

In August of 1981 the Indiana Black Exposition was held in the central city. The fair, or better yet, the black world's fair, brought hundreds of thousands of African Americans to the area to support a vast assortment of black entrepreneurs, entertainers, organizations, scholars, and activists. For one week blacks controlled the city of Indianapolis. If there was a "chocolate city," Indianapolis was it. Usually one of the greatest attractions for a black exposition was the appearance of a major social, political, or economic black leader as speaker. Imam Wallace D. Muhammad, the new head of the "old" Nation of Islam, renamed the World Community of Al-Islam, was the guest speaker of the event. Farrakhan, not to be outdone, called on Minister J. D. to secure a venue for him to speak.

Brother Minister J. D. located a local Baptist minister who agreed to allow the Muslims to use his church to host Farrakhan. However, the buildup to Farrakhan's evening lecture was greater and more effective than the actual event. On the Saturday morning of the scheduled lecture Captain Joseph ordered me to Indianapolis for a "fishing" and security detail. The fishing activity was composed of selling *Final Call* newspapers, passing out flyers advertising the event, and verbally harassing people to attend the Farrakhan lecture.

When I reported to the mosque and Captain Joseph, he immediately ordered me to meet and escort Farrakhan's five-car caravan into the city from approximately five miles out of the downtown district on Interstate 465. Brother Joseph told me that I was responsible for leading the minister safely to the downtown Hilton Hotel and that in the event of any emergency I was to sacrifice my automobile and body for the leader. At that time I felt honored yet frightened by that duty. Nonetheless, I followed the directive. Years later I learned that one of the reasons I had been chosen to meet the group was that I drove a very good-looking Delta Royale Oldsmobile 88 and that I was the most expendable. I was not from Indianapolis, did not have a family, and held no job that I could lose.

Leading the way for Minister Farrakhan was a surprise and an honor. As I drove slowly I continuously looked in my rearview mirror for Farrakhan's white, four-door, 1980 Lincoln Continental. I was afraid that I would lose the leader and be sentenced by Elijah Muhammad and God to eternal damnation. Every police car that I saw made me think that the "white devil" was on our heels to stop the messenger of God from speaking. Despite my paranoia, no negative incident occurred.

When we reached the Hilton, I formally met the national leaders. They were Supreme Captain Theron X, Chicago Captain Michael X, National Assistant Larry X, National Secretary William X, FOI guard

Benny X, and Farrakhan's son, Mustapha. My initial meeting with the national heads was dignified, polite, but firm. I was greeted in Arabic, As-Salaam-Alaikum by Captain Michael X. He promptly asked me to state my name and the name of my captain. Captain Theron X then ordered me to go with him to inspect the minister's sleeping room for bombs, telephone bugs, or anything that looked out of the ordinary. Well, I did. But having been in college all my adult life and a product of a typical West Indian middle-class environment, I did not know what to look for. Nevertheless, I searched the room for twenty minutes, looking for anything unusual. Months later I learned that I was being tested for the national security team because Minister J. D. X had told Chicago about my being a university student, as well as an expert full-contact karate fighter.

The search completed, I was sent to the lobby to meet more FOIs coming in from other cities. According to the protocol of the Nation, when Elijah Muhammad or Louis Farrakhan was scheduled to speak, all Muslims from a five-hundred-mile radius were instructed to be there for security, as an audience to insure against a poor showing, and for a regional meeting. Thus, in the lobby I met FOIs from Wisconsin, Michigan, Kentucky, Missouri, West Virginia, and Ohio. As a member of the local mosque I was treated as a VIP guard and was supposed to know everything about the city—where blacks hung out, shopped, and danced. But I was not from the city, so this caused a few problems.

That afternoon I had a detail, in other words a Muslim job. I was to spread the news about Farrakhan's evening lecture at the black exposition. As I was performing my duties, Brother Michael of Chicago instructed me to lead a seven-member squad through the black community for "fishing." I told Brother Michael that my local home was in West Lafayette. His response was swift and hard. "Nigger, this is your damn city. I don't care what suburb that you live in. Men of Muhammad must know every section of the devil's landscape. Nigger, what's general order number one?" He was referring to the general orders that a Fruit of Islam soldier must know before holding a post. The response was, "General Order Number One, sir, is to hold my post until properly relieved." Michael was attempting to make a connection that Indianapolis was my post and that I should know everything about the city. Brother Michael's demeanor, as I would find out, was typical of FOI leaders. They were demanding, rude, and arrogant.

Just as Brother Michael gave me a rude awakening about the relationship between the foot soldier and the Chicago officers, I met a passionate brother who would later work as one of my soldiers or FOIs. Brother Gilbert X was the captain of Muhammad's Mosque of Columbus, Ohio. He was a gentle and benign man who had made a tremendous impact on the building of the Nation in central Ohio during the tenure of Elijah Muhammad. As Michael took joy in humiliating me in front of a group of FOIs, Gilbert had the courage to rescue me from additional rage of the Chicago officer. He told Michael that I was needed for a special kitchen detail. What he did instead was to take me to an office at the church and explain the meaning of the FOI. In addition, he gave me a glass of water so that I could relax and absorb his informative and kind words. However, as things sometimes work in the Nation, at a future date the kind Brother Gilbert with several other FOI members would terrorize me and my family and destroy one of my automobiles.

Farrakhan's lecture started at 7:00 P.M. Farrakhan spoke openly on "Elijah Muhammad and the Risen Christ." At this time the minister's theology focused on how Elijah escaped death and that he was the Christ, Messiah, and Mahdi. The subcontext of his thesis centered on Wallace Muhammad as the great hypocrite. Although the meeting was poorly attended, it laid the foundation for the growth of the Nation in the Midwest. Although only 150 non-Muslims came out to hear Farrakhan, at least 300 self-proclaimed registered members of the Nation attended.

After the lecture the leaders of the Nation held a "hold back/regional" meeting at the church. Larry X, William X, and Theron X addressed the membership on the role they must play in rebuilding the Nation of Islam. In an atmosphere like a high school pep rally they indoctrinated the group, telling them they were warriors for Allah and that Farrakhan was the divine leader of the entire black world. They stressed that helping Allah build the Nation of Islam required hard work, dedication, spiritual development, and most important, money. Members were instructed to give one-third of their salaries to the Nation under Farrakhan.

When the meeting was over, the believers congregated at the local storefront mosque for fish sandwiches, bean soup, candied carrots, and the Nation's staple and cash dish, bean pie. At the mosque the Muslims ate and talked about their service to Allah and the great teachings of Minister Louis Farrakhan. In this congregation of believers and warriors I developed a renewed and more fervent determination to support the

Nation. Later that evening I was ordered to leave the mosque for the Hilton to assist in manning an all-night security post in the lobby. There I learned how verbally violent and potentially dangerous the FOI could be.

Brother Benny of Chicago, one of the most dangerous FOI activists in the entire organization, verbally confronted a biracial couple who were buying a magazine in the hotel's guest shop. Benny walked straight to the black woman and asked, "What are you doing with this devil?" While I was bracing for a fight, the woman walked away quickly, and her male white associate literally ran out of the lobby. I am convinced that if her male companion had responded in a different manner, Benny would have physically attacked him. Unfortunately, episodes like this would become a common practice as the Nation continued to grow in strength and numbers.

My indoctrination into the Nation was an exciting time. Even though there were blatant signs of racism, bigotry, and plain theological hogwash, I became increasingly committed to the overall theme of racial solidarity and the self-help principles espoused by the Nation. I devoted my remaining tenure at Purdue to academic activism for the Nation of Islam.

5

Seventy-Ninth and Emerald

In June 1982 I received my master's degree in history from Purdue University. I then returned to St. Petersburg, Florida, to work with my father and to spread the teachings of Elijah Muhammad, Minister Farrakhan, and the Nation of Islam. During this brief time in my life I sold religious supplies to individuals who believed in Haitian Vodun, Cuban Santeria, Trinidian Shango, and Brazilian Condomble in the family store. However, on the weekends I donned my suit and bow tie to sell the *Final Call* newspaper and the goodness of Louis Farrakhan. As Farrakhan's lone representative in the Tampa Bay area, I had the distinction of meeting a diversity of individuals in several types of places—parks, churches, and bars. Unfortunately, I was viewed by most people as a throwback to the old days of the Nation of Islam.

At that time Farrakhan was not very well respected in the black community outside of New York or Chicago, and representatives of the Nation were treated very badly. In St. Petersburg haters of Muhammad and the minister cursed and sometimes assaulted me. Once, in a St. Petersburg park, I was forced to beat two assailants who attempted to take my papers. The only positive aspect of the episode was my statement to the police: "I was forced to beat them in the name of Allah." The three months I spent in St. Petersburg as a Muslim gave me the foundation to become a strong and independent Muslim in Chicago.

In August 1982 I moved to Chicago for two reasons: to work with the Nation of Islam and to marry a Muslim sister named Gwendolyn. My activities as a husband and a member were filled with excitement, tension, and confusion. However, the majority of my activities stemmed from the Nation of Islam's Headquarters, located on Seventy-ninth Street and Emerald.

Gwendolyn was a pretty, dark-skinned, and intelligent sister whom I had met at Purdue. As a mechanical-engineering major, she represented the high-quality individual that the university sought; however, what separated this woman from the others was her commitment to the African American community. During the summer breaks she went back to Chicago to work in a variety of volunteer agencies. This was an activity that very few, if any, young black university students considered. Because she was committed to the political struggle of African Americans and a Muslim, we decided to marry. Both of us realized that we were one of a very few couples in the country who believed in the liberation of black people through the teachings of Mr. Muhammad.

Before my arrival in Chicago Gwendolyn had become quite active in the Muslim Girl Training and the General Civilization classes with the Nation. On any given week she would attend three to five Nation of Islam services. However, her primary service to the Nation was teaching science and math to children. Because of her educational prowess and her profession as an engineer for Commonwealth Edison, she was given special status in the Nation.

My arrival was greeted a little bit differently. Although I held a master's degree in history, most of the believers did not know what I was going to do with this degree or how it could possibly benefit the Nation. For example, in one FOI class all the brothers were asked what skills they possessed. When I responded that I had a liberal arts background, the questioner stated frankly that the NOI needed electricians, engineers, and farmers, not "college niggers."

The reason the Nation focused on skills training for the men was because of its original focus and its relationship with the Booker T. Washington school of racial uplift. From 1895 to 1915 Booker Washington, the founder of Tuskegee Institute and the foremost leader of black America at that time, argued that African Americans must devote their time and energies to an industrialized education. Such an education would assist blacks to respond economically to racism. Washington believed that blacks must devote themselves to the skills of the hand. He felt that occupations in agriculture, carpentry, brick masonry, and mechanics were much more beneficial to the progress of the African American than political agitation for civil rights. He considered it better to have money and to own a business than to have no money and the right to eat in white establishments. Elijah Muhammad, a product of Marcus Garvey's Universal Negro Improvement Association, followed the ideas of Washington and continued promoting the theory of hard work, self-sufficiency, and black capitalism. Farrakhan's early Nation followed the same course. Thus, because I was considered a young intellectual, the brothers had no position or job for me, at least according to their views and attitudes.

Having a master's degree and being a member of the FOI was an acute paradox. Although the minister spoke openly and vividly about professionals and intellectuals joining the movement, his sentiments were not echoed by the Muslim brotherhood. In order to stay calm and relatively sane, I deliberately challenged many of the lessons that the believers were forced to learn. For instance, registered members of the NOI had to memorize and recite several lessons that had been given by Master Fard Muhammad to Elijah Muhammad. These recitations were designed to equip the formerly "deaf, dumb, and lost Negro" with "Supreme Wisdom and Knowledge." In reality, the lessons were elementary courses in math, reading, and writing—with a smattering of history, geography, and religion. I used to agitate the brothers, especially the FOI captain, by stating the materials were not factual or up-to-date. In particular, when asked the population of planet Earth, one was expected to give the memorized answer: "The population of the Original Nation in the Wilderness of North America is 17,000,000; adding 2,000,000 Indians, it makes it 19,000,000. All over the Planet earth is 4,400,000,000." Well, in 1983 there were more than seventeen million black people in the United States. In fact, the U.S. Census gave the figure as thirty-four million. I continued to tell the brothers the information was wrong. The frustrated brothers would reply that when Master Fard Muhammad told them differently, then they would change the figures. Just forcing the FOI to call on the name Fard Muhammad was a victory. It temporarily afforded me the opportunity to gain strength to endure the blatant ignorance of the brotherhood.

Although ignorance flourished among the brotherhood, a few men attempted to forge a relationship with me based primarily on my intellect and international experiences: Brothers William Muhammad and Akbar Muhammad. Brother William, the national secretary of the Nation of Islam in the early 1980s, was a light-skinned, very thin man who had an innate ability to understand the most elaborate and complicated issues. A self-taught man, well versed in accounting and calculus, William enjoyed holding stimulating discussions about the Nation and entrepreneurship. Having the ability to quickly and easily grasp complex mathematical formulas, William could easily have attained a graduate degree and become a successful businessman. Nonetheless, he labored diligently to keep the business records and financial reports of the NOI balanced for proper growth and accountability.

Brother William had been a trusted friend of Farrakhan's since the mid-1960s, when he labored with the minister at Temple Number Seven in Harlem. William was rumored to have been one of the men who encouraged Farrakhan to leave Wallace and to rebuild the Nation of Elijah Muhammad. William, in contrast to Farrakhan, was a hard-working, honest man who had no ambition for material wealth. As the national secretary, he handled literally millions of dollars, but at no time did he give the impression that he was keeping any of the money. In fact, he did not even look as if he were receiving a salary. Brother William drove a secondhand Cadillac, wore suits from thrift stores, and had shoes that were at least seven years old. The only thing that looked good on him was his young and beautiful wife. Even though William had little material wealth, he always seemed content with his life and more than happy to utilize the services and expertise of new Muslims, like me, in developing the Nation of Islam.

Larry X Prescott, later known as Abdul Akbar Muhammad, the national assistant to Farrakhan, considered himself a self-taught scholar. Having an interest in history, he opened a bookstore in Harlem that featured materials on Africa, the Caribbean, and black America. In the 1960s his store was a pillar in the black community; African Americans, especially in the Nation, frequented the establishment. As a scholar, or, as many would say, the "Historian in the Nation," he easily made friends with the black intelligentsia. Leroy Jones, C. Eric Lincoln, and John H. Clarke became professional associates of Brother Larry's. Because I was a young graduate student, Larry took time to allow me to demonstrate and exercise my skills in the Nation. Because Larry saw himself as a scholar, and because he was my mentor, he persuaded FOI leaders to let me teach a course on black history to the Chicago Fruit of Islam.

Every Saturday morning I presented a black history lesson to the brothers at the Final Call Building. I lectured on various aspects of the history, culture, and life of African people on the continent and the Diaspora. In addition, I taught the FOI brotherhood note taking and the importance of reading several types of history, such as women's, European, medical, and ancient Greek. The FOI membership enjoyed my portion of the training very much. In fact, several informed me that if not for my presentations, they would not have attended FOI training. Teaching the class was not only beneficial to the male membership but also to me.

Teaching history to the FOI in Chicago immediately improved my status in the Nation. More than a foot soldier, I became Brother Vibert, a scholar and a very important person in the organization. There were several reasons for my elevated status. First, I taught a special class in Chicago, the capital of Islam in the United States. Second, I taught under the watchful eyes of Minister Farrakhan. If I had not been approved by him, I would not be teaching the class. Third, I was now considered a special, educated brother who had decided to follow the teachings of Elijah Muhammad, through the works and deeds of Minister Louis Farrakhan. In fact, my history class to the FOI was duplicated throughout temples, mosques, and study groups in the Nation. Another benefit I received was the constant and direct tutoring given to me by Larry X (Abdul Akbar Muhammad).

Akbar was an excellent teacher. Weekly he instructed me to read volumes of literature on black nationalism, Pan-Africanism, communism, Marxism, capitalism, democratic values, Islam, Christianity, and Judaism, after which we discussed the materials. Ultimately, the sessions served two purposes: they kept me academically focused and motivated, and they gave Akbar scores of notes that he could use in his lectures and discussions. However, one of my proudest moments as a student member of the Nation came when Minister Farrakhan observed one of my history lectures. As I was speaking to the FOI, the minister entered the room, stood in the back, and showed his approval with smiles, gestures, and a question. At that particular moment I felt like a true disciple of God. Akbar told me that the minister was pleased with my work but not with my appearance. At the time I had a gold crown on one of my front teeth. When I spoke, the gold tooth made me appear gap-toothed. Akbar and the minister arranged for me to see Dr. Salaam, the personal dentist of the Messenger, to correct the problem. By the next Saturday the gold crown had been replaced with an ivory substitute.

Another characteristic that defined me as special was my prowess in the martial arts. During this period Akbar, William, and the national staff struggled to keep the motivational level of the FOI high. In addition, they needed something to control the aggressive nature of many of the believers. Thus, I began to teach kickboxing to the Fruit.

During this period members of the Nation of Islam believed they were at war with Wallace Muhammad and the World Community of Al-Islam. Farrakhan's polemical rhetoric encouraged the idea that Wallace was an evil conspirator who worked with the government to kill Elijah Muhammad and to destroy the Nation. His labeling of Wallace Muhammad as a hypocrite, the anti-Christ, and a rebellious son incited many to talk of attacking members of the rival Muslim sect. Minister Farrakhan did not want bloodshed between the two groups but merely wanted to develop a warlike mentality among the FOI. The logic of producing such an attitude stemmed from encouraging members to adopt a zealous view of the Nation. The typical brother, however, could not separate fact from fiction or rhetoric from a direct order. Knowing this, the national staff encouraged me to teach the brothers basic martial arts skills. As Akbar stated to me, "White boys have ice hockey to exploit their aggression, perhaps we could use the martial arts to do the same."

On Monday, Wednesday, and Friday mornings at 6:00 the FOI karate classes began. However, out of a membership of two hundred FOI in Chicago, only twenty-five consistently attended the sessions. The brothers who were serious about the martial arts eventually proved to be some of Farrakhan's most trusted, militant, and dedicated followers. These men were quite different from the typical FOI. They were not motivated by materialism or money, and the majority of them were unemployed, only getting money from the selling of papers or from generous family members and friends. They viewed Farrakhan as a Christ-like figure and considered his words divine. If you attacked Farrakhan, you were assaulting God; they were religious warriors, zealots. They were the most devout followers in the Nation. This select group prayed five times a day; read the Quran, the Bible, and the books of Elijah Muhammad at least three hours every day; and strictly followed the diet of Elijah Muhammad, which meant maintaining a vegetarian lifestyle and eating once every other day. For greater spiritual and physical purification, these men occasionally would not eat for several days.

Last, they were fighters. They had a battle history as former members of gangs, boxers, hit men, and barroom brawlers. These were the men of Farrakhan. Yet these brothers were some of the nicest, most honest, and most peaceful people on earth. In exchange for my services the brothers, my karate students, made sure that I had money for fuel, that I served on the best squads, and that I was not harassed by Nation officials. They were not only excellent students but also leaders among the FOI. Ultimately, they funneled their energies into continuing the positive work of helping Farrakhan build the Nation by selling the *Final Call* newspaper and by living a religious life rather than by beating up their fellow Muslims.

As I became more entrenched in the Nation's structure, certain personalities and characters began to introduce themselves to me. One of these was Louis Farrakhan Jr. The younger Louis, a young man of slight build, was quite emotional. He carried an element of rebellion toward his father and the Nation. His views of his father's ministry and the structure of the Nation developed from his lack of having a traditional father. Farrakhan's position in the Nation required total devotion to Elijah Muhammad. Unfortunately for Louis Jr., his father, who loved him, could not demonstrate the parental emotions that he needed. C. Eric Lincoln, author of *Black Muslims in America*, illustrated Farrakhan's devotion to Elijah, as opposed to his son:

> Louis seems indefinable. On one occasion he returned from a speaking engagement in New York to find that one of his five children was seriously ill. He took the child to the hospital and returned at once to work. Asked how he could concentrate on his tasks without apparent concern, he explained, "Mr. Muhammad teaches us not to grieve over what we can do nothing about. I have prayed to Allah. If Allah takes my son, it is because Allah is wiser than I and he knows better than I whether he should continue to live. But whether or not my son lives, the Messenger's work must still be done."[1]

I first noticed Louis in our Saturday morning FOI meetings. The FOI leadership demanded that everyone be on time. Most brothers who were late had to do pushups, yet Louis Jr., who always was between ten and thirty minutes late, was never reprimanded. As I noticed this practice, it became obvious that this young man was close to the power structure in the Nation. In addition, in our classes Brother Louis constantly challenged the FOI leadership. For instance, he protested loudly that the "Actual Facts" lessons were antiquated. He objected to the wearing of Class B uniforms—dark suit, white shirt, and bow tie—as being unattractive. In fact, on one particular Saturday Louis wore a purple, green, red, and blue African dashiki shirt. Although everyone was shocked, I could not hold back my laughter. Another episode of Louis's uniqueness came during a Savior's Day celebration at the Chicago armory. The majority of the FOI were on some type of detail—security, selling the Nation's products, or patrolling the parking lots. Louis, however, was seated in the VIP section of the lecture hall eating bean pies. Between bites he cried out to his father, "Teach us, Brother Minister!"

Louis Jr. was a strange fellow, but he illustrated a certain brilliance, cunning, and cleverness. Willingly or unwillingly he forced the leaders in the FOI to become independent thinkers. His antics attacked the very soul of the Nation, showing that rhetorical jargon, intimidation, and archaic methods of teaching Islam failed with the more sophisticated and educated young black generation.

Brother Louis became quite friendly to me, perhaps because we were both New Yorkers who happened to be living in the Midwest. On occasion he would drive me in his father's Lincoln to my south-side apartment. On these rides he openly spoke about his difficulty in relating to the political and religious structure of the Nation.

Louis was a very complex and smart man. On the day that I permanently left Chicago, I boarded the Seventy-ninth Street bus en route to the Dan Ryan L station. On the bus I saw Louis with a strange non-Muslim woman I did not know. Louis was obviously high; I had heard he was an occasional user of cocaine, but I had never paid attention to the rumors. Nonetheless, he acknowledged me with a hint of embarrassment, saying that when he got himself together he was going to rejoin the brotherhood. I responded, "Louis, you never left the fold." We embraced, and I disembarked at the station. The next time I spoke to Louis was in 1995 at the Nation's Salaam Restaurant; the younger Farrakhan told me he had built a million-dollar-a-year wholesale-travel agency. He stated that his wife, Sister Lisa, was the manager of the "only Muslim travel business in the Nation of Islam." It's true that Lisa runs the Windows to the World Travel Agency but not that it was built by Louis Jr. Rather the donations of thousands of Muslims laid the foundation for the enterprise.

Louis Jr. was not the only person connected to the elite at the power center of the Nation. In 1983 Minister Rockman, the leader of the Atlanta temple and a personal friend of Minister Farrakhan's, had rejoined the Nation. Rockman, a forceful speaker with a southern accent, spent a lot of time in Chicago. He was part of a group of former leaders of Elijah Muhammad that Minister Farrakhan was attempting to recruit to the

"New" Nation of Islam. Rockman became one of the first of the few to reenter Farrakhan's Black Muslim organization. However, although the Atlanta Muslim became a VIP within the mosque, it was his son who received a special welcome and admiration from the FOI and the larger Muslim community. At the age of twenty-five, the younger Rockman had earned an MBA and JD from Georgetown University. Farrakhan, thinking that Rockman's son would bring his skills to the Nation, introduced him to the NOI amid a chorus of fanfare and excitement. I remember several brothers and sisters who had joined the Nation with various college and university degrees in multiple disciplines becoming quite upset because they were forced to sell newspapers, whereas Rockman Jr. was guaranteed a position of influence and power. But unknown to Farrakhan, the young Rockman had other plans. He departed from the confines of the Muslims to join the ranks of the Central Intelligence Agency.

Although some members of the NOI received special status because of their blood relationship and personal friendship with Farrakhan, the majority of the FOI were willing to make their way to the top through hard work, honesty, and dedication. James Booker was one of these men. Brother James X, later to be known as Brother Wali, was a brilliant writer who had earned a graduate degree from Howard University. The son of the nationally acclaimed journalist Semion Booker, Wali was raised in privileged circumstances. As a young boy he attended academically strong elementary and high schools. A brilliant youth, Wali had benefited from a diversified lifestyle. His friends ranged from Jewish to Catholic. His parents had hoped that James would become a humanist, as well as a professional, but never a black nationalist follower of Louis Farrakhan.

But unlike his father, a political liberal activist who did not agree with Farrakhan's views on religion and the destiny of African Americans, Wali was a militant black nationalist. He brought to the Nation the education, skills, and diplomatic talents usually reserved for the American elite to serve their country and class group. Shortly after joining the Nation in 1978, Wali became the editor of the struggling *Final Call* newspaper. Within one year he transformed the paper from a second-rate tabloid into an outstanding monthly journal filled with news about Africa, Latin America, Europe, and America. Under his leadership the *Final Call*'s circulation increased to such an extent that it was being billed as the most popular black newspaper in the United States. Farrakhan rewarded him with trips throughout the world and later the position of assistant minister of Mosque Maryam, the National Center of the NOI.

However, for all of his brilliance Wali was deluded by the words of Farrakhan. He could not analyze or recognize the inconsistencies in the Nation's leadership. Wali thought Farrakhan was God's ambassador. "Farrakhan," according to Wali, "could do no wrong." Wali and I held intense marathon conversations about Farrakhan's direction and the thesis of the NOI. Wali often told me that if I had been a member of the Nation during the 1960s, I would have been killed because of my questioning of Farrakhan's logic. In response I jokingly stated that if this had been the 1960s, we both would have been dead because of the Vietnam War. Surely, we both would have been drafted. Our heated arguments occasionally could be heard from his office throughout the Final Call Building. The last major conversation we had was during a trip to Libya. This argument concerned the succession of leadership in the Nation. At the time Wali favored Dr. Minister Alim Muhammad of Washington, D.C., the spokesperson for Louis Farrakhan and the minister of health for the organization. I supported Akbar Muhammad. From the time we left Kennedy International Airport in New York City, during our stop in Malta, and until we reached Tripoli, our final destination, we argued, laughed, and jokingly fought. Unfortunately, just before his untimely death of heart failure in 1992, Wali had confided in me that he was having second thoughts about the future of the Nation. Much of his new attitude stemmed from his forced resignation as the assistant minister of Mosque Maryam and the lack of financial support that the Nation had supplied to him and his growing family.

Unfortunately, the great editor of the Nation, Wali, lived in poverty. His small apartment that housed his wife and children resembled a Third World shanty. The family slept on box springs, dined on secondhand tables, and leisured on worn-out sofas. For this dedication to Farrakhan's Nation, according to insiders, he died with no life insurance policy or organizational annuities. He left his family not only fatherless but broke.

Wali could not possibly have predicted his death or the dilemma that the Nation placed him in. Like scores of others Wali was groomed for NOI leadership through selected organizational classes. Like Wali I was placed in the ministerial sessions.

During my time with the FOI I directed my energy toward learning the theology, structure and organizational development of the Nation. Like many of my peers I was placed in leadership/religion classes that groomed me for future ministry in the organization. There were classes for future secretaries, captains, and ministers. Akbar and Farrakhan, as I have stated, enrolled me in the class for future clergy. Every Wednesday evening the future ministers met with Akbar to discuss such issues as the relationship between the Bible and the Quran, the role of Jews in the religion of black Americans, and the difference between orthodox Islam and the Nation of Islam. At the conclusion of these sessions we joined the general membership, who studied from Farrakhan's audiotape series "Respect for Life."

The "Respect for Life" series was a collection of Farrakhan's speeches. The lectures focused on the Nation's theology and the role of Minister Farrakhan as Elijah Muhammad's representative. During the 1980s the series became a prerequisite for anyone wishing to join the Nation of Islam. Farrakhan's "Respect for Life" and the ministry classes were extremely important to my evolution in the Nation. Like many others I believed that my destiny was to be a minister for Farrakhan and Muhammad. Eventually, I became a member of Farrakhan's clergy. However, I soon began to question my alleged "divine calling."

Future leaders were selected primarily by Akbar, Wahid/William, Farrakhan, and selected staff members. These leaders incorporated creative measures that tested the devotion and dedication of candidates for leadership positions. During the early 1980s the Nation was a small unit, and FOI members could be used and tested in a variety of ways. Several types of assignments were given to test the physical and spiritual strength of future leaders. In my case I received calls as early as 5:00 A.M. directing me to meet an arriving dignitary at O'Hare International Airport by 6:30 A.M. Other times a buzz, at my home in the middle of the night, assigned me to work security at the Final Call Building immediately. Sometimes I would arrive for Sunday meeting only to be told to work a special detail to recruit members to join the NOI and thus would be unable to enjoy the Sunday service. Still I might be told after services to assist in cleaning the building and to stay afterward for a special meeting that could last several hours. Often my friends, mother, and wife had to wait in the lobby for me to take them home long after the Sunday lecture ended. Most humiliating of all was arriving a few minutes late for a meeting and being told to sit or stand in a corner, as if I were an unruly child in elementary school. This practice severely tested one's dignity and patience with the organization. However, if you passed or functioned without complaint or hostility, the chances of earning a leadership position within the organization increased.

The first direct statement from Minister Farrakhan about my role within the Nation came in April 1983 while I worked backdoor security at the Final Call Building. My job was to frisk individuals who entered, including Farrakhan, and to check incoming packages for weapons, explosives, and drugs. After Minister Farrakhan entered the structure, he asked me questions about my family, upbringing, and education. However, his most pointed question came when he asked, "Do you have a vision about becoming a member of the clergy?" I responded in the negative. Recalling a painful story of my father's activities within the AME Church, I stated that the religious world had exploited my family, forced us to live in poverty, and never honored my father for his good work. In fact, the church used its power in an attempt to destroy my father as a man, husband, and leader. Therefore, I would never become a member of the clergy. Farrakhan stated that he understood. Later I learned that several of his children felt the same way. Nevertheless, despite my misgivings, I became a minister in the Nation of Islam.

Several events occurred that provided me the learning experiences and diligence that I needed before I embarked on preaching the gospel of Elijah. First, I needed a clear understanding of the structure of the Nation. During the early 1980s the organization was run primarily by Akbar and Farrakhan. Although they preached the ideas of Elijah's governance, they seldom followed or even recognized those ideas. Their basic concern was to recruit new members by any means necessary.

During the tenure of Elijah Muhammad individuals who wished to become members of the group had to write a "Savior's Letter," which asked Fard Muhammad's (Allah) permission to join the Nation and to receive a holy name. A holy name is an Arabic name that replaces one's birth or Christian identification. Usually, after several years of dedicated service to the Nation, Elijah Muhammad created a special name for the person. For example, the name *Farrakhan*. Muhammad's genius expressed itself in *Farrakhan*. He used English and Chinese to develop a new Islamic word. The first part, *Farr*, illustrated that Louis X was a product of Western civilization. He is not of Eastern ethnicity; however, even though he is "far away from [the] East/the Holy Land,"[2] he knows Islam better than Arabs. *Khan*, a Chinese term for militant leaders, implied, according to Muhammad, Louis's aggressive and bold style as a minister. Thus, the new name—*Farrakhan*.

The savior's letter had to be written perfectly, the letters, punctuation, even the date on the script had to be exact. Most candidates simply traced the letter and returned it to the mosque's secretary, who then mailed it to Chicago for approval. If the letter passed inspection, the candidate was granted an X after his first name and was considered a registered Muslim in the Nation of Islam. However, in most cases under Farrakhan, a person simply attended special classes that taught the theology of Fard and Elijah Muhammad. Once a candidate completed the classes, which lasted anywhere from one to six months, he was granted an X.

In many instances, however, membership was granted to people in a haphazard manner. For example, if an individual was an entertainer, friend, business personality, or professional, and was liked by the Nation's powerful elite, that person was granted an X and an Arabic name by Farrakhan without any preliminary letters or classes. Leonard Searcy, now Leonard Farrakhan, chief of staff (former owner of a Popeye's Chicken franchise in Chicago), and Benjamin Chavis, currently Benjamin Muhammad, a former head of the National Association for the Advancement of Colored People (now special assistant to Louis Farrakhan), were among those selected with no prior preparation.

I also learned the rules of cooperation within the confines of the Nation. The general belief is that before a man is given a leadership role, he must be tested in battle under a tough commander. This lesson came in several ways. The first examination came from individuals who were often intellectually inferior but who held positions of power. These brothers instructed me to do things that were often archaic and illogical. For instance, to prepare for the 1982 Savior's Day celebration in Gary, Indiana, a lieutenant took several brothers to Gary to post bulletins in windchill temperatures of minus 45 degrees. If this was not bad enough, he ordered us to take off our gloves so that we could place the bills more quickly and efficiently on walls and light posts. During the convention a captain and several national leaders placed ten brothers and me in military formation outside the Gary Convention Center and ordered us not to leave our position until we were properly relieved by a commanding officer. We stood in subzero temperatures for over one hour.

A favorite method of testing was through embarrassment in front of other FOI members, family, and visitors. Often commanding officers used harsh intimidation tactics to see if a soldier was going to break. For instance, Supreme Captain Abdul Sharrieff Muhammad, the current leader of the FOI, often used terms such as *Nigger* and *Motherfucker* or threats such as "I'll bust your ass" to frighten people into submission. If the victim responded to these actions without anger or without talking back, he was described as a good soldier.

The ultimate way to show one's allegiance to the Nation was through financial donations. This was the most dangerous and devastating. Potential and standing leaders were expected to give financial assistance to the Nation despite the hardship it may have on a family.

The Nation held fund drives at least four times a year. Mosque leaders, as well as registered Muslims, were expected to give $1,000 or more to the campaigns. Ministers were also required to influence their congregations to make charitable contributions to several of the Nation's various financial agencies, such as the Number 2 Poor Treasury, the Billion Dollar Economic Development Plan, the Savior's Gift Drive, and the Three Year Economic Program.

Although members were often willing to sacrifice for the Nation, they occasionally ignored basic responsibility to their spouses and families. It was not uncommon for ministers and other major leaders to lead their families into financial ruin. I know of five cases where individuals lost their homes, businesses, or vehicles because they supported NOI fundraising drives.

Two examples are when Akbar Muhammad suffered his first heart attack in 1988 in New York City and when Wali Muhammad died in 1993. Because of the NOI's laissez-faire and the constant diminishing of family resources, both families suffered insurmountable financial burdens. The Nation did not encourage members to purchase health or life insurance policies. Akbar and Wali represent the Nation's elite, but lesser-known and poorer believers suffered even greater distress. As a member and potential leader, and later as a minister, I gave greatly to the financial growth of the organization. On many occasions I also placed my family in jeopardy because of my willingness to open my bank account and wallet to Farrakhan. For my sacrifice I was considered a "good brother."

In one way or another I passed the Nation's examinations. In retrospect I allowed my emotional needs, perhaps my emotional immaturity, to position me as one of the many exploited members of the NOI. Nonetheless, it would take some time for me to realize that the current structure of the Nation was based on the complete subjugation of its members.

One of the reasons I found it difficult to leave the temple of confusion, hostility, and exploitation was my fascination with the individuals who were attracted to Farrakhan. In one month I might see activists such as Stokely Carmichael (Kwame Toure), Robert Williams, Dr. Van Sertima, attorney Lewis Myers, Prince Ben Israel, Al Sharpton, attorney Johnny Cochran, Dr. William De Bois Jr., and Steve Cokley or entertainers such as Craig Hodges, Mike Tyson, Public Enemy, and Burning Spear walk through the doors of the Nation's buildings. To observe black advocates and entertainers visit Farrakhan's south-side office was exciting. As a young Muslim I, like others, believed that we were connected to something special, spiritual, and revolutionary. Therefore, even though I felt misused, I rationalized that "believers would suffer much for the word and work of Allah and his messenger." I suffered from this delusion.

Although race activists found their way to Seventy-ninth and Emerald, I became more impressed with former leaders of the old Nation of Islam who came to Chicago to join forces with Farrakhan. Leaders like Emmanuel Muhammad, John Muhammad, Askia Muhammad/Charles 67X, Donald Muhammad, Khallid Muhammad, Abdul Allah Muhammad, Jabril Muhammad, Moses X Powell, and Theron X embodied a very special spirit for young brothers and sisters.

Emmanuel and John Muhammad were blood relatives of Elijah Muhammad. Emanuel was the oldest of his children, and John was the Messenger's brother. Both men illustrated their unique love for Elijah and his theology, and both favored Farrakhan's attempt to rebuild the Nation. When these individuals entered the Final Call Building, they manifested the light of divinity.

Charles 67X, later to become Askia Muhammad, was the editor of the famed *Muhammad Speaks* newspaper. Charles was an important personality because he printed and illustrated the ideas of Elijah Muhammad for millions of blacks throughout the world. Also, Charles knew every major player and plot within the structure. Meeting him was like communicating with the intellectual thoughts of the Messenger. Donald Muhammad of Boston represented the new age of Elijah's teachings. Less confrontational and extremely moderate, unlike many of his colleagues, Donald was diplomatic and businesslike. Abdul Allah Muhammad, the direct opposite of Donald, illustrated the hard-core manipulative style of many of the old Muslim leaders. He could be counted on to say what the Messenger or Farrakhan wanted to hear. Abdul signified the pillar of the movement during the 1960s. The Messenger in many ways needed yes-men to keep things moving and in perspective. But unfortunately, Abdul illustrated the type of corruption that Minister Malcolm had identified prior to his untimely death in 1965. Bernard Cushmeer or Jabril Muhammad was the theologian of the movement. He, more than anyone else, connected Elijah's teachings to traditional Islam, Sufism, and Christianity. But paramount was his connection to Louis Farrakhan. According to Farrakhan, Jabril reintroduced him to the teachings of Elijah Muhammad. After the death of Elijah Muhammad and the restructuring of the Nation of Islam by Wallace Muhammad, Farrakhan maintained that he had lost interest in being a race and spiritual advocate. He had decided to go back into show business. En route to California from New York City, he spoke to Minister Jabril. Jabril asked to meet him at a hotel in Hollywood. At the hotel Jabril gave Farrakhan a copy of his book, *This Is the One*. The book, stated Farrakhan, confirmed that Elijah was the Christ, and he must not renew his career as a singer or professional actor but must devote his time and energy to rebuilding the Nation of Islam. Under the leadership of Louis Farrakhan the Nation's theology changed frequently. Therefore, meeting Jabril was similar to being introduced to the apostle Paul.

There were also several other major players in the Nation, such as Theron X, the former captain of the FOI, who helped train the FOI of Elijah and Moses X Powell, one of the enforcers of the Nation. Brother Moses was a well-known karateka and a member of *Karate Illustrated*'s Hall of Fame. It was surprising to find that he followed Louis Farrakhan.

My time in the Final Call Building involved working not only with men but also with Muslim women. Registered Muslim women were members of one or all of the following female groups: the General Civilization class, the Muslim Girl Training class, and the Vanguards. Although these groups had different titles, they all had the same objectives—teaching women to function as proper Muslim ladies, mothers, and wives. However, like their male counterparts in the FOI, the women were expected to secure and defend the mosque. They searched females before allowing them to enter NOI functions and even occasionally served as Farrakhan's personal bodyguards.

Contrary to the image of female Muslims being security guards, they primarily functioned as housewives. However, most held ambitions of attending colleges and universities. Unfortunately, the majority never achieved degrees in higher education. These women, who never reached their academic potential, became diligent workers for the Nation, substituting their desire for education with labor for the Nation. They became pillars in the structure of the organization. The Muslim sisters served as secretaries, treasurers, organizers, and occasionally as ministers in the Nation. Unfortunately, during the early years of the Farrakhan movement, no matter how diligently the sisters worked, they were not respected as equal partners with the men.

A prime example was Sister Dabney, who served as Wahid's secretary in the Final Call Building. Dabney, a tall, beautiful, light-skinned woman, had two postgraduate degrees, a doctorate of philosophy, and a doctorate of law. However, the only position that the Nation found for her was typing and filing papers. Like most sisters in the Nation, she worked long hours without complaint or bitterness. Members of the FOI, instead of thanking Dabney for her excellent clerical support, treated her as a nuisance or a "bitch." FOI members often remarked that she was insensitive and cold toward men. But the harshest male comments toward Sister Dabney were made when a male officer made extremely degrading sexist remarks about Dabney to FOI members.

The Black Student Union scheduled Minister Farrakhan to speak at Northern Illinois University. The officer in charge of the FOI blatantly told twenty-five male Muslims that Dabney disrespects the brotherhood. The issue arose when Sister Dabney inadvertently crossed in front of the commanding officer as he spoke to the FOI. The commander stopped his comments about Muhammad, Farrakhan, and the Black Nation to begin a tirade about women being inferior to men and about their being rude and childish by nature. He concluded that "women must be spanked." He used an example of how he forced his wife to bend over his knee to receive punishment and beatings like their children.

Another example of the total disregard for the professional status of black women in the early 1980s was illustrated by the Nation's use of my wife, who holds an engineering degree from Purdue University. Instead of placing her on major mechanical and electrical projects, they often assigned her to the kitchen to bake cakes and cookies.

My tenure with the Nation in Chicago was a turning point in my life. It became apparent that if I continued to live in the Windy City and to serve in the Nation, I would never realize or accomplish my goals as a man. In late 1983 I applied to the Ohio State University Graduate School to pursue a Ph.D. in twentieth-century American history. In the fall of 1984 I was admitted to the history department. However, my Muslim life in Columbus, Ohio, continued to illustrate the widespread hypocrisy of the movement.

6

Conflict, Religion, and the Ministry

The experience that I gained in Chicago broadened my understanding of organized groups, institutions, and religious communities in black society. Regardless of the theology and theory, African American organizations are often led by insincere and self-promoting individuals. Unfortunately, these bandits used corruption, intimidation, and hypocrisy to erode the spiritual strength of rank-and-file members. In the mid-1980s the Nation had begun an internal decline, and destruction of the movement seemed imminent. Paradoxically, as I witnessed the beginning of the death of the Nation, I, like other Muslim ministers, encouraged unsuspecting blacks to join the dying Nation of Islam.

In 1984 Gwendolyn and I moved to Columbus so I could attend Ohio State University's graduate school. As I contracted with the history department to work toward my doctoral degree, my wife landed a position at the university as the lead engineer in the Facility Plants Department. Although we both viewed our new surroundings with excitement and optimism, there was a tinge of sadness in leaving the warm, though hostile, surroundings of the Nation of Islam in Chicago.

When we arrived in the capital city of Ohio, there were three major items on our agenda—find lodging, meet with professors in the history department, and find the local mosque. Two of the greatest facets of the Ohio State University were its size and its commitment to integrated, comfortable family housing. With the help of the graduate school we found housing at the Buckeye Village Community. The one-bedroom apartment was a modern unit with central air conditioning, far superior to the hot one-bedroom flat we left on Sixty-ninth Avenue and Merrill Street in Chicago. The meeting with my new professors went equally well. The individual who recruited me to the history department was Dr. Warren Van Tine. Professor Van Tine was one of the younger and brighter scholars of the department. At that time the history department was ranked among the top five in the nation, and Dr. Van Tine was considered one of the nation's leading scholars in the fields of labor and social history.

Dr. Van Tine was the first professor I met. I went into his office, introduced myself, and thanked him for aiding my quest to join the history department. The smiling little man, who looked liked a cross between a sixties flower child and Einstein but sounded like a brilliant politician, responded that he was happy to see me, and I believed him. This was significant because I was still under the spell of Farrakhan, who taught that whites are generally liars and that Germans and Jews are the greatest storytellers. Regardless of what I was taught by the Nation, Dr. Van Tine became not only my mentor but my friend. Later that week he invited me out for donuts at the favorite local academic and radical hangout, Buckeye Donuts. We discussed politics, race, and gender issues. When Professor Van Tine asked how I identified myself politically, without hesitation I gave a typical Black Muslim answer, "I am a black nationalist, Marxist, Muslim." It appeared that he did not know what to think of my answer.

My years working under Van Tine were filled with joy, excitement, and optimism. As I labored with love in the history department, my hopes for the Nation of Islam in Columbus would gradually turn to disappointment.

On our first Sunday in Columbus we found the local mosque. Unlike Chicago, which had a large and newly remodeled Final Call Building filled with more than one hundred FOI members each Sunday, the Columbus Muslims worshiped in a classroom at an elementary school. What was even worse was the size of the congregation. Including myself and my wife, there were only ten people in attendance. To say the least, we were extremely disappointed. However, although the numbers were disturbing, the engaging smile, lecture, and good spirit of the local minister were encouraging signs. Minister Donnell, the young, good-looking, and polished orator of the Muslims, exhibited passion and sincerity toward Elijah Muhammad and Louis Farrakhan. After the service we introduced ourselves to the local believers. Minister Donnell, his wife, Shirley, and other members, including Brother Howard, Sister Callie, Brother Gilbert, Brother Kevin, Brother John, Brother James, Sister LaTonya, and Brother Jack, embraced us and welcomed us to the black community in Columbus.

The relationship with the Muslims went well until Minister Akbar

Muhammad of Chicago suggested that I organize a Muslim student study group at the university. Without hesitation I did so. I posted flyers and spread the news by word of mouth of the Nation of Islam's study group on campus. The information spread like wildfire. A number of university students attended the first meeting at the Buckeye Village Activity Center. Unfortunately, unknown to me at the time a number of disgruntled Nation of Islam members also attended the meeting. They posed as neophytes who wanted to learn about Farrakhan and the Black Muslims.

The attending renegade Muslims believed that the study group could spark the development of a rival Columbus mosque. These individuals, who loved Farrakhan, hated Minister Donnell passionately. For several weeks the Muslims merged with the increased number of students who attended the meetings. Everything seemed to be going well until an upset, hyperactive Minister Donnell showed up at a meeting with seven gun-toting FOI members.

The chain of events that followed was hectic, fast, furious, and life-threatening. Brother Donnell and his FOI came into the venue like a Mafia hit squad. The students, and those who were former members of his mosque, literally ran out of the complex. My friend Brother Jack, a member of the mosque in good standing with Donnell, ordered his wife, Maryam, and Gwendolyn into an adjacent room. Gwendolyn protested; she wanted to stay and fight. As a Chicago girl, Gwendolyn had the courage of a tiger. She was a very good martial artist and knew how to use knives and sticks in combat. Reluctantly, she left the room. Ultimately, it was Brother Jack and me against the hit squad. Minister Donnell then went on a marathon tirade about his position as minister, the problems of the temple, and my activities in setting up a rival mosque. I tried to explain to him that Chicago instructed me to recruit and organize students for Muhammad. But Donnell did not want to hear my explanation. I attempted to explain this to his captain, Brother Gilbert, who had helped me out of jams years earlier in Indianapolis. Unfortunately, my former savior responded by showing me his gun. As a result of the Buckeye Village raid I complied with Donnell's request to stop the meetings and promised to refrain from associating with Muslims in bad standing. Ultimately, the fighting Muslims of Columbus departed, feeling victorious over the new brother from Chicago. I felt relieved that I settled an issue without any bloodshed. Gwendolyn was furious that I did not assault the goons. The four of us—Jack (who was an expert in judo), Maryam (who always carried a weapon), Gwendolyn, and me—could have beaten the Donnell group. I remember thinking that it was good that Gwendolyn was locked in the back room. If she had not been, several members of the Nation may have been seriously injured.

Afterward, I called Minister Akbar to tell him about the incident. He told me to remain calm and that organizing for Muhammad would be filled with many obstacles. He instructed me not to hesitate in using martial arts to enforce rules and regulations.

The problem that surfaced in the Columbus mosque did not originate entirely from the local membership but was partly the fault of the national headquarters. Columbus, as with most other temples, was part of a loosely federated community of Muslims. These satellite temples operated without any leadership or direction from the National Center. The only time that the central office contacted the various Muslim outposts was in regard to financial matters. These included obligations to the centralized operational funds in Chicago for the support of national salaries, travel, building projects, the purchasing of property, conferences, rallies, and the support of the *Final Call* newspaper. In return the general body believed that they were connected to an organization that respected their participation and membership. The Muslim faithful were fond of bragging that they held privileges and rights in the Nation. But in reality the National Center felt no obligation toward the general operation of local mosques. Local ministers, secretaries, and other officials did not receive salaries, retirement pensions, insurance benefits, or legal assistance. Local mosques did not incorporate themselves as members of the Final Call or Nation of Islam but as independent churches or temples. For example, the Columbus mosque incorporation papers once read, "The Body of Christ, Incorporated." Most members, however, did not realize that their mosques were independent religious entities. Those who did know were usually members who held a position in the local mosque. The title of their position was more important to them than exposing the legalities of the operation. Apparently, they were not concerned about the exploitation of Muslim followers.

Minister Donnell was in this class, but unlike many other ministers, Donnell did not have to take this route. He came from a middle-class upbringing, was an outstanding student in high school and college, and married into a prominent middle-class family. If he had not become involved with the Nation, Donnell might have had a career as a politician, business executive, or attorney. Although the Columbus minister illustrated flashes of organizational brilliance, he tended to rule by force, intimidation, and corruption.

The Columbus mosque was in a state of confusion and division. Muslim members had divided themselves into several political groups. For example, some individuals believed that the organization's laws should be enforced strictly. Others thought that the new "Nation" represented an air of liberalism and moderation. The different thoughts manifested themselves in the administration and activities of the temples. The conflicts within the mosques paralleled the religious conflicts between the Persians and the Arabs over who were the true followers of the prophet Muhammad (PBUH [Peace and Blessing Upon Him—used in Islamic literature to give honor and respect to the prophet Muhammad]).

During the 1980s the Columbus mosque was one of the most aggressive within the Nation. When Minister Farrakhan contracted to give lectures in New York City, Philadelphia, Miami, St. Louis, or Los Angeles, the Columbus temple was always the first to provide security. But even when united in a mission, they were divided. It was common for members to issue charges and countercharges against each other. On a normal Sunday after the main lecture it was common to have a "holdback" meeting to hear Muslims recite acts of hostilities against each other. Some of the alleged crimes were embezzlement of the temple's monies, fornication, adultery, and domestic issues of spouses refusing to be gainfully employed. Because of the Nation's rhetoric that whites are devils, many Muslim men refused to work for white companies. It became common to hear brothers brag, "I work for no one but God—myself."

One of the most eccentric Muslim hearings involved a minister's borrowing the panties of a mosque secretary. The alleged incident occurred in Chicago during a Savior's Day convention. The minister maintained that the request was made in innocence. It occurred when he was staying at the Chicago Hilton. He stated he failed to pack additional briefs so he innocently asked the mosque's secretary if he "could borrow one of her panties." The problem was that the borrower and lender were both married but not to each other.

An equally provocative case occurred when a Muslim woman exposed an alleged affair between a major eastern minister and herself. The woman testified that she and her lover once met in a hotel during a

Muslim convention. The minister propositioned her, and she responded, "If you want to make love, pick up the Quran and throw it across the room." Allegedly, the minister did so.

The National Center was well aware of these problems. On several occasions Minister Akbar traveled to Columbus and other cities to negotiate peaceful settlements within the mosque. On these visits he listened to complaints, changed officers, and reaffirmed the Nation's support of the local minister. Usually, this tactic temporarily suppressed the hostilities. The prime objective of the Chicago office was to stop local conflict before it had a negative impact on financial support to Chicago. This was the case with the Columbus mosque.

The Columbus mosque soon became a thorn in the side of the National Office. Muslims from Columbus sent scores of letters, placed hours of long-distance telephone calls, and traveled to meet with any national officer who would listen to complaints about their local temple. Members repeatedly warned the Chicago staff that violence would develop if the National Office did not quickly intercede. The warnings became a reality between 1984 and 1987.

In 1985 Minister Akbar manipulated me into accepting the post as minister of the local mosque. He did so in an elaborate sequence of events that took approximately four months to complete. During this time Minister Donnell was suspended from his role as the pastor. His top assistant, James X, a former Baptist pastor, was given temporary charge of administrative duties. However, in a matter of several weeks he also was relieved of his duties. The parishioners did not accept James's leadership because of his close attachment to Donnell. Minister Akbar then called a special meeting in Columbus to decide on the next course of action. The Columbus conference included not only registered Muslims from the capital city but also ministers and officers from such cities as Cincinnati, Cleveland, Springfield, and Dayton. Normally the visiting Muslims served as witnesses and security if violence occurred.

In a meeting that lasted several hours Akbar Muhammad announced that the temple would not have a local leader but that everyone would be tested to see if they qualified for the vacant position. These examinations were based primarily on lecture style. Every Sunday a different brother would present the main sermon. During this time Akbar Muhammad made me the administrative adviser to the temple. I was responsible for the local operation of the temple, including its relations with the National Center. I had to choose an administration, develop an organizational structure, create an atmosphere of cooperation and freedom in the temple, and establish a working relationship with the black community of Columbus. The only responsibility that was not placed on me at the time was presenting the weekly sermons, although that would come later. In reality I was the local minister.

Akbar, a master administrator, understood that if he or Minister Farrakhan had asked me outright to become the Columbus minister, I would have declined the offer. The administrative changes effected a period of intimidation, terror, and violence within the mosque. The violence began with acts of vandalism against my vehicles, but other temple members faced worse.

For example, one disgruntled member, who had accused members of the former administration of destroying his life as a father, husband, and breadwinner, assaulted one of the former leaders with a knife. The incident occurred when a brother went to the home of the believer to talk about the shake-up at the mosque. The respondent went into the kitchen, grabbed a knife, and attacked the former officer, chasing him out of his home and down the block. Fortunately, no damage was done. Still later the violence entered the mosque itself.

One Sunday a brother was lecturing when two Muslim men walked toward the rostrum and told him to sit down. The two male members stated that if he would not sit down peacefully, then they would put him down. At this time the women and visitors in the mosque ran out of the storefront building. Meanwhile, the brothers had divided themselves into rival gangs. I remembered thinking that this was a scene from *West Side Story*, with two squads of the FOI replacing the Sharks and Jets. In a matter of seconds sticks, broom handles, and chairs were being thrown and swung while I sat safely in a corner of the storefront watching and taking notes for the National Center. At this particular juncture, I took full advantage of being the adviser and not the minister. If I had been the minister, I would have had to risk my body to stop the fight; as an adviser, I could sit back and watch the battle. After about thirty minutes of battle, with no one seriously hurt, the fight ended with verbal threats. That evening I called Akbar in Chicago to inform him of the violence. In response Akbar called for a special meeting to be held on Wednesday of the coming week. At that meeting the believers would be in for a great surprise.

The secretary of the mosque phoned all registered Muslims in the city to attend a special meeting that would tell the fate of the NOI in Columbus. The announcement spread quickly. Members who had not attended a temple service in months, in some cases years, crowded into the small storefront mosque. The mosque filled with more than a hundred people, and all nervously awaited Akbar's statements. However, it would not be Akbar making any statement this evening; it would be Farrakhan.

Unknown to the membership, Farrakhan had decided to handle this problem personally. He arrived at the small building in a three-car caravan. When the three luxury vehicles pulled up, the few FOIs standing outside the building realized who was going to lead the meeting. The men who emerged from the cars were Mustapha Farrakhan, the son of Louis Farrakhan; Abdul Allah Muhammad, longtime friend and assistant to Minister Farrakhan; Moses X Powell, karate expert and personal bodyguard to the minister; several FOIs from Chicago; and, of course, the minister. The format of the special meeting was a mixture of a Baptist revival tent service and a criminal hearing.

The minister went into a separate section of the storefront to meet and speak to the local officials. He instructed them on the proper way to handle conflict among the parishioners and how extreme local problems could negate the positive appeal of Elijah Muhammad's work. Meanwhile, Minister Abdul Allah Muhammad led a revival session that he called "What Islam Has Done for You." Members stood up to testify about their past and to declare that Allah, Muhammad, and Farrakhan had changed their lives for the better. The session was both sad and comical; individuals who usually showed no emotion or connection with God or the temple, other than wearing bow ties or long dresses, stood up to cry, moan, and express their faith in Allah. Many performed as if they were featured stars on Broadway or in Hollywood. The actors did not conclude until the minister gave word that he was finished with his fact-finding mission.

When Farrakhan approached the rostrum to address the Muslims, the moans and cries stopped immediately. Farrakhan started his presentation on the meaning of Islam, the importance of the NOI, and the enemies within the movement. As he developed his argument, he asked several rhetorical questions. But not quite understanding the rhetorical nature of the questions, several Columbus believers raised their hands to answer. One particular brother, who considered himself an expert on the

Quran, the Bible, the teachings of Elijah Muhammad, astrology, and Islamic Sufism, presented an answer that dumbfounded even Louis Farrakhan. Farrakhan asked, "How do we know that the coming of Christ is at hand?" The responding Muslim's answer dealt with the angle of the Moon to Earth and the Sun, the relationship of the planets to the great pyramids of Giza, and the birth date of Elijah Muhammad. Farrakhan, not wanting to embarrass the man, responded in a simple statement, "That's good; you have a point, brother." But most of the meeting was devoted to far more practical discourse.

The minister asked one of the leaders of the mosque rebellion who had instructed him to "sit the brother down." When the rebel replied that Master Fard Muhammad had told him to, Farrakhan began to shout. When had Fard Muhammad told him that? Where had the brother last seen Fard Muhammad? Had Fard Muhammad told him about his calculated blunder? The minister reprimanded the plotters harshly, telling them they were wrong to attempt to "coup de tete." He then asked if anyone could give a broader review of what took place on the previous Sunday. Because I had taken notes, I was more than happy to oblige. Many members then groaned because they did not want me to tell Farrakhan what had occurred. At the end of the meeting Farrakhan reprimanded the Muslims for their actions. A few weeks later, in the aftermath of the hearing, I was appointed the new minister of Muhammad's mosque in Columbus.

I was named the minister despite my reluctance and the objections of several local Muslim members who viewed me as an outsider, too connected to Chicago, and too strict. They knew I would enforce the Nation's laws, something the parishioners were not accustomed to. Several Muslims who blamed me for the hearing attempted to embarrass me by arranging a debate between the local Nation and the Wald Community of Al-Islam. During this period Nation ministers had been ordered not to publicly discuss Islam with the other Muslim groups. Nonetheless, the Columbus mosque ignored the orders. Secretly, the former minister arranged a debate between one of the sons of Elijah Muhammad and me. The thesis of the forum was, "What is [the] true plan?"

Wali Muhammad, son of Elijah Muhammad and former son-in-law of Louis Farrakhan, represented his elder brother, Warith Deen Muhammad, as the local imam of the World Community of Al-Islam/American Mission Muslim Association. During this period in the development of the Nation, Minister Farrakhan stressed the importance of self-development and nonconfrontational encounters with Muslims of different persuasions. Nonetheless, the Columbus leadership did not listen to the directives of the central office. As the new leader I attended the debate but did not know the format or the objectives of the meeting. When I arrived, I was placed opposite Imam Muhammad. The pastor of the church announced to the gathering that this was the first of several religious debates between the various "schools" of Islam. The announcement caught me off guard. However, following the orders of the central office to refrain from debate and arguments, I attempted to direct the discussion toward the similarities and the common problems that we had as Muslims, black people, and as political minorities in the United States. Unfortunately, the Muslims and the general black community wanted a confrontation. They directed questions to Muhammad and me that focused on obvious differences. Because I refused to address these differences, many in attendance believed that I lost the argument. One Nation of Islam member told me that I had been "crushed by the infidels."

Although several believed that their new minister was manhandled by our enemies, many recognized that I had been set up and promised their support to my administration. A few Muslims favored confrontation, but most preferred to focus on the development and growth of the Nation of Islam.

One of the first activities we implemented was a service that provided security escorts for the black elderly who lived on the east side of Columbus. In 1986 the *Columbus Dispatch* reported that gang violence had increased in the city. Gang members, reported the newspaper, were assaulting women and senior citizens. In response to the report the local branch of the National Association for the Advancement of Colored People, the National Urban League, and the city council organized a town meeting at the Millrose Community Center to discuss these problems. Sensing the potential of the meeting for the Nation, I instructed our members to attend the conference in full force. Surprisingly, they did. At the town meeting I committed the Nation's FOI to provide security escorts for a five-block area from 6:00 A.M. to 11:30 P.M. The program was quite successful. The Columbus mosque was the first group under the leadership of Louis Farrakhan to enact a street protection program.

Our second major activity focused on youth. The local administration, which included myself, the captain, and secretary, decided to have a skating party that would feature a rap and break-dance contest. The membership was split on the decision to schedule the function. Several Muslims argued that rap music and break-dancing ran contrary to the teachings of the Honorable Elijah Muhammad. They maintained that the Messenger stopped Farrakhan from engaging any longer in the entertainment industry. I responded that Farrakhan had produced calypso ballets and plays aimed at recruitment and retention of young adults. Finally, ignoring the criticism, we held the dance/skating party. It was a successful event. Interestingly, Minister Farrakhan, two weeks after the Columbus event, invited the British reggae band Burning Spear to perform at the National Center in the Final Call Building.

My third initiative centered on the family, specifically the women. Many wives in the temple were disgusted because of their husbands' refusal to assume any domestic responsibilities. Specifically, many men refused to work, citing the Muslim work code of entrepreneurship. Instead, they sold *Final Call* newspapers and bean pies. Their ideal of self-help focused on quitting the "Devil's job" and promulgating the philosophy of Elijah Muhammad. In response to female complaints the FOI decided to hold an appreciation dinner for the sisters. The dinner was a black-tie affair. The FOI transformed the mosque into a lively eatery that featured fine cuisine and classical music. The dinner helped resolve much of the domestic tension in the mosque. It appeared that both genders appreciated the event.

The three programs succeeded, but anger, resentment, and hostility still smoldered in the mosque. These emotions emerged in very subtle ways. For example, the FOI had a habit of forgoing all local responsibilities when Farrakhan was scheduled to speak within a five-hundred-mile radius. Members often ignored the fact that the temple needed finances to pay its rent, telephone, electricity, insurance, and other pressing bills. Unfortunately, temple leaders habitually used temple monies to pay travel expenses to Farrakhan's lectures. In response to this I implemented a "traveler's letter" for members who wanted to be with the minister.

The letter was modeled on the travel letter that Elijah Muhammad had implemented during the 1960s. Muhammad, believing that the Nation was infested with government agents, created the form to reduce surveillance of the organization. My letter, like the Messenger's, stated that a person was in good standing with the local mosque and should be treated as a respected member of the Nation when visiting other temples. My definition of good standing was that the person contributed to the financial upkeep of the local mosque. However, several members reported to the National Center that I did not want the FOI to provide security for Farrakhan. The central office ignored the complaints against me, especially when the National Center instructed me to provide FOI security for the minister in Youngstown, Ohio.

However, the activities of the Nation in Youngstown proved hostile to my administration. Farrakhan's lecture in a theater in downtown Youngstown went on as planned. Attendance was sparse, perhaps five hundred people at best. Nonetheless, the minister impressed the attendees with his passionate plea that they help rebuild the Nation of Islam. After the lecture the Muslims congregated in the home of the local minister to socialize and eat. Before we left for the pastor's house, I informed members of the Columbus mosque of our departure time. However, the former leaders of the Columbus mosque decided to show their pique by refusing to honor the departure time. Instead, they caused several members and all of the school-age children to be tardy for their institutions. Unfortunately, a few of the adults lost their jobs because they were too tired to go to work the next day.

Petty hostility and anger became the norm of the mosque because members were angry at the National Center and at me. The surest way to keep corruption among the believers was to misuse mosque finances. The Columbus Muslims had a penchant for deliberately not honoring bills. They were constantly behind in rent, in payments for electric and telephone services, and in payments to the National Center.

Like members in several temples throughout the Nation, members in Columbus displayed a low regard for handling the financial responsibilities of the local mosque. In Columbus and several other cities, believers were commonly forced to move from one venue to another because of nonpayment of rent/mortgage. Between 1984 and 1986 the Columbus mosque moved five times. Religious venues included an elementary school, hotel conference rooms, storefront properties, and residences. In fact, this is why it still is difficult to locate temples throughout the country. They must constantly change their addresses because of evictions. Regarding the other debts, it was bad enough that a religious institution carried excessive balances that forced utility and phone companies to terminate services but worse that accounts were in the names of individuals and not the temple. Unfortunately, several members earned bad credit ratings because of this practice. Often, as in Columbus, individuals refused to complain about this sort of treatment, fearing they would be ostracized by the organization. Although the refusal of the mosque to pay local creditors was bad, the National Center never attempted to intercede. However, when Columbus Muslims experienced difficulty in their financial commitment to Farrakhan, swift and immediate action was taken by the National Center's administration.

In 1984 the National Center allowed temples to receive products on consignment. The major items given to members to sell were the *Final Call* newspaper and the whiting fish that was sold under the Blue Seas Fish label. At that time the Columbus mosque was required to sell a minimum of five thousand newspapers a month. Often the temple did not have the money to buy the papers directly from the National Center; however, the center would send the papers anyway, with the agreement that the balance would be paid by the beginning of the next month. For the most part this never occurred. The believers and the mosque often fell further in debt until the local administration developed a way to pay the Chicago office.

Primarily, the weight of the problem was placed on the FOI to sell the papers. The FOI were taught that the newspapers were the swords and guns of Messenger Elijah Muhammad and Minister Louis Farrakhan. These weapons must be used to destroy the white world and to uplift the black kingdom on earth. To accomplish these goals, the warriors, the FOI, must be fanatical in selling the papers. In fact, one of the quickest ways to increase one's status within the mosque was through the promulgation of the *Final Call* newspaper.

Unfortunately, many FOIs did not have the time to sell newspapers or were not good salespersons, so they often purchased the papers themselves. The practice caused financial problems for several members. It was not uncommon for Muslims to have stacks of unsold papers in their vehicles or homes.

The National Center and local administrations cared nothing about the burdens associated with selling the products. Their interest rested only on the purchase. It did not matter if the buyer was an FOI salesman or a legitimate client. In fact, it was virtually impossible for some members to sell papers because of their work schedule or the nature of their jobs. For instance, Muslim men in Chicago were expected to be at city bus stops and the L-train stations before 6:00 A.M. This was quite difficult for FOIs who had the responsibility of a family and a job. The only ones who could possibly meet these obligations were unemployed men.

As for the Blue Seas Whiting Fish, members were again expected to buy thousands of pounds yearly. Just as with the newspapers, members often did not have the money to buy the fish directly from the Final Call. Thus, consignment arrangements were made between the temples and the National Center. Again, members were placed under a financial burden. Eventually members refused to buy the fish. Because of this policy, Blue Seas failed as a money-making enterprise. In 1991 the company filed for bankruptcy.

The economic problems created by the Nation of Islam greatly affected the stability of Muslim families. Most Muslims had only a high school education. The majority worked as laborers and service employees, whereas scores of others, permanently unemployed, received some form of government assistance. Contrary to Muslim rhetoric, Nation members were recipients of subsidized housing, welfare checks, and food stamps and participated in Women's Infant Children (WIC) programs. These families, devoted followers of the Messenger and Louis Farrakhan, often gave 60 percent of their monthly income to the mosque. As a result family members often went without proper medical care, nourishment, and amenities that an average American family expected. To compensate for lack of funds, family members often hustled to make ends meet. For example, women sold baked goods, hand-made clothing, or babysitting services for extra income. The men used their personal automobiles as taxis. But on occasion desperate members used illegal means to compensate for monies lost to the Nation. In cities like New York, Philadelphia, Atlanta, Columbus, Cincinnati, Chicago, and Los Angeles, stories of insurance fraud were common. Members would claim that their car had been stolen and destroyed. Credit card scams and even illegal NOI drug busts were also frequent. But perhaps even more troubling was the level of sophistication that characterized criminal financial practices at the highest levels of NOI leadership, as when Minister Khallid Muhammad falsified documents to obtain a bank loan to purchase property in Atlanta.

Minister Khallid Muhammad, the fiery pastor from Los Angeles, had by 1986 become the second-most charismatic leader in the Nation. Muhammad, who held a doctoral degree from Xavier University in New Orleans, had been preaching Islam since the mid-1970s. Before Farrakhan had legally formed the Final Call Nation of Islam, the West Coast Muslim evangelist lectured under the alias Minister Malik Rasheedeen. As Rasheedeen he made headlines debating issues such as "Evolution versus Creation," "The Intelligence of the Black and White Race," and "Who Came First—Whites or Blacks?" Dr. Rasheedeen, an assistant professor of African American Studies at one of the local universities in the Los Angeles area, soon had a large following. In the early 1980s Farrakhan persuaded Rasheedeen to join him in the Nation of Islam. By 1983 Farrakhan had given Rasheedeen the new name of Khallid Muhammad and had promoted him to the position of minister of the Los Angeles membership and national captain of the Fruit of Islam.

Minister Khallid Muhammad used charisma, leadership skills, and the ideas of Louis Farrakhan to create a sizable and devoted Black Muslim community on the West Coast. Under his direction the Muslims built a million-dollar mosque and created a business that sold Khallid's lectures on audio- and videocassettes. He had also formed one of the Nation's largest and most militant FOI groups. Combining the rhetoric of black nationalism and capitalism, Khallid attracted national attention from both Muslims and non-Muslims. Once, during a period of local unrest, Khallid Muhammad slowly drove his white stretch limo, a Rolls Royce, through the streets of black Los Angeles with more than one hundred FOI members dressed in white military suits jogging beside and behind the vehicle. Khallid's display of financial stability and military arrogance promoted a black brand of Americanism; he was using illegal tactics to augment his and the mosque's income. In 1986 he was convicted and imprisoned for running a scam in which he acquired funds by deceiving the Social Security Administration and then used the money to purchase homes in Atlanta. Khallid was not the only member of the Nation who operated from the dark side of the law—just the most prominent to do so.

Farrakhan and the national administrators realized that activities like Khallid's had to cease. Even though the Nation took no formal stand on Khallid's legal problem, Farrakhan understood that excessive bad news reflected negatively on the Nation's mission. To keep local leadership under control and to establish renewed commitment to his leadership and objectives, Farrakhan held a mass naming ceremony for the Nation's officers.

Members of the Nation of Islam are given the letter *X* to attach to the end of their first names. The *X* represented the carrier's unknown surname and African ethnic group of origin. It was taught that after bestowing the *X*, Allah, Master Fard Muhammad, would ultimately grant a holy name to the believer. However, in the absence of Allah (Master Fard Muhammad), the Honorable Elijah Muhammad granted divine names. Between 1933 and 1975 Messenger Muhammad gave names to very few Muslims. For example, in 1975 the Nation had a membership of slightly more than three hundred thousand, and less than 1 percent had an Arabic or holy name. Some of the few who received holy/Arabic names were Muhammad Ali, Raymond Sheriff, and Louis Farrakhan. Interestingly, Muhammad had not given even his greatest and brightest student, Malcolm X, a holy name. Malcolm's Arabic name, Malik El-hajj Shabazz, was presented to him by Middle Eastern Muslims when he made his holy pilgrimage, or *hajj*, to Mecca. But the tradition of selectively bestowing holy names died under Minister Farrakhan's Final Call administration.

One day before the 1985 annual Savior's Day lecture, Minister Farrakhan called all the laborers together at the convention site for a special meeting. The preconference was slated to explain Farrakhan's recent activities and his vision of the Nation of Islam. But the minister had other objectives. In a sweeping move the minister acknowledged the diligent service of the local leaders in promoting the ideas of the Final Call Nation of Islam. For their services he rewarded the five hundred ministers, captains, lieutenants, and secretaries with the surname Muhammad. In a scene similar to group marriage ceremonies of the Hare Krishna, the Muslim leaders went wild, hugging, crying, kissing, and jumping around like school-yard children. Instantly, everyone was calling each other Brother or Sister Muhammad.

I found this event quite interesting. In one broad gesture Farrakhan cheapened the integrity of granting holy names. During the tenure of the Messenger, receiving a holy name was a rare event and a most special affair. During the early days of the Nation, Farrakhan gave new names to a select few, such as family members, special friends, top assistants, and devoted workers. But now anyone could receive a name. The only requirement was that one be an officer in the Nation or be in attendance when the minister decided to rename individuals. Despite the jubilation of the newly named individuals, Farrakhan's ceremony restructured the traditional format of the organization, cheapened the mystical image of the *X*, and lessened the appeal of an Arabic name. Two members of the Columbus mosque received new names: the secretary and me. While the secretary hugged me and laughed, I could only think how the name Muhammad was common in the Muslim world, no different from English-speaking countries naming a child Bob, Jane, or Susan. It was, therefore, difficult for me to replace a unique Caribbean name like Vibert with a generic Arabic name like Muhammad. However, in selected communities and situations, my new name would come in handy.

After the convention I gave serious thought to the direction the Nation was taking. I realized that naming individuals *Muhammad* was a ploy to encourage greater loyalty among Farrakhan's followers. I decided it was time to gradually separate myself from the political structure of the organization. First, I made another Muslim brother my assistant minister to ultimately replace me as the minister of the temple. Second, I devised an economic program that focused on individual economic development to help group members become self-sufficient within the Nation's structure. Third, I encouraged members to register at local colleges and universities for courses in history, English, and business. I believed that with a little motivation several Muslims could earn college degrees. Fourth, I sent a letter to Akbar Muhammad and Louis Farrakhan informing them that my obligations with the Ohio State University were too intense for me to devote the quality time needed to govern a growing mosque.

My resigning as minister suited many members of the Columbus mosque quite well. Former rivals became good friends. Brother Minister Donnell, who had blamed me for his forced resignation from the ministry, became quite close to me. For over a year he studied kickboxing under my tutelage; we communicated often about the works of the Messenger; and he occasionally counseled me on the role of the Quran in modern society. In retrospect, Minister Donnell, despite his early 1980s organizational failures in the Nation, was a deeply sensitive and spiritual man. He was one of the best-read students of Quranic studies in the entire Farrakhan organization.

Even though I had demoted myself, I continued to have a certain status within the group that constantly placed me at the center of the storm. In fact, my activities within the Nation continued to grow. What ultimately occurred was the development of a strange duality between me and the structure. Although I despised its blatant exploitation of its members and the black community, I appreciated and valued its practical message of black pride and self-help.

I clung to an emotional belief that there was still hope, that the Nation would be the vanguard black America. The "twoness in one strange body" that Du Bois remarked in America's race situation at the beginning of the twentieth century became the same dilemma I experienced in the NOI.[1] Could I be a Black Muslim and still review and condemn the policies of the Nation, or must I restrict myself to silence in a body yearning to speak the truth?

7

Farrakhan Speaks

Conventions, Rallies, and Savior's Day

Since the formation of the Nation of Islam in 1930, major conventions, rallies, and Savior's Day celebrations have functioned as major political promotions for the support of the organization's infrastructure. These activities are used to motivate members to follow the direction of the leader, to raise money for the organization's activities, and to illustrate to Muslims and African Americans the numerical size of the Nation.

In 1974 Elijah Muhammad held the last Savior's Day convention of his forty-four-year tenure as patriarch of the movement. During the convention the Nation demonstrated its wealth and growth to the world. The national secretary announced that the membership had reached an unprecedented figure of five hundred thousand members, who attended temples in every major city in the United States and several cities in Latin America and the Caribbean. Members learned that the Nation was worth $75 million and that its corporate empire included several businesses: a trucking firm, farms, restaurants, newspapers, grocery stores, apartment buildings, a fish enterprise, and a fleet of airplanes. The faithful also learned that the leadership planned to build a hospital on Chicago's south side and to purchase a historical black college or university. The rally illustrated the magnitude of the Nation as a vibrant entity of black capitalism and the general good health of the American economy for African Americans. Last, the affair reminded believers of the goodwill of Fard Muhammad as Allah to deliver to black America the last messenger of God, Elijah Muhammad, so that he could guide them to self-sufficiency and independence.

However, under the leadership of Minister Farrakhan the rallies, the conventions, and the annual Savior's Day event became assemblies to showcase Farrakhan's talents as orator, entertainer, and warrior against whites, Jews, and the American government and to show the world that Farrakhan was the leader of African Americans.

On February 22, 1981, Louis Farrakhan held the first Savior's Day convention after the death of Elijah Muhammad and Farrakhan's resignation from Wallace Muhammad's new World Community of Al-Islam, later to be known as the American Muslim Mission. The convention, held at the Conrad Hilton Hotel, was designed to promote Elijah Muhammad as the Christ of the Christians and the Mahdi of the Muslims and to show that Farrakhan was Elijah Muhammad's appointed leader of the Black Muslims.

Farrakhan lectured on an elaborate conspiracy by Wallace Muhammad, alleging that Jews, Arabs, and the American government were out to destroy the Nation. The theme, "A Savior Is Born for the Black Man and Woman of America," echoed the ironclad tradition of Elijah Muhammad, issuing threats against whites for their evil toward the black world.

Minister Farrakhan spoke at length about the killing of black children in Atlanta, Georgia, referring to the serial murders of twenty-six black children in Atlanta by Wayne Williams. The minister alleged that whites were responsible for the Atlanta killings. With typical Islamic bravado the minister shouted, "You better start finding the killer of our babies or some of your white babies will begin to die." For the traditional Black Muslim, black nationalist, and so-called militant African American these were sweet words. However, the greatest story that echoed through the crowd was Farrakhan's announcement that the Messenger was "alive and well" and that the "Nation is back!"

The 1981 convention was the most important rally in the history of Farrakhan's Nation of Islam. It laid the foundation, political and theological, for the first few years of the new movement. It encouraged dissenters of Wallace Muhammad and Silas Muhammad, one of his chief rivals who also was the head of a branch of the Nation of Islam, to join the charismatic preacher. In addition, it captured the minds of black students and the militant underclass to join an organization that offered them a psychic escape from the rigors of white bigotry and hostility. The three thousand people who attended the four-hour lecture were treated to the best of Farrakhan, who displayed intelligence, wit, and charisma as he explained his vision for the Nation to the excited audience. Interestingly, although the new organization represented a return to Muhammad's program, which had been unwilling to work, align, or negotiate with other black groups, Imam Wallace Muhammad encouraged many of his followers to attend Farrakhan's convention. Wallace allowed his people to decide individually whether Farrakhan represented the true tenor of Islam.

In February 1982 the Nation held its second consecutive Savior's Day in Chicago. This convention was more elaborate than the previous rally. Showing the Farrakhan appeal for excitement, showbiz, and lights, the three-day convention incorporated twelve workshops designed to solve the problems of black Americans. The community action leaders, political activists, and black nationalist scholars who conducted the workshops shouted silly rhetoric on such subjects as religion, politics, law, military science, economics, health, education, culture, communications, counterintelligence, history, law enforcement, and international relations. The panels were nothing more than gripe sessions about the evils of whites and reactionary blacks. Muslims and underclass blacks listened to inspirational and emotional jargon that gave the impression that the Nation was the Black Vanguard.

Farrakhan and Akbar, the real designers of the convention, completed a brilliant scheme that ultimately served the interests of the group by touching the emotions of the audience. Black attendees displayed feelings ranging from black pride to white hatred. The planners wanted to manipulate the fears of African Americans for the black nationalist promoters of the Nation. When individuals left the convention, the majority believed that they seriously discussed and found answers to the plight of black America. However, the real climax of the event was Farrakhan's lecture "Has America Entered Divine Judgment?"

The minister had given thousands of lectures since 1977, but to most observers the 1982 Savior's Day address was Farrakhan's best. The lecture described the logic, scope, and theological framework of the Nation. For four hours the minister traced the development and history of Fard and Elijah Muhammad's theology and its relationship with America's political and social structure. The logic and appeal of Farrakhan's talk followed typical Muslim fashion, with esoteric symbols, eccentric mysticism, and prophecy of destruction for the white world at the end of the millennium. The ideas and arguments of the lecture conflicted with traditional religious concepts, ideas, and conclusions. However, it followed typical Muslim thought.

In 1983 Farrakhan announced to the Muslims in Chicago that the Nation was moving the Savior's Day convention from Chicago to Gary, Indiana, a small black town twenty-five miles east of Chicago. Through negotiations with Gary's black mayor, Richard Hatcher, the Nation was allowed to use the city's new convention site, the Genesis Center. Five thousand Muslims arrived in the city of Gary for the three-day meeting, whose theme was "A Savior Is Born for the Black Man and Woman of America." This meeting lacked the creativity, excitement, and glamour of the first two conventions. Farrakhan, who lectured for five hours, had to plead with the audience to stay and listen to him. The workshops were copies of the previous conventions and offered no new orators or conspiracy theories. The only sign of surprise came from the Nation's top California minister, Harold X, later known as Khallid Muhammad. The outspoken West Coast pastor brought one hundred Fruit of Islam Muslims from his Los Angeles temple to Indiana. The California Fruit electrified the congregation in their sparkling white uniforms and white combat boots. The Californians excited the audience with their discipline, precise machinery drills, and devotion to Khallid, not Farrakhan. By far, the most talked-about Muslim leader in Gary in 1983 was not Louis Farrakhan but Minister Khallid Muhammad.

Overall, the convention was a failure. The Nation never held a February annual meeting outside of Chicago again. However, the next annual meeting catapulted the Nation into the national limelight. In 1983 Farrakhan toured and lectured in thirty American cities. The majority of his addresses focused on Elijah Muhammad as being the Christ and on the significance of the Nation. In most areas he was received warmly but not always as jubilantly as expected. Between April and December several developments occurred that radically changed Farrakhan, the Nation, and the organization's relationship with blacks, Jews, and white Americans. In April Farrakhan moved the Nation from its apolitical position into the arena of traditional American politics. Contrary to the activities of Fard and Elijah, Farrakhan, as the new leader, endorsed Harold Washington, Chicago's black mayoral candidate. In fact, he encouraged Chicago Muslims to campaign, register to vote, and to cast their ballots for Washington. Ultimately, Washington won the election and rewarded Farrakhan with praise and admiration.

In August of the same year Farrakhan was one of several black leaders who spoke at the march on Washington, D.C., a celebration and protest commemorating the original march in 1963. The march was symbolically important for the Nation for several reasons. During the first march Elijah Muhammad and the Nation were not given an invitation to the event, which provided a stage for all the other major black groups in the country. Second, Malcolm X, the national spokesperson of the Nation, branded the march on Washington a farce because it was run, financed, and controlled by whites, Jews, labor unions, corporate America, and the Kennedy administration. But now, Coretta Scott-King, the widow of civil rights leader Rev. Dr. Martin Luther King, the star of the first march, granted Farrakhan an invitation to the latest march. This opportunity to speak at the march's anniversary validated Farrakhan as one of the major black leaders in the United States. In the August edition of the *Final Call*, the lead story was titled "The Five Minutes That Shook the World," referring to Farrakhan's five-minute address before the Washington Monument.

In November the minister delivered the keynote address to the nation's oldest civil rights organization, the National Association for the Advancement of Colored People. The group, started by a biracial group of liberal Americans in 1909, had been a target of Farrakhan's for several years. He considered it nonproductive, class conscious, conservative, and Jewish-controlled, yet the organization allowed the fiery minister to address its members in Washington, D.C. Apparently turning over a new leaf, Farrakhan spoke on the great history of the organization and its importance to the struggle for racial equality and equal rights in the United States. A humble Farrakhan told a moving story of how, as a young boy, he had been allowed by his mother to read the association's paper, the *Crisis Magazine*. In this paper he learned of the horrible treatment that blacks suffered in the South—house burnings, race riots, and lynchings. After reading of such horrid activities, according to Farrakhan, he cried and asked, "Why do they treat us in this manner, Mommy?" The sincerity and emotion that Farrakhan expressed gained for him a new sense of respect from professional and less-militant black groups who now saw Farrakhan not as a militant racist but as a gracious and God-fearing black leader. In December the minister's fortunes continued to improve.

Rev. Jesse Jackson, the founder and leader of People United to Save

Humanity, or Operation PUSH, invited Farrakhan to be a member of a coalition of black leaders traveling to Damascus, Syria, to negotiate the release of black Air Force pilot Robert Goodman, who had been shot down after illegally entering Syria's airspace. Jackson, the premier civil rights leader of the decade, joined forces with Farrakhan, giving credibility to the Muslim as a major player in black political activism. Although Farrakhan played a minor role in Goodman's release, the *Final Call* touted the minister as the leading advocate for the release. It was reported that the Syrians were impressed with his knowledge of the Quran, fluency of Arabic, and understanding of Arabic history. Wali Muhammad, former editor of the *Final Call*, stated that if it had not been for Minister Farrakhan, "Goodman would not have been released."[1] Although Wali Muhammad's remarks were subjective and questionable, it became apparent that many in the black community held the same view. In February 1984 Mayor Marion Barry of the District of Columbia proclaimed a Minister Louis Farrakhan Day in recognition of his leadership in the release of Goodman. It was during this period that the minister had his first and only visit to the White House, when the Jackson delegation was ordered to brief President Ronald Reagan and Vice President George Bush on the Middle East trip.

Only four years removed from the Nation's first Savior's Day, Farrakhan had secured the admiration and respect of thousands of Americans, both white and black, who saw him as a rising star for civil and human rights. However, as quickly as he presented himself as a responsible leader, Farrakhan's fiery and emotional oratory forced the larger American audience to question his logic and wisdom and required his supporters to justify his inexcusable rhetoric.

On February 25, 1984, the Nation held its Savior's Day convention at the Richard Jones Armory. The Chicago, Illinois, building was packed with ten thousand screaming followers and supporters of the minister. It was the largest audience to attend a Nation's rally since the death of Elijah Muhammad. The atmosphere was electric. The minister had just completed the successful Syria trip, he was being touted by many as a responsible black organizer, and he was encouraging people to vote—an unprecedented direction for a Black Muslim. Farrakhan focused on Jesse Jackson's decision to run in the Democratic primaries for the party's candidate for the presidential election. The Muslim leader not only verbally supported Jackson's campaign but provided financial support and physical protection. But in his three-hour Savior's Day lecture, the minister assumed the mantle as Jackson's bodyguard and as God's personal emissary against the "wicked Jews." Jackson had allegedly received death threats from American Jews who were incensed over his overtures to Palestinian leader Yasar Arafat and at his referring to New York City as "Hymietown." Farrakhan told the audience that Jackson could meet with anyone he chose and that black candidates were really complimenting the Jews about their power and prestige in New York City by calling it Hymietown. He insisted this was not a negative statement because Jews call themselves Hymie. But in the same breath he threatened that if Jews harmed Jesse, he would be the last one they harmed, implying that he would lead a campaign to physically assault Jewish Americans.

The Jewish community was not the only target of Farrakhan's rage. He lashed out against the black reporter from the *Washington Post* who had broken the story of Jackson's anti-Semitic statement. Branding journalist Milton Coleman as an Uncle Tom and traitor to his race, Farrakhan urged the black community to purge him from their ranks:

> What do [we] intend to do with Coleman? At this point, no physical harm. But for now, I'm going to get every church in Washington, D.C., to put him out. . . . Wherever he hits the door, tell him he's not wanted. If he brings his wife with him, tell his wife she can come in if she leaves him. But if she won't leave him, then you go to hell with your husband. That he's a traitor and [if] you love to sleep in bed with a traitor of your people, then the same punishment that's due that no good filthy traitor, you get it yourself as his wife. One day soon, we will punish you with death. You say when is that? In sufficient time, we will come to power right inside this country. One day soon. This is a fitting punishment for dogs. He's a dog. We don't give the bread of Jesus to dogs. We just throw him out with the rest of the dogs.[2]

Minister Farrakhan's language forced Nation observers to reflect on the harsh words he spoke of Malcolm in the early 1960s. However, the minister later maintained that he had not threatened Milton Coleman but had related a story of historical fact, saying that is how traitors are treated in nation-states and adding that because the Nation is not really an independent state, he, Farrakhan, had no power to sentence Coleman to death. Coleman, however, took no chances and notified the FBI and the District of Columbia police that Farrakhan and the Nation had threatened his life.

Farrakhan's militant language increased with every inhalation. During the same lecture he bluntly accused the American Jewish community of leading a conspiracy to murder Jesse Jackson. Blaming the Jews for the death of Jesus, Malcolm X, and every major biblical and human rights activist who represented oppressed people, Farrakhan took the liberty of responding to a militant faction of the Jewish community who did not like Jackson:

> I am saying to the Jewish community who may not like our brother, it is not Jesse Jackson that you are attacking. Remember this now. You're not attacking an individual. Jesse's gone past that now. When you attack him, you attack the millions that are lining up with him. You're attacking all of us. That's not an intelligent thing to do. We know that blacks and Jews have had a good relationship in the past. We've gotten along well, because you're a suffering people and so are we. But my dear Jewish friends, you understand that everything comes of age.[3]

The lecture immediately placed the faithful in a position to attack all Jews as evil exploiters of the black community. For example, shortly after Farrakhan's speech, I met Minister Khallid Muhammad in a small room that was used as a snack bar for the Savior's Day convention. While there, I asked Khallid why the minister was opening up a can of worms that he would not be able to close. Without hesitation Khallid defended the minister, arguing that the Quran speaks out against Jews and that Jews, as sworn enemies of the black race, developed the NAACP to destroy blacks. In one sweeping move the major enemies of the Nation were not racist whites but Jewish Americans.

On March 11 of the same year Farrakhan continued his anti-Jewish rhetoric. At the movement's headquarters on Seventy-ninth Street in Chicago, Farrakhan boldly stated that "Hitler was a great leader." Calling Hitler "great" was the problem. It was like the Kurds calling President Hassan great, South African Zulus calling de Klerk great, and black Americans calling Klansman David Duke great. Farrakhan erred in calling Hitler great. Speaking to a packed house at the Final Call Building and to a radio audience that numbered in the thousands, he described how Hitler used his leadership skills to rebuild Germany's economic and political structure following its defeat in World War I. Farrakhan's historical facts were correct. *Time* magazine in 1930 named Hitler its "Man of the Year." But what concerned many blacks, Jews, and whites was not the historical accuracy of the statement but its implications about the general attitude of Black Muslims toward Jews. During this period the Nation's publications included the notoriously racist *Protocols of the Elders of Zion,* which argued that Jews had forged a conspiracy to take over the world. Unfortunately, the majority of Muslims believed *Protocols* to be true and correct in the same manner as they viewed Hitler as a "great" world leader. Ultimately, the Muslims began to challenge the authority of the Holocaust.

Unlike any other period in the history of the Nation of Islam, believers, blacks, nationalists, and many in the black community supported the Jew baiting of the group, showing open disdain and hatred toward people of Jewish dissent. There were several cases throughout the country in which Muslims used intimidating tactics against Jews, such as following identifiable Jews through airports, verbally attacking them in primarily black audiences, and speaking about them in racist terms in public. Regardless of whatever historical events motivated these Muslims, such actions cannot be justified. In fact, during this period I wrote a letter to Minister Farrakhan, asking him to cease the barrage of negative language against the general Jewish community. In my note I stated, "while it is true that certain Jewish groups like Western European Jews merged with White Americans to exploit, rape and murder blacks as well as Native Americans, the majority of the Eastern European Jewish community did not have a heavy hand in exploitation of black Americans. In fact, like blacks, they were victims of tar and feathering, beatings and lynchings."[4] The letter did not alter his views or activities toward Jewish Americans. If anything, Farrakhan's anti-Semitism increased. The minister's oral response to my concerns was curt: "I received your letter."

Farrakhan and the Nation of Islam enjoyed the publicity that they received from a supportive black community and an angry Jewish community. Almost overnight the national press remarked on Farrakhan, the Jews, and the broken alliance between the nation's two most important and strongest minority groups. To continue manipulating the press and the African American community, the Muslims aggressively stressed that the ills of the black community were caused by Jewish people. On June 24, 1984, Farrakhan attacked the very foundation of Judaism, the Torah. In a highly emotional address, recounting his most recent tour of Libya, the minister called Judaism a "dirty" or "gutter" religion. The exact words are unintelligible because the tape that was used to record the message is garbled. However, the Muslims argued that Farrakhan said "dirty," and Jewish Americans maintained he had said the latter term. Nonetheless, neither description is flattering when discussing another person's ethnicity or cultural belief system.

American Jews, whites, and even many blacks repudiated Farrakhan for his statement. Jesse Jackson, the presidential candidate that Farrakhan supported, even had to distance himself from the racist language of the Muslim. Jackson, ever the diplomat, stated that he would have to separate himself from the words of Minister Farrakhan but not from the man. In defense of the minister, Black Muslims such as historian Hakim Shabazz of Buffalo maintained that Farrakhan had used words like *dirty* to describe a lifestyle of religious devotees, that is, religion as a way of life. Members of the Nation agreed with Professor Shabazz but also stated that Farrakhan's words were taken out of context. According to this view, the minister's lecture argued that Jewish nationalists had taken land from Palestine through corrupt policies using terrorism to oppress the Arab Muslims. Thus, according to Farrakhan and his followers, the press, Jews, and others who criticized the minister were manipulated by the Jewish-dominated American press. To defend the argument, they pointed to Farrakhan's own words: "Now, that the Nation Israel, never has had any peace in 40 years and she will never have any peace because there can never be any peace structured on injustice, thievery, lying and deceit and using the name of God to shield your dirty [gutter?] religion under his holy and righteous name."[5]

Although the language that Farrakhan used to describe Judaism was vile and vicious, he continued to bait the Jewish community into having a "showdown" with him. In addition, he seemed to encourage the federal government to challenge him and the Nation on broad allegorical statements about political and social issues. On July 14, 1984, Farrakhan told a cheering New York City audience that the United States was the greatest criminal nation in the world and that the problem country of the world was not China or Russia but America. The statement was in line with the theology of Fard and Elijah Muhammad, that America is the biblical Babylon—the evil empire. Now, however, Farrakhan broadened the theology to claim that Jews were responsible for African American plights. It appeared that Farrakhan's thesis was intended to infuriate whites and Jews.

As Farrakhan's war of words continued, his relationship with Colonel Qadhafi of Libya became increasingly closer. In September 1984 he left for the North African nation to attend its fifteenth-anniversary celebration of Qadhafi's revolution. Akbar Muhammad, Khallid Muhammad, and several high-ranking officials of the Nation attended the celebration with Farrakhan. The trip to Libya played a significant role in Farrakhan's development as the head of the Nation. Within twelve months the North African visit paid off for Farrakhan.

In February 1985 the Nation again held its annual convention in Chicago. Savior's Day brought an international dimension to the Chicago audience. First, there was the introduction of foreign revolutionaries and diplomats like Ahmed Ben Bella of Algeria, Ghana's president, Jerry Rawlings, and Colonel Mu'ammar Qadhafi, who addressed the fifteen-thousand-member audience via satellite. The Libyan leader shared his plans for the Nation and urged the black community to rebel in armed struggle against the "yoke of American oppression." He added that Libya would aid the revolution with military and economic support. Farrakhan responded that the North African leader could assist the Nation with financial support. However, the Nation did not issue military discourse in America. The public discussion between Qadhafi and Farrakhan clearly illustrated that the Black Muslim used extreme and radical language to influence the North African, as well as other revolutionary states. Nonetheless, the militant Libyan leader promised to support black Americans militarily and financially in their fight against the racist and imperialist regime of white America.

The majority of Black Muslims supported Farrakhan's conservative views of resisting military support but welcoming international financial aid. Unknown to the Muslim audience, Farrakhan had already made plans to travel to Libya in May 1985 to pick up $5 million from the Libyans to start a program called POWER (People Organized Working for Economic Rebirth). The financial aid of Qadhafi permanently intertwined and connected him to the leadership, internal structure, and theological and political direction of the Nation.

While Farrakhan was traveling overseas, especially to Islamic states in the Middle East, and getting closer to the Arabs and the Libyan leader, prominent members in the Nation of Islam complained quietly of Farrakhan's apparent shift from black nationalism to Arab nationalism and from Black Islam to traditional Islamic values. It seemed to many that Farrakhan was gradually turning away from Elijah's message. These individuals firmly believed that Allah was Fard Muhammad, that Elijah was the last messenger of Allah, that the white man was the devil, and that a spaceship occupied by twenty-four black scientists orbited the earth.

Belief in this UFO, or mother plane, is central to the theology of the Nation. Between 1981 and 1984 Farrakhan delivered scores of lectures on the mother plane. Sensing the criticism of his activities with Qadhafi and other Arab leaders, Farrakhan temporarily went back to Elijah's teachings of the mother plane. Farrakhan's return to the issue of UFOs was illustrated in an alleged vision of Elijah Muhammad and the mother plane.

Farrakhan claimed at a 1984 press conference in Washington, D.C., that during one of his frequent vacations at his Mexican villa, he was beamed aboard the mother plane. Stating that this was a vision, he maintained that he met with Elijah Muhammad. The Messenger, reported Farrakhan, was alive and in good health. More important, however, Elijah stated that President Reagan, Vice President Bush, and General Colin Powell and other members of the Joint Chiefs of Staff had developed a plan to attack Libya and to exterminate black Americans. Thus, the press conference, according to Farrakhan, was ordered by Elijah Muhammad so that the world would know of America's "evil plans." Two years later in December the Reagan administration attacked Libya. According to the Nation's *Final Call,* this was a testimonial to Farrakhan's vision. In addition, Farrakhan argued that the crack explosion in black America was a part of the government's plan to murder black Americans. Years later the minister maintained that he actually was transported to the spacecraft.

In the midst of the Libyan controversy, the Jewish confrontation, and the spaceship journey Farrakhan found the time to function as a traditional Muslim. In August of 1985 he made his first religious pilgrimage, or *hajj,* to the Islamic Holy City of Mecca. However, unlike most Muslims, after making the journey, Farrakhan did not take or use El-hajj as a preface to his name.

Shortly after the alleged vision and hajj, Farrakhan made plans to hold the Nation's first October Savior's Day. The minister taught, in the weeks prior to the convention, that Elijah Muhammad was a savior to the black community; he also taught African Americans how they themselves could be saviors for their own liberation. The October event, different from past major conventions, was held outside the Midwest. The lecture was held at Madison Square Garden in New York City, where fifty thousand people packed the Jacob Javits Center to listen to the gifted Muslim speaker. But the reason for the convention centered on the economic growth of the Nation and on the continued controversy with Jewish Americans.

The theme at the New York lecture was "Power! At Last, Forever." During his three-hour lecture Farrakhan announced that the Nation of Islam had developed a line of beauty and body products called Clean-N-Fresh. The cosmetic company began with excitement and optimism. Black enterprises such as John H. Johnson Corporation, the owners of *Ebony* and *Jet* magazines, and Fashion Fair Products promised to support the venture with a generous financial investment, as well as with technical support. The Nation's line promised to offer the black community products at competitive prices. Farrakhan reasoned that the Nation's product would stimulate economic development by providing jobs. Unfortunately, the affordable body products and employment opportunities never materialized. The Clean-N-Fresh items typically cost twice what competitors charged. The employment opportunity for African Americans was a dismal failure. Except for a small number of Muslim salesmen, Clean-N-Fresh did not have any jobs to give to the unemployed masses.

While the Nation continued to promote its new cosmetic firm, Farrakhan continued to promote racism and anti-Semitism in the United States. For the first time in American history, a United States representative, Mark Siljander (R-Michigan), introduced a resolution to condemn the anti-Jewish comments made by Louis Farrakhan. Although the Nation and Farrakhan publicly denounced the congressman, they secretly basked in the free publicity. The minister increased his town circuit, bragging at each stop of Siljander's proposal. However, most of the minister's towns were international.

Farrakhan set out on one of his many world tours, traveling to the Caribbean, Central America, Africa, and the Middle East. The latter two regions would become the oratorical hot spots that highlighted the war of words between Farrakhan, the federal government, and Jewish Americans.

In early 1986 President Reagan ordered a restrictive travel ban to Libya. Farrakhan believed that the ban was a conspiracy to stop his proposed trip to Qadhafi's international revolutionary conference. In a lecture prior to his departure he stated, "I am a free black man. The U.S. Government does not control or tell Louis Farrakhan where to go. Only Allah and the Honorable Elijah Muhammad can control my travel."[6] The cheering Chicago black audience voiced its approval of the fiery Muslim leader. On February 6, 1986, the minister challenged the ban. Deliberately testing the will, resolve, and influence of the U.S. government, Farrakhan's itinerary called for him to stop in England, where he would speak, and then to continue on to Nigeria and, finally, Libya.

Great Britain, one of the strongest and fiercest allies of the United States, had other plans. First, the British Parliament, utilizing its Exclusion Act, did not allow Farrakhan and his twenty-member traveling group to enter the United Kingdom. In fact, British authorities held the minister in a holding chamber at Heathrow International Airport for over eleven hours. The delay was designed to intimidate and harass Farrakhan until he was able to board his connecting flight to Nigeria. England, with considerable influence in the West African nation, urged the government not to honor Farrakhan's contract to speak in Lagos, the capital of Nigeria. When Farrakhan arrived in Nigeria, the British request was granted. Before a large audience at the National Center, armed soldiers roughly removed the minister from the stage and ordered him out of the African nation. Farrakhan, not used to this type of treatment, became shaken and confused until President Jerry Rawlings of Ghana, Nigeria's regional neighbor, sent a plane to transport the Muslim and his group to Accra. For four days Farrakhan met with anyone who would speak to him in Ghana. Ultimately, Akbar Muhammad influenced the Ghanaian president to give the minister a grand introduction to Ghana. Farrakhan was able to rebuild his damaged ego and continue his African adventures to Libya.

In Libya Farrakhan addressed Qadhafi's Mathabah Conference of the Third World. In a highly charged lecture to international revolutionaries Farrakhan warned the United States to cease its war against Libya and to stop its escalation of a world war. In addition, he predicted the United States would destroy itself because of its reckless behavior toward Libya and other African states. More confident than ever, Farrakhan left Libya for Egypt, where he again had a vision that instructed him to order the Nation of Islam members to observe the traditional month of Ramadan—fasting with the world community of Muslims. This was new for the Nation of Islam. Under the leadership of Elijah Muhammad, the Nation did not observe the Muslim month of Ramadan. Rather, December was designated by the NOI as its religious month. Different, however, from Christians, who celebrate the birth of Jesus, the Black Muslims fasted the month to illustrate the hypocrisy of Christians. Elijah Muhammad argued that Black Muslims fast during December because Christians overindulge in eating and drinking. He claimed that during this month so-called Christians get drunk and kill in the name of Jesus. Before returning to the United States, the Muslim delegation stopped in several nations in the Caribbean.

During the remainder of the year Farrakhan continued his intense schedule of lectures. Although he gave more than one hundred lectures in this year, the only domestic one that really generated excitement was the October 7, 1986, Savior's Day event, where he and Imam Warith Deen Muhammad, Elijah Muhammad's son and leader of the American Mission Muslim Organization, appeared onstage together to celebrate the legacy of Elijah Muhammad. Farrakhan and Warith Deen Muhammad agreed to respect each other and to work together on projects that would equally benefit both organizations. Shortly after the apparent show of solidarity, Farrakhan purchased from Warith Deen Muhammad the Stony Island Mosque and School that Elijah Muhammad had used as the National Center for the Nation of Islam. With each believer of the NOI donating $1,000 to purchase the $2.5-million structure, both leaders lived up to the promise that they would support programs of mutual benefit.

Warith Deen Muhammad's organization was overwhelmed by debt, and it had to streamline and sell obsolete holdings. Finances were also a crucial concern for Farrakhan. Since 1982 he had collected millions of dollars from his followers to raise money for the building of a National Center complex, school, bakery, and adult educational facility. However, for unknown reasons the money was never used for the announced purposes. He apparently hoped that he could avoid embarrassment and state and federal investigations for fraud by purchasing the dilapidated mosque.

In 1988 Farrakhan continued the policy that by now was his trademark—presenting scores of lectures in the United States, making worldwide exotic trips, and waging a war of words against the government and American Jews. But in this year another element became part of the Muslim arsenal—Tawana Brawley. On November 28, 1988, the Associated Press reported that fifteen-year-old Tawana Brawley had been kidnapped, raped, and sodomized by white New York City police officers. Al Sharpton, a Christian minister and civil rights advocate, together with attorneys C. Vernon Mason and Alton Maddox, brought the case to national attention by charging that there was a major coverup to avoid bringing the police to justice. The three fought diligently to defend the rights of the young girl, who was accused by a grand jury of making up the event. Utilizing the legal system, Sharpton, Maddox, and Mason attempted to sue the New York City Police Department, the mayor's office, and the state's attorney general for violating the rights of the young black victim. Farrakhan threw himself into the debate by lecturing about the viciousness of the incident, the racism of New York police, and the city's failure to assist in finding the criminals.

In the next eight months Farrakhan made several trips to New York to attend rallies in support of Ms. Brawley. In addition, many of his lectures during this time focused on Brawley and the New York Police Department.

Farrakhan also began speaking on the May 13, 1985, bombing by the Philadelphia Police Department of the MOVE Headquarters in Philadelphia. MOVE, a militant black group, promoted a holistic lifestyle and antigovernment objectives. Except for one survivor, all of the men, women, and children were killed in the inferno that destroyed a full city block of homes. When the destructive fire occurred, Farrakhan denounced the Philadelphia mayor, the city council, and the police department. However, by 1987 the Muslim had become quiet on the MOVE incident. But in an open letter to black mayor Wilson Goode, who ordered the bombing of MOVE, Farrakhan challenged him to correct the wrong that he had done. The minister wrote in the *Final Call:*

> Since the county grand jury has found your actions of May 13, 1985
> morally reprehensible, though not legally culpable, I appeal to you

on moral grounds to help the victims of the MOVE tragedy. Arson is a crime. Murder is a crime. State arson and state murder were perpetrated against citizens of the United States and the City of Philadelphia. Eleven members of the MOVE Organization are dead and the one survivor of that holocaust is in prison on false charges of complicity in the burning and killing of her own family. Will you heed the cry of this family? . . . As your brother, I appeal to you to correct the wrong done by accepting your responsibility in this tragic event and seeing that justice is done.

Farrakhan's appeals in both the Brawley and MOVE cases were remarkable gestures by a national black leader. But compared to what Farrakhan had claimed of his own stature and standards, they did not measure up to his rhetoric. A more fitting standard for the Nation would have been to assist in the legal representation of the two victims or at least to unleash the organization's investigative crew to assist in finding information for the victims' cases. But this was not done. It had become evident that Farrakhan talked a good fight but that he would not put his money or his legal team in motion to help victims of discrimination and racism. As for Brawley, besides promises of support from the Nation, she received a Muslim holy name from Farrakhan. On October 9, 1988, at the seventh annual Savior's Day convention, Tawana was "blessed" before twelve thousand people with the new name Maryam Muhammad.

The next year was an uneventful period in the Nation. Farrakhan continued his heavy lecture schedule while attacks on Jews continued to be the modus operandi of the organization. The only new developments were a campaign against black gang activity and the beginning of all-black male lectures. The theme of 1989 was "Stop the Killing." To Farrakhan's credit he was able to inspire several black gang leaders in organizations such as the Bloods, Disciples, and Gangster Disciples to cease their activities in the black community. The Nation's programs among the gangs were the most positive events for the Nation in several years. The national media wrote in admiration of the minister's ability to work with young black and Hispanic gangs in cities such as Chicago, Los Angeles, New York City, and Miami.

The 1980s ended on a positive note for the minister, but the 1990s would be filled with uncertainty, eccentric ideas, and internal strife for Farrakhan and the Nation of Islam. The new decade started in typical fashion with the minister lecturing at a hectic pace, occasionally giving as many as three presentations in three different cities in a week. Farrakhan's first major lecture during this period was at the three-day convention sponsored by the Nation in Detroit, Michigan, on December 14, 1990. In front of twenty thousand people he harshly criticized the proposed war in the Persian Gulf between the United States and Iraq. He argued that the war's purpose centered on oil and money for wealthy Americans. In addition, the fiery minister stated to President Bush, "If you want to see American blood flow through the sands of Iraq, then send your son!"[7] Apparently, the minister's aggressive language toward the United States and his supportive tone toward Iraq gained him an invitation by President Saddam Hussein to Iraq to address the International Scholars Conference in Baghdad. The American Muslim took full advantage of this special invitation by supporting the Islamic delegates' call for a holy war against the United States and by branding America the great Shaitan (Satan).

To elaborate on America as notoriously evil and on Jews as the authors of America's desire to conquer and control the world, Minister Farrakhan endorsed the Nation's controversial book *The Secret Relationship between Blacks and Jews.* The manuscript, written by a group of Muslims from Boston, used selective articles to argue that Jews played a major role in the slave trade that ultimately destroyed the foundation of the African American community in the New World. A critical review of that book noted that the authors did not separate the types of Jews in the exploitation of blacks from those who supported the concept of black self-determination. Reviewers also maintained that the Nation's book wrongly branded the Jewish people as perpetrators against the human family. As one Cincinnati rabbi stated, "We were blamed for the death of Jesus, the economic problems of Germany after World War I, and now the enslavement of blacks."[8]

The Secret Relationship between Blacks and Jews ultimately put many black scholars in the storm of the debate. Intellectuals, who considered the book offensive, racist, and just bad history, were targeted by a new breed of militant students and the Nation as reactionaries against the liberation movement. Unfortunately, several scholars attempted to ride the Farrakhan problack and anti-Jewish wagon to success. For example, Caribbean scholar Tony Martin embraced the Farrakhan theme and wrote and lectured extensively on the "controlling Jew." Professor

Leonard Jeffries, head of the Black Studies department of City College in New York, lectured frequently on the Jewish conspiracy to control the media and black organizations. And Professors Ron Karenga and Maliefa Asanta, the two leading scholars of Afrocentric thought, promoted Jew baiting by remaining politically silent on the controversy. On the other hand, scholars like Henry Taylor of the University of New York in Buffalo, Darlene Clarke-Hine of Michigan State University, and Robin Kelly of the University of New York in Manhattan spoke openly against *Secret Relationships*. These scholars went on record condemning pseudo-scholarship to justify ethnic negative behavior by blacks toward another race.

For my part Professor Benny Kraut, orthodox Jew and head of the Department of Judaic Studies at the University of Cincinnati, and I developed in 1992 through 1993 the first and only upper-level course in the United States that traced the historical relationship between America's two most important minority groups. Unfortunately, radical members in both groups accused Professor Kraut and me of being too liberal and soft with the enemy. Even the head of the Black Studies department at the University of Cincinnati asked me in a hostile tone why I was teaching a class with a Jew. Sadly, other members of the department under the Farrakhan spell silently supported the anti-Semitic views of the Nation. Nonetheless, the course ran successfully for two years. As for Farrakhan, the Nation's book was proof that Jews hated blacks and that it was time to tell the Jews how blacks felt.

While scolding Jews, Farrakhan was secretly fighting prostate cancer. Throughout the Nation people were wondering about the extent of the illness and the health of the minister. Farrakhan's bout with cancer influenced members to talk about the next line of leadership. I found this period quite interesting. For years prior to the reports of Farrakhan's illness, many believed that he would live forever. Many Muslims actually argued that it was inconceivable and impossible for Farrakhan to die. Unfortunately, the Muslim leader promoted this view by claiming that he was incarnated with the spirit of Elijah Muhammad. But now there was a real possibility that the minister could die prematurely.

The thought of Farrakhan's death created an unsettling feeling among the faithful. The Nation quietly partitioned behind several major leaders who might possibly head the organization after the death of the supreme minister. The major contenders for the top post were Minister Akbar

Muhammad of Ghana, Minister Alim Muhammad of the District of Columbia, Minister Khallid Muhammad of Atlanta, Minister Don Muhammad of Boston, Minister Jabril Muhammad of Phoenix, and Minister Abdul Muhammad of Chicago. Each of these leaders held significant power and influence among the body of believers. Sensing this problem, Minister Farrakhan, like former President Marcos of the Philippines, showed his personal workout schedule by video to an audience of over fifty-five thousand people at the Georgia Dome in Atlanta and by satellite to thousands more viewers at home. The audience witnessed the minister running the one-hundred-meter dash, lifting weights, and stretching. With each stride on the track and weight lifted or pulled, the audience cheered. I could only imagine what his rivals who aspired for his position might be thinking of the apparent good health of their leader. Although the minister succeeded in temporarily destroying the rivalry among his top ministers, there was one sad note to the affair. The African American doctor from Chicago who first told Farrakhan of the illness was severely criticized by many members of Farrakhan's inner circle who maintained that he did not know what he was talking about. Farrakhan then consulted a white physician who found the same problem his black colleague had diagnosed. Sad to say that the Black Muslims, like many black Americans, valued the advice of a white professional more than that of an African American professional.

After the physical education video Farrakhan declared to his followers that he had been healed of all traces of prostate cancer. It was a well-known fact that the minister believed in herbal and root medicine, often practiced in the Caribbean and Latin America as Roots, Vodun, Santeria, or Obeah. He employed similar concepts practiced by Native Americans to resolve his suffering with cancer.

In 1993 Farrakhan not only fought off internal strife and cancer but also new allegations from the black community, white media, and Dr. Betty Shabazz that he was responsible for the murder of Malcolm X. The controversy began with the 1992 theatrical release of Spike Lee's biopic *Malcolm X*. The film capitalized on a cultural nationalist rebirth of Malcolm among African American youth. In 1993 and 1994 the American youth later to be known as "Generation X" became fascinated with the image of Malcolm as a bold, strong, and defiant black leader. As the image of Malcolm X grew among media personnel, Farrakhan's image and that of the NOI diminished. Lee branded Elijah Muhammad and the Muslim inner circle as the group who murdered the Black Muslim leader. In addition, the director/producer characterized Elijah Muhammad as a feeble old man who took sexual advantage of teenage secretaries. At this time Malcolm's widow gave several interviews to the New York press accusing Farrakhan in the murder of her husband. In a feeble attempt to answer Lee's *Malcolm X* and Dr. Betty Shabazz's charges, Farrakhan advertised that at the annual Savior's Day convention he would tell the world what really happened. The lecture was titled "The Honorable Elijah Muhammad and Malcolm X, 25 Years Later: What Really Happened?"

Because of the popularity of Lee's movie and the renewed interest in Malcolm X, the auditorium at the University of Illinois Pavilion was packed with at least twenty thousand people to hear Farrakhan's lecture. The talk centered on Farrakhan's relationship with Malcolm X as a student, as a friend, and, later, as a protector of Elijah Muhammad. Unfortunately, Farrakhan's presentation did not offer anything new to the discussion. The only segment of the three-hour-long talk of any interest was the introduction of four of Muhammad's alleged wives and their children to the audience. The former secretaries and widows elaborated on how Malcolm was a liar, hypocrite, and disbeliever in the labor of Elijah Muhammad. Although these women spoke about the great will of Muhammad and the evil of Malcolm, I found it interesting that none of the offspring of Elijah and Clara Muhammad, his first and only legitimate wife, spoke at the event. It appeared to many in attendance that Clara and her children were ignored in the theological and historical discourse on the Nation of Islam.

Farrakhan would be vindicated of his alleged role in the assassination of Malcolm X when, in 1995, the Federal Bureau of Investigation uncovered a plot by Qubilah Shabazz, one of the daughters of Malcolm X, to hire someone to kill him. The Nation of Islam quickly alleged that the plot was inspired by the government to create a deeper wedge in the black community between the followers of Farrakhan and the admirers of Malcolm. During a press conference at the National Center in Chicago the minister stated, "I am personally saddened over the indictment and arrest of Qubilah Shabazz. The same forces that denied Malcolm X protection after his house was fire-bombed as a result of a hostile environment created by the government, have now exposed Malcolm's daughter, Qubilah, to a similarly hostile environment."[9]

Betty Shabazz responded that she was surprised at the extent of the minister's humanity in understanding that Qubilah had nothing to do with this. In May 1995 the Nation of Islam hosted a legal fund-raiser for the Shabazz family at the Apollo Theater in Harlem, New York. The affair healed the wounds that had kept the Shabazz family and the Nation of Islam separated. It represented an end to the thirty-year animosity between the followers of Elijah Muhammad and Malcolm X. The minister eloquently maintained that Dr. Betty Shabazz, the widow of Malcolm X, and he had become symbols that reflected concerns and issues of black America far greater than their individual lives. He added, "At this point in time, we must deal with these great concerns—government entrapment and misconduct, attacks on black leadership, and justice for Qubilah Shabazz. At some point healing must begin. Even though we believe Qubilah Shabazz is a victim of government entrapment, I also believe that Allah (God) permitted these circumstances to give us an opportunity to do that which would allow the healing process to begin."[10]

As the minister desperately attempted to begin the healing process between the Nation and the supporters of Malcolm X, an unexpected dilemma occurred that overshadowed the Malcolm issue. On November 23, 1993, Khallid Abdul Muhammad, the National Representative of Louis Farrakhan and the Nation of Islam, minister of defense and the former supreme captain of the Fruit of Islam, delivered an extremely inflammatory anti-Jewish lecture at Kean College, a small liberal arts institution in New Jersey.

Minister Khallid Muhammad, self-described as Farrakhan's flame-thrower, represented the rough side of the Nation. He spoke in terms of Elijah Muhammad and the NOI as being bold, militant, and aggressive, a force for violent revolution. With his dark black complexion, shining bald head, and muscular body fitted in designer suits, Khallid inspired the young ghetto dwellers who believed that no one was interested in their affairs. As stated by a Los Angeles gang member, "Khallid is a well-dressed gang banger."

Like many of his ministerial colleagues, Khallid had a checkered past that flowed through the corridors of higher learning and the correctional institutions of the United States. Khallid, affectionately referred to as "Dr. Khallid" in the Nation, allegedly earned a doctorate degree from Dillard University in New Orleans and later taught at the University of California at Long Beach in the African American Studies department. However, Dillard University has no record of Khallid or Harold Moore Vann, his birth name, ever having earned an advanced degree from the university, and the University of California denied that he ever taught at the university as a professor. Nonetheless, whether or not he had earned a degree or taught at a university was not important to the Nation of Islam. The real significance to the organization was that he demonstrated a gift for articulation, intelligence, and organization and that he was a defiant defender for Louis Farrakhan.

Khallid had been a supporter of the Nation since the early 1970s. When Warith Muhammad restructured the Nation, Khallid labored solo as a Black Muslim evangelist. In 1980 Farrakhan recruited him as an organizer for the new Nation of Islam. During the early years he served as one of the minister's most trusted supporters, traveling with him throughout Latin America, Europe, Africa, and the Middle East. Speaking on Khallid's defense of him, Farrakhan stated, "Harold X [Khallid] is a beautiful black man who is a natural warrior for our God Allah and his Christ, Elijah Muhammad. When Brother traveled with me, I used to wonder why he always carried that big Bible with him. I later found that the Bible was a case for his gun. Brother had cut out the inside of the book for his piece [gun] to protect me. I told Harold that we don't need any weapons because Allah will protect us."[11] However, Farrakhan recognized and enjoyed the militant spirit of his younger disciple. But Khallid's Kean College speech would forever alter their relationship.

At Kean College the aggressive and loose cannon Minister Khallid Muhammad used every racist, political, historical, and theological barb in his arsenal to attack the Jewish community. He blamed the Jews for the destruction of the black community through the renting of slum housing, the selling of pork and liquor, and the promotion of drug abuse and prostitution. He claimed that Jews controlled the Federal Reserve, libraries, the entertainment industry, and the political arena. But worse, according to Khallid, the people who called themselves Jews were impostors. The original Jews were black. Jewish Americans, stated Khallid, always attempt to appeal to the emotions of the black community. He roared that Jews had claimed to share the sufferings of blacks, but according to Khallid, the Jews had used black Americans for their own selfish political goals. More astoundingly, he blamed the Jews for the Holocaust:

> Everybody always talk[s] about Hitler exterminating six millions Jews. . . . But doesn't anybody ever ask what did they do to Hitler? They went there, in Germany, the way they do everywhere they go, and they supplanted, they usurped, they turned around [Germany] and a German, in his own country, would almost have to go to a Jew to get money. They undermined the very fabric of the society. Now, he was arrogant, no good, devil bastard, Hitler, no question about it. . . . He used his greatness for evil and wickedness but they [the Jews] are wickedly great, too, brother. Everywhere they go and they always do it and they hide their head.

At Kean College Khallid's fury was that of a madman. He attacked everyone and anyone he considered an enemy. He called Jews savages who ate juniper roots; he called the Pope "a no good cracker" and implied that he was a homosexual. Khallid said, "Go to the Vatican . . . [and look at] the old, no good Pope, you know that cracker. Somebody needs to raise that dress up and see what's really under there."[12] The Nation's spokesperson was in rare form. In fact, combining all the antiwhite, anti-Jewish, and anti-Arabic polemics of Fard Muhammad, Elijah Muhammad, Malcolm X, and Louis Farrakhan, none were as vicious and hostile as Khallid's charges. However, the most horrific and reactionary of all his statements articulated his contempt of whites in South Africa:

> If we want to be merciful at all, when we gain enough power from God Almighty to take our freedom and independence from him, we give him 24 hours to get out of town by sundown. . . . If he won't . . . , we kill everything White that ain't right in South Africa. We kill the women, we kill the children. We kill the babies. We kill the blind, we kill the crippled, we kill 'em all. We kill the faggot, we kill the lesbian, we'll kill them all. . . . Why kill the babies? . . . Because they gonna grow up one day to oppress our babies. . . . Why kill the women? . . . Because they are the military or the army's manufacturing center. They lay on their back and reinforcements roll out between their legs.

Khallid continued to rant:

> Kill the elders, too. God damn it, if they're in a wheelchair, push 'em off a cliff in Capetown . . . or Johannesburg . . . or Port Sheppiston or Durbin. How the hell you think they got old? They got old oppressing black people . . . and when you get through killing 'em all, go to the God damn graveyard and dig up the grave and kill 'em again. 'Cause they didn't die hard enough. And if you've killed 'em all and don't have enough strength to dig 'em up, then take your gun and shoot in the goddamn grave. Kill 'em again. Kill 'em again, 'cause they didn't die hard enough.

Soon after the lecture, the B'nai B'rith's Anti-Defamation League ran a full-page advertisement in the *New York Times* featuring excerpts of Khallid's speech and asking the reader to decide if Farrakhan and the Nation had become more moderate and tolerant of other ethnic and religious groups. As soon as civil rights leaders read the advertisement, they immediately denounced Khallid's statements. Abe Foxman of the Anti-Defamation League; Benjamin Chavis of the National Association for the Advancement of Colored People; William H. Gray of the United Negro College Fund; Kweisi Mfume, Maryland Democrat and head of the Congressional Black Caucus; Charles Rangel, Harlem's Democratic Representative; and Jesse Jackson of the Rainbow Coalition quickly condemned Khallid's remarks and asked Farrakhan to make a statement on whether the Nation's spokesperson was speaking on behalf of the Nation of Islam.

Benjamin Chavis, who later became an enemy to Khallid, was one of the first to publicly criticize the Muslim minister. He stated at a lecture at the Smithsonian on the birthday of Martin Luther King:

> I am appalled that any human being would stoop so low to make violence-prone anti-Semitic statements. . . . [Khallid's statements are] a slap in the face to the memory of Dr. King, Medger Evers, Malcolm X, Viola Liuzzo, Andrew Goodman, James Chaney, Michael Schwerner, and countless others who devoted their lives to the liberation of African Americans and others who have been oppressed. Our struggle for racial justice must never be diverted or derailed by the senseless expressions of anti-Semitism and other hatred.[13]

National leaders, white and black, now turned their attention to Farrakhan, asking what he was going to do about Khallid. As the National Office of the NOI considered what to do about the Khallid problem, rank-and-file Muslims quickly rallied around the spokesperson. They viewed Khallid Muhammad as a defiant spokesman of the black nationalist philosophy of Elijah Muhammad. Most Muslims had for years viewed Khallid as the straight shooter of the Nation. Thus, his statements were consistent with the rhetoric of the organization.

Initially Farrakhan attempted to adopt the perspectives of the believers. On February 3 Farrakhan announced in a press conference that Khallid's statements were "vile, repugnant, malicious and mean-spirited," yet, he stated, "Khallid spoke truths about the Jews, Whites and the Catholics."[14] The punishment for Khallid's terrible attitude, but not his racist and repugnant religious comments, was a suspension from his position as a minister and the organization's spokesperson. Internally, Farrakhan dismissed Khallid from the Nation, yet the general public, NOI members, and even Khallid Muhammad would not find out about his expulsion until late 1995.

The Khallid issue brought Farrakhan a great deal of hostility from the white and Jewish communities; however, many in the black community embraced the minister's defiant public stand against Jews, whites, and the American government. Because the majority of black Americans saw Farrakhan as a major political leader who should be heard by the larger white majority, the minister enjoyed invitations from talk-show hosts like Phil Donahue, Barbara Walters, and Arsenio Hall. As for the Nation's conventions, they became larger and increasingly anti-Jewish, antigovernment, and antiwhite. Throughout 1994 and 1995 Farrakhan's public appeal to African Americans was overwhelming. He attracted eighteen thousand for the Only Women's lecture in Atlanta, twenty-five thousand for the Only Men's lecture in New York, and almost two million for the Nation's Million Man March on Washington, D.C. However, Farrakhan's popularity would begin to wane because of internal organizational squabbling, mismanagement of finances, blatant mistreatment of its own membership, the Khallid problem, and a changing religious theology.

Figure 1. Pittsburgh, Penn. Clockwise from back row left: Mustapha Farrakhan, son of Louis Farrakhan and assistant supreme captain of the FOI; Khallid Muhammad, supreme captain of FOI and personal bodyguard to Louis Farrakhan; Louis Farrakhan; Salaam Muhammad, personal driver and bodyguard to Louis Farrakhan; two unidentified FOI members; signer.

Figure 2 (a–b). The former business office and clothing shop is now a venue for billboard signs and advertisements. The structure was purchased in the early 1990s by the Nation of Islam.

Figure 3 (a–e). The flagship temple of the Nation, Mosque Maryam, was once the largest Islamic religious venue in the Nation of Islam. The beautiful structure that houses the University of Islam, a secondary school, was purchased and refurbished by members of the Nation in the 1980s. In the front of Mosque Maryam is one of the trucks of the Leotis Fleet. The fleet transports newspapers, videos, and foodstuffs to various Muslim temples across the country.

Figure 4 (a–b). The Salaam Restaurant opened in 1995. Members of the Nation of Islam had to give a minimum $1,000 donation toward the construction of the eatery. In May 2000 the establishment was closed for repairs, according to the Nation. However, according to insiders, the Salaam has been operating in a sea of debt and financial mismanagement.

Figure 5. The intersection of Seventy-ninth St. and Emerald Ave. was a popular strip for Muslim activities in the 1980s and early 1990s. Today it is a deserted area with closed NOI businesses like the Salaam Restaurant, office buildings, and bookstores. In the foreground is the Final Call Building, which still houses the offices of the *Final Call* newspaper.

Figure 6. Dr. Vibert White (left), an adviser to the Million Man March, Inc., organized the transportation of hundreds of black men from Cincinnati, Dayton, and Columbus, Ohio, as well as from West Virginia and Michigan, to attend the Nation's march on Washington. Courtesy of Laurence Williamson, Columbus, Ohio.

Figure 7. Million Man March. Dr. White (right) giving last-minute instructions to his group. Courtesy of Laurence Johnson.

Figure 8. A few of the many Fruit of Islam members who attended the Million Man March. Men of all ages, religions, and social classes brought their hopes and prayers to Farrakhan's event. Courtesy of Laurence Johnson.

Figure 9. One of the many Cincinnatians who attended Farrakhan's Million Man March. This gentleman was the first person to book passage on the bus caravan from Cincinnati to Washington, D.C. Courtesy of Laurence Williamson.

Figure 10. The Cincinnati contingent watching and enjoying the MMM activities. Courtesy of Laurence Williamson.

Figure 11 (a–b). Welcoming celebration of Nation of Islam delegates to President Qadhafi's Mathabah Conference in 1988. Nation of Islam participants cruised from the island of Malta to Tripoli, Libya. They were welcomed in a harbor in Tripoli.

Figure 12 (a–b). The Black Man's Think Tank. University of Cincinnati, Cincinnati, Ohio. Minister V. L. Muhammad, representative of the Nation of Islam, 1991.

Figure 13 (a–b). Damage from a bomb to the office of the *Cincinnati Herald*, a black newspaper. The attack was done a week before Minister Khallid Muhammad was to speak in Cincinnati. Speculation was that a Jewish group may have been responsible for the bombing; however, later arguments surfaced that this may have been the work of Muslims in the NOI who were loyal to Louis Farrakhan. Within a month after the bombing Minister Khallid Muhammad was shot in California.

Figure 14. Minister V. L. Muhammad (left) and former heavyweight boxing champion James "Bone Crusher" Smith. Washington, D.C., 1994.

Figure 15. Minister V. L. Muhammad (foreground) and Dr. Leon Sullivan, organizer of the African and African American Summit meetings held annually in Africa. Washington, D.C., 1994.

Figure 16. Nation of Islam restaurant in Columbus, Ohio, 1987.

Figure 17. Prison Ministry of Minister V. L. Muhammad (center) and the Nation of Islam. Two Muslim inmates at the maximum security prison in Dallas, Penn., 1988.

Figure 18. Former editor of the *Final Call* newspaper, Wali Muhammad, visiting the "old city" in Malta, 1988.

Figure 19. Dr. Vibert White (left) with head sheik of the Layenne Islamic Brotherhood in Yoff, Senegal, 1994.

Figure 20 (a–b). Dr. White (top: left in gateway; bottom: right) leaving the Layenne mosque after religious Friday prayer, Yoff, Senegal, 1994.

Figure 21. The ship to Tripoli, Libya, included not only Nation of Islam delegates but also Canadian Aryans. Occasionally the Mathabah Conference organizers do not adequately review organizations past their basic ideology of contempt of Jewish Zionism and American imperialism.

Figure 22 (a–b). Tripoli, Libya. The welcoming of Black Muslims to the 1988 Mathabah Conference.

Figure 23. Minister Louis Farrakhan (second from right) and Dr. V. L. White (third from right) with various Cincinnati Muslims at the Ghana Savior's Day event, 1994.

Figure 24. Minister Farrakhan (right) enjoys a light moment at the Ghana Savior's Day event, 1994.

Above: Figure 25. Minister Farrakhan enjoys a drink while personal bodyguards observe the surroundings at the Libyan-owned Libada Beach Hotel Resort in Accra, Ghana. Minister Farrakhan and the Nation of Islam enjoyed their first Savior's Day celebration outside the United States in 1994. *Left:* Figure 26. The personal dining area of Louis Farrakhan inside the Salaam Restaurant, Chicago.

Figure 27. Inside the refurbished mosque of the Nation of Islam. The mosque was first purchased in 1972 by the Honorable Elijah Muhammad, was closed in 1978 by Imam Wallace Deen Muhammad, and was purchased in 1988 by Louis Farrakhan. The mosque is the flagship religious venue of the Nation of Islam.

Figure 28. The Nation of Islam advertised the Salaam as a multipurpose establishment, comprising a bakery, fast-food service, and fine dining. This photo shows the Salaam's fine-dining establishment.

Figure 29. The Fruit of Islam, besides being the security force of the Nation of Islam, consisted of the organization's salesmen. Many FOIs quit their full-time jobs to sell the Nation's products for meager wages. FOI, Cincinnati, Ohio, 1994.

Figure 30. The Muslim Girl Training Group (MGT) represented the female wing of the Nation of Islam. The MGT comprised the General Civilization class and the Vanguards. MGTs promoted the ideals of proper female behavior as Muslim wives and mothers. In the 1980s and 1990s the MGT held national women-only conferences. Columbus, Ohio, 1987.

8

Cain and Abel

Division in the Brotherhood

And the Lord said unto Cain. Where is Abel thy brother? And he
said, I know not: Am I my brother's keeper? And [the Lord] said,
what hast thou done? The voice of thy brother's blood crieth unto me
from the ground. And now art thou cursed from the earth, which
hath opened her mouth to receive thy brother's blood from thy hand.

Gen. 4:9–11 AV

And relate to them with truth the story of the two sons of Adam,
when they offered an offering, but it was accepted from one of
them and was not accepted from the other. He said: I will certainly
kill thee. (The other) said: Allah accepts only from the dutiful.
At length his mind made it easy for him to kill his brother, so he
killed him; so he became one of the losers.

Holy Quran, chapter 5—Al-Masidah: The Food, section 5:27, 5:30

The Holy Bible and the Holy Quran both detail the story of Cain and
Abel, two brothers who presented separate offerings to God. Cain, a
farmer, presented the Lord with a gift of vegetation. Abel, a herdsman,
offered God meat and fat. The Lord accepted both offerings and thanked
the men but remarked that he appreciated the meat more than the vegetables. In a rage of jealousy and envy Cain murdered his brother, Abel.
The Nation of Islam, like the two rival brothers, has a history of express-
ing love, sincerity, and loyalty to its members. However, since the
middle 1980s, rumors of political power brokers using their prestige to
undermine, exploit, and oppress fellow Black Muslims have increased.
In the early 1990s several episodes surfaced that supported the stories of
internal mechanisms within the structure to suppress the activities of
grassroots and undisciplined Muslims.

The personality that represented the grassroots members, an undisciplined side of the Nation of Islam, was Minister Khallid Muhammad. Since his acceptance into the Muslim fold, Minister Khallid has characterized himself as a warrior for the street brother and sister. As the minister of mosques in Los Angeles, Atlanta, and New York City, Khallid created a cult-like following that embraced gang members like the Crips and Bloods of south central Los Angeles, the Gangsta Disciples of Chicago, and the Zulu Nation of Miami and the Bronx. More than any other Black Muslim, including Farrakhan, Khallid's devotion ran deep into the hip-hop generation of musical rap star entertainers. Hard-core rap artists and groups like Public Enemy, Niggas With Attitude, Ice Cube, and Tupac Shakur, to name a few, viewed the controversial Muslim with admiration and respect as the leader of Generation X.

The young militant members of the FOI also respected Khallid tremendously. Although these young warriors respected Farrakhan as the overall leader of the movement, they followed Khallid as their "general of arms," the person who fought with them in the trenches and on the streets of America's ghettos. The skillful orator and brilliant teacher labored diligently to create a special relationship with the young militants in and outside the Nation. His method was based on one-on-one relationships, blunt and nonspiritual language, aggressive and sometimes racist dogma, and the personal style of Malcolm X, Fred Hampton, Huey Newton, and a Mafia hit man all rolled up in one person. However, whereas the larger grassroots membership of the Nation supported the colorful minister, the leadership despised his ability to organize and promote himself as the most popular leader, except for Farrakhan, in the Nation of Islam.

As a member of the Midwest region and student of Akbar Muhammad, I, like many in the upper echelon of the movement, viewed Khallid as a loose cannon who was dangerous to the overall objectives of the movement. Minister Khallid's behavior seemed too reckless for a religious movement. His court conviction for falsifying tax documents and for operating a social security scam to obtain mortgages for buying homes placed the Nation in jeopardy. I agreed with the Chicago office's condemnation of Khallid as "non-religious, arrogant, and foolish" for a Nation of Islam minister.[1]

The campaign to disguise Khallid by the Nation's leaders started in

1983. The fiery and colorful Khallid brought one hundred of his top Los Angeles Fruit of Islam soldiers to the Savior's Day celebration in Gary, Indiana, in 1983. His troops, dressed in white FOI uniforms with white helmets, boots, and gloves, gained attention with their strict discipline and attention to Khallid's orders. In fact, his men only recognized one other leader besides Khallid, and that was Farrakhan. Again, major officers and ministers in the Nation argued that Khallid was "arrogant, brash and wrong to show up the Chicago [Farrakhan's] FOI."[2] Hostility continued when Khallid created a media company to produce and market his own lecture tapes, articles, and books. The West Coast regional minister complained to Chicago that Khallid was attempting to start his own Nation of Islam in California. But Khallid's greatest mistake to the Nation's leadership class was building the first modern mosque of the Nation under the leadership of Louis Farrakhan. The beautiful religious structure was built in the heart of black Los Angeles. The structure cost an estimated $3 million. Designed in traditional Islamic style, the mosque was lined with stained glass and plush carpeting, creating an overall royal splendor that outshone every temple mosque in the Nation of Islam. The organizational talents that Khallid displayed in the funding and building of the Los Angeles mosque overshadowed every minister, including Farrakhan, at this particular stage in the development of the Nation.

Embarrassed, frustrated, and jealous at the quick rise of Khallid, by the mid-1980s several ministers had complained to Farrakhan that Khallid was a potential threat to the overall growth of the movement. They convinced the leader that something must be done about this "crazy man," whom many described as brash, thick-headed, and non-negotiable. Bowing to the pressure of many of the Nation's ministers, Farrakhan acted on the "Khallid problem." First, in 1983 for unspecified reasons Farrakhan, according to Khallid, busted or silenced him as the Los Angeles minister. In 1985 Minister Farrakhan transferred Khallid from Los Angeles to Chicago. The reason for the relocation, according to Akbar Muhammad, was to have "Khallid organize the Chicago Fruit [Fruit of Islam] into a better-equipped force for the Nation."[3] However, the real reason was to keep Khallid close to headquarters for observation. In fact, when I learned of Khallid's relocation and position as the supreme captain of the Fruit of Islam, I immediately sent a letter to Farrakhan stating that the "transfer of Khallid was a well thought out move," adding that "our perusal of Khallid was a priority that we could not ignore."[4]

There was also jealousy toward Khallid because of his lavish lifestyle. Khallid operated what was at the time the only black-operated business on Rodeo Drive in Hollywood, a $600,000-a-year enterprise. He resided in a $300,000 home, drove a $90,000 Rolls Royce, and wore $2,000 designer suits. Other ministers, who lived in rented shanties, dressed in $80 suits, drove Buicks, and struggled to make ends meet, were incensed with Khallid's materialism. Khallid responded that they "were jealous and envious, they waited for the Nation and Farrakhan to take care of them. Me, I take care of myself!"[5] But, like an obedient child, Khallid uprooted his family and moved to Chicago. To the anger of his enemies within the Nation, he made the best of the situation. In a matter of weeks he transformed the FOI from a passive group of newspaper sellers to aggressive entrepreneurs and students of cultural historical events. According to Brother Malik, former lieutenant of Khallid, "Khallid taught us how to be revolutionaries. The FOI became more than paper pushers [sellers of the *Final Call*]; we became the black Mafia!"[6] Members throughout the Nation were talking about Khallid's work with the Chicago Fruit. Young FOI members from around the country traveled to meet with Khallid to talk about his philosophy of the Nation's military structure. Unfortunately, although he was popular among the soldiers, he was disliked by his peers. According to several employees who worked in the Final Call Building, where Khallid had an office, there were constant arguments between Khallid and Akbar Muhammad, Wali Muhammad, and Leonard Farrakhan, NOI chief of staff. Observers said that these in-house fights included hostile profanity and that they bordered on physical confrontation. Privately, all of these men told several individuals of their hatred of Khallid. Khallid, for his part, did not hide his disgust with his brothers.

According to many of the FOI brothers who studied under Khallid in Chicago, they were happy to labor with Supreme Captain Khallid. Through Khallid the brothers gained a sense of empowerment that they desperately needed. The FOI purchased an FOI building, as well as automobiles. They were instructed to meet with gang members, dope pushers, prostitutes, pimps, and other so-called outcasts. Khallid's forte was being a street-wise minister. For this role he encouraged FOI members to go into the worst sections of the city to recruit men for Muhammad. He believed that the worst, toughest, dirtiest, and meanest individuals made the best FOIs. Because they had been living so badly for so long, working for Muhammad through Khallid's leadership was a step up from their ghetto lives. Apparently, Khallid's recruitment style worked. These new recruits worked tirelessly under his leadership. Fearing no one but God, they patrolled three of the worst housing projects in the United States: the Ida B. Wells, the Cabrini Green, and the Robert Taylor Homes. During Khallid's tenure in Chicago the FOI were responsible for a decrease in criminal activities in these dilapidated killing fields called apartments. In only three months the Chicago FOI's membership tripled. But once again jealousy raised its ugly head in the National Center. Within a few months Khallid was transferred to Malcolm's and Farrakhan's former mosque in Harlem, New York—Muhammad's Mosque Number Seven.

During the mid-1980s the former flagship mosque of the Nation, Temple Number Seven, was beset by corruption, lack of productivity, and an inefficient minister. In the country's largest city, with a population of thirteen million, the Nation's membership was less than two hundred. The temple was a one-level flat on the third floor of an old run-down theater next to a steamy, smelly, second-rate boxing gym. But more embarrassing, the New York Muslims consistently sold fewer *Final Call* newspapers than many of the Nation's smallest temples and study groups. Before Khallid's move to the Big Apple, Farrakhan experimented with Akbar Muhammad as the interim minister. Akbar, the best organizer in the Nation, was overburdened with dividing his duties as national assistant to Farrakhan in Chicago, as the Nation's ambassador to Africa, and as the minister of the New York temple. Ultimately, Temple Number Seven suffered, and Akbar's physical health declined when he was stricken with the first of three heart attacks.

Khallid looked to his move to New York with excitement. He was finally in the city, on the streets, and under the star and crescent that brought Malcolm X and Louis Farrakhan admiration, fame, honor, and prestige. Like a runaway train Khallid sped to New York to begin his new mission. Harlem was a special place for Khallid. As a skilled street orator and organizer, he knew that the five boroughs of the city offered him the opportunity to once again become the Nation's most popular leader. Like his predecessors Khallid formed alliances with several members of the

black community. He introduced himself and shared the stage with individuals like Professor Leonard Jefferies, Professor John Henry Clarke,
Rev. Al Sharpton, activist Lenora Fullani, Dr. Yusef Ben Jahannan, and
Congressman Charles Rangel. Khallid, a personable and socially polished individual, impressed many in Harlem as being a brilliant, talented, and responsible black leader. As he made his rounds among the
black elite and powerful in New York, he also sought out villains, ex-
cons, and socially disadvantaged individuals to join the Nation. As he
had in Los Angeles and Chicago, Khallid transformed the Harlem
mosque from a degenerate, nonproductive entity into the Nation's strongest mosque. But again, as with Cain and Abel, jealous members of the
brotherhood conspired to remove Khallid from Temple Number Seven.

According to internal mosque discussion, part of the conspiracy to
remove Khallid came from Philadelphia's Mosque Number Twelve.
Philadelphia was one of the fastest growing mosques in the Nation in the
mid-1980s. It was led by a young fiery minister named Anthony, who
was only in his mid-twenties. Different from many of his peers who
aspired to prestige and a national office, Minister Anthony was dedicated
to the growth of the Nation and the restructuring of the black community. Located on Broad Street, a couple of miles from Temple University
and Father Divine's Lorraine Hotel, the mosque was filled with hard-
working and dedicated members. However, the membership was affiliated with Farrakhan's youth minister, Conrad Muhammad.

Conrad Muhammad, who branded himself the young Farrakhan, had
ambitions to become the minister of New York. He, like Khallid, realized the importance of Temple Number Seven to a young minister who
longed for influence and power within the Nation of Islam. Several of
Farrakhan's top ministers spoke openly about Conrad's assertiveness
and ambition to become Harlem's minister. Akbar Muhammad was
amazed that Minister Conrad worked so diligently and openly to get the
New York mosque. It would not be strange, according to Akbar, "if
Conrad manipulated his way into the ministerial post of New York."[7]
Predictably, the young college minister left Philadelphia for the bright
lights and popularity of New York City.

Conrad Muhammad knew that by moving to New York he would be
placed in the limelight before the Muslims. As the National youth minister, he was given the privilege of sitting on the rostrum with host minister Khallid. Occasionally he was given the opportunity to lecture or

teach on Sunday. Conrad took advantage of these luxuries. Quietly he forged a cadre of supporters within the mosque and the National Office, and they eventually helped him become the main minister of the mosque. However, before Khallid was removed from his ministerial post, he too had created a network of allies within the Nation, and these allies stayed with him for several years.

Khallid, considered by many the bad boy in the Nation, continued to build for Farrakhan but also continued to receive grudging admiration and negative attention from his enemies. Critical attacks escalated during his brief tenure as the minister of the Atlanta mosque. The southern city proved to be Khallid's undoing. In an uncharacteristic manner Minister Khallid attempted to use another person's social security number to secure a loan to purchase a house. Convicted of violating federal laws, Farrakhan's "flamethrower" was sentenced to the federal penitentiary.

Khallid's adversaries rejoiced in the minister's conviction. However, contrary to the hopes and prayers of Muhammad's enemies that Khallid would be isolated from the Muslim fold, the FOI rallied in support of him. Black Muslim men, along with thousands of other African American males, visited, telephoned, and wrote to the jailed Muslim. Again, capitalizing on his situation, Khallid told the brotherhood that he was a "victim of White racism and a government conspiracy to destroy the Nation."[8] The brotherhood viewed Khallid as a political prisoner and expressed their personal dedication and loyalty to him. Because Khallid was the first major Muslim leader since Malcolm X to be jailed, he vividly pointed out the connection between himself and Malcolm as a member of the legacy of great black leaders who fought against American oppression and racism. He occasionally used the case of Marcus Garvey of the Universal Negro Improvement Association, who was sentenced to federal prison for mail fraud, to further illustrate the connection. Khallid's thesis focused on his innocence. However, like his predecessors Malcolm and Garvey, Khallid was guilty of the crime.

It appeared that no matter what situation Khallid was in, he came out ahead. His release from prison made him a Black Muslim icon. Between 1988 and 1995 he became the most sought-after speaker in the Nation of Islam except for Louis Farrakhan. One reason Khallid was so popular within the Nation was his grassroots style of talking and acting. No matter what town or city Khallid visited, he sought out the most black ghettos. He entered crack houses, wine dens, places of prostitution, and gang quarters. His fearlessness in addressing the worst in the black community gained him the respect of the lowest of the black underclass. In the temple he enjoyed meeting the rank-and-file membership who were often ignored and mistreated by the brass of the Nation of Islam. For example, during the Savior's Day celebration of 1984, unlike several ministers in the Nation who sat on stage while Minister Farrakhan spoke, Khallid roamed the stadium meeting and shaking the hands of poor Muslim followers. He understood that these people needed to feel important and close to the leaders. During another event Khallid met with the faithful in a snack bar area while Farrakhan addressed the crowd.

Not only did Khallid attempt to empower the masses by his egalitarian approach, but he also labored to bridge the gap between splinter groups within the Nation of Islam. In 1977 Farrakhan had decided to leave the World Community of Al-Islam; another devout follower of Messenger Elijah Muhammad had done so a few months earlier. Silis Muhammad, former business manager of the Nation of Islam under the leadership of Elijah Muhammad, declared a holy war on Imam Warith Deen Muhammad's organization and vowed to rebuild the Nation. Silis, far less articulate than Farrakhan, created a solid association, also called the Nation of Islam, which was dedicated to the old tenets of Fard and Elijah Muhammad. Unlike Farrakhan, who used mass rallies to attract followers, Silis engaged in a patient, diligent struggle to build businesses and housing projects for his followers and for underclass black Americans.

Since 1977 Silis and Farrakhan have continued a religious battle in which each would declare himself the true leader and stigmatize the other as the "great hypocrite." Each group, through its own newspaper—Farrakhan's *Final Call* and Silis's *Muhammad Speaks*—promoted the greatness of its leader and the significance of its organization. There are only three things that the groups agreed on: (1) Fard Muhammad came as God to black Americans, (2) Wallace Muhammad destroyed the Nation of Islam, and (3) Elijah Muhammad sanctioned only one person to lead the Nation after his birth.

In spite of the rivalry between Silis and Farrakhan, Khallid decided to mediate and to build a benign relationship between the two leaders. Working with Silis's national spokesman, Kuba Abu Koss, Farrakhan's minister Khallid ultimately held several meetings with Silis Muhammad to establish a dialogue between the two groups. Minister Silis Muhammad, although slighted by Farrakhan's cancellation of several scheduled meetings and broken promises, agreed to Khallid's atonement communiqué and said he would be willing to sit down with Minister Farrakhan.

Khallid's overall objective was to begin the process of unifying the Nation of Islam. He viewed Silis and Farrakhan as great disciples of Messenger Elijah Muhammad and believed it was imperative that individuals like himself get the two Muslims together. He also believed that if Farrakhan and Wallace Muhammad could communicate and embrace at the 1992 Savior's Day event in front of thousands of people, surely Silis and Farrakhan could meet and talk. Khallid thought Farrakhan had more in common with Silis than with the Messenger's errant son, Wallace.

In 1993 Silis Muhammad published a letter entitled "Silis Muhammad Seeks Forgiveness" in the *Muhammad Speaks* newspaper. The author maintained that neither he nor the Nation of Islam still considered Minister Farrakhan the biblical "Second Beast" [devil] and asked forgiveness for such errant and arrogant statements. In 1982 Silis Muhammad had accused Farrakhan of being a false prophet. The head of the rival Muslims sect had maintained that Farrakhan had deviated from Elijah Muhammad's philosophy. Therefore, he was a hypocrite and a "declarer." Silis argued that Farrakhan must follow him as the leader of the Nation of Islam. Silis's justification rested with the notion that he left Wallace's Al-Islam before the formation of Farrakhan's Final Call, Inc. However, although Silis extended an olive branch, it had conditions. Silis would stop the verbal attacks on Farrakhan if Elijah Muhammad's Muslim Program was implemented within the structure of the Final Call Nation of Islam.

Silis's most pressing concern was with the issue of reparations. Elijah Muhammad had called for the United States government to repay blacks for their labor and sufferings for having been an enslaved group. Farrakhan at first seemed interested in Silis's idea and objectives and invited him to the Nation's Savior's Day event in 1994 in Chicago.

Minister Silis Muhammad accepted Farrakhan's invitation. However, instead of attending the event, Silis sent his wife, Misshaki Harriet Muhammad, attorney general of the Nation of Islam, and Minister Dhoruba Asadi, a top aide, to represent his organization. Before an audience of ten thousand Mrs. Muhammad announced that Silis Muhammad planned to file a petition for reparations at the United Nations on behalf of all African Americans and that her husband called on Louis Farrakhan to assist him in attracting ten thousand blacks to march on the United Nations. Realizing Farrakhan's great oratorical skills, Silis knew it would be easier for Farrakhan to attract a mass audience himself. But instead of supporting Silis's march on the United Nations, Farrakhan announced plans for his Million Man March on Washington. According to Minister Asadi, Silis felt betrayed that Minister Farrakhan would undermine him in front of an international audience. Minister Silis Muhammad believed that the call for a march on Washington was not a divine calling, as suggested by Farrakhan, but a countermove to the planned march on the United Nations.

On September 25, 1994, Farrakhan finally responded to Silis's numerous letters and phone calls. Minister Farrakhan apologized for his long delay in responding and extended an invitation to Silis to address the Million Man March crowd. However, the invitation was tainted with Farrakhan's clear demands that there be no discussions about Elijah Muhammad's appeal for reparations from the United States. Farrakhan wrote, "[T]he terms for your participation for the March are unacceptable; [but] if [you] decide to attend you will be welcomed and accorded honor and respect."[9] On October 3, thirteen days before the Million Man March, Silis responded to Farrakhan's letter, asking which terms were unacceptable and why. Silis neither attended nor addressed the crowd.

Minister Khallid's attempt to bring the two Black Muslim leaders together failed. It became apparent that the largest Black Muslim sects would continue to be separated. The animosity that continued to plague the two nations became symbolic of the relationship between Louis Farrakhan and Khallid Muhammad.

On November 29, 1993, Khallid Muhammad told a small audience of 150 at Kean College in New Jersey that Jews were evil, that the Pope was a homosexual, and that all white South Africans should be killed. Civil rights leaders, politicians, theologians, members of the U.S. Congress, and virtually every sane person in the United States thought the speech was vicious, mean-spirited, and uncivilized. Ultimately, Louis Farrakhan terminated Khallid as a minister and national representative of the Nation of Islam. However, Farrakhan's actions against Khallid departed from the typical rhetoric of the Nation, in which hostile language toward enemies was the rule. The former national spokesperson was simply following the precedent of the Nation and specifically Farrakhan's example.

Khallid's speech was publicized by the Anti-Defamation League of B'nai B'rith in a full-page advertisement in the New York Times. Farrakhan ignored the issue, hoping that it would miraculously go away. But the minister's friends and enemies, the Black Congressional Caucus, and the Anti-Defamation League demanded that he address Khallid's statement. Maryland congressman Kweisi Mfume and several others wanted to know if Khallid's views represented the ideas of the Nation of Islam.

The question was embarrassing to Farrakhan. It might expose the fact that he had one message for his followers and another for the larger number of more moderate black leaders and the Islamic community. Throughout his ministry Farrakhan had described whites, Jews, Arabs, and moderate blacks as the authors of crime, vice, and evil in black America, as well as in much of the world. He had attacked Christianity, Judaism, and traditional Islam as nonprogressive and nonsupportive of the growth of African Americans. The ideas that he preached were aligned with rhetoric of the Nation of Islam from its inception. Therefore, many people who joined the organization were attracted to the problack language and the harsh bigoted language toward other groups. The racist and intolerant tone toward other groups served a dual purpose not only for the Nation but for local and federal law enforcers as well. The Nation filled a void that allowed people to be passively angry. They could take out their frustrations in the Muslim halls by exposing the evils of whites while remaining peaceful within the larger community. Second, law enforcement agencies, such as the Federal Bureau of Investigation, knew that the Nation had a penchant for harsh language but lacked the stomach for violence toward whites or the government. According to FBI reports, the Nation of Islam had no history of violently attacking whites or the government in any organized fashion. The Nation has used violence against its own members. The only threat was that the Nation, under a militant and aggressive leader, had the potential to become an agent for revolutionary activities that possibly could create a problem in the United States. The FBI overwhelmingly believed that the Nation served as a forum for blacks to vocalize their hostility toward whites and the government but that within the structure of the temple blacks were taught to become model citizens and to embrace the concepts of the conservative Protestant work ethic. For all the diatribes of

Farrakhan against Presidents Nixon, Ford, Reagan, and Bush, he is a staunch Republican. The problem is that the minister must behave in front of his followers like a Huey Newton or a Malcolm X militant.

In contrast to Farrakhan's theatrical pose as a revolutionary, he had attempted to moderate his racial tone for sympathetic whites, blacks, and Jews who supported the Nation's position on family values, self-help programs, education, and an end to Affirmative Action. In addition, he desperately sought to expand his Islamic popularity to traditional Muslims who did not embrace the claims that Elijah Muhammad was the last messenger, that Caucasians are devils, and that blacks are the chosen people of God. As a result, after Khallid's Kean College lecture Farrakhan had to address openly these contradictions to his followers, enemies, and allies.

On February 4, 1994, the *New York Times* published an article titled "Farrakhan Repudiates Speech for Tone, Not Anti-Semitism." Reporter Steven A. Holmes stated that in a rare press conference Farrakhan maintained that Khallid's speech was filled with several truths. According to Minister Farrakhan, Jews owned 75 percent of all African slaves in the United States, so Khallid's statement on Jewish involvement in the slave trade was correct. Farrakhan stated, "I found the speech, after listening to it in context, vile in manner, repugnant, malicious, mean-spirited and spoken in mockery of individuals and people, which is against the spirit of Islam. [Although] I stand by the truths that he spoke, I must condemn in the strongest terms the manner in which those truths were represented."[10]

However, a few nights before that press conference Farrakhan had spoken at a Black Man's Rally in Harlem. There he told the fifteen thousand member all-male audience that Jews conspired in an elaborate scheme to separate Khallid from his teacher. Unfortunately for many of the Nation's moderate black and white allies, Farrakhan continued with the same theme at the press conference. Waving an alleged secret and internal document titled "Mainstreaming Anti-Semitism: The Legitimization of Louis Farrakhan," the minister argued that the Anti-Defamation League, threatened by his popularity, had decided to use every possible tool to undermine his credibility among African Americans. He stated that the Jews wanted to exploit black leaders who envied Farrakhan's appeal among the black masses. Thus, the whole brouhaha about

Khallid's speech was inspired and concocted by American Jews. In response to Farrakhan's repudiation of Khallid and his description of the controversy as instigated by Jews, many black Americans voiced their approval. But within three months after the affair many in the Black Muslim fold quietly began to question Farrakhan's reasoning. During this period Farrakhan had quietly ordered the Nation of Islam to separate itself from Khallid Muhammad.

On April 2, 1994, Khallid Muhammad was invited to speak in Cincinnati by Tres X Brown, Ronnie X Black, and me. The event was to advertise the Nation of Islam's upcoming Savior's Day celebration in Ghana, West Africa. We hoped that Khallid's visit would spark interest among people wishing to attend the West African nation. Tres, Ronnie, and I would arrange the trip with a wholesale travel agency.

Although we knew of the problems Khallid's Kean College lecture had created, we did not realize that there existed a tainted relationship between Khallid and the National Center. In fact, Tres and Ronnie viewed Khallid as a Muslim leader who had been reprimanded by Louis Farrakhan for violating the spirit of Islam. Also, a few weeks earlier we had met Khallid at Western Kentucky University, where he had been invited to speak by the Black Student Union. The auditorium was filled with Nation of Islam personnel and the FOI, who supplied the orator with security. There was no indication that a problem existed between Khallid and Farrakhan. Except for a few devotees who quietly questioned Khallid's relationship to the leader Farrakhan, it appeared that the Kean College controversy had subsided, at least in the Nation of Islam. However, this was not the case. A couple of days before Khallid's scheduled lecture in Ohio, the National Center gave several indications that Khallid was not wanted in the Nation.

Two days before Khallid was to speak in Lincoln Heights, a small black city aligned with the Cincinnati district, the local black newspaper office, the *Cincinnati Herald*, was firebombed. The paper, which had run favorable articles about the Nation, Farrakhan, and Khallid, had advertised the Lincoln Heights meeting. Individuals associated with the paper, along with many members of the black community, speculated that the local Jewish community was responsible for the attack. Realizing the tension that existed between Farrakhan and Jewish Americans, I sent a fax to Minister Farrakhan and the *Final Call* advising them of the bombing and of the potential threat to Minister Khallid Muhammad. For unknown reasons neither the National Office nor the chief editor, James Muhammad, a native of Cincinnati, responded to the urgency of my message. I believed that the bombing was a dress rehearsal for an attack on Khallid. It was designed to see what type of response the Nation would make if one of their own were harmed.

Khallid's Lincoln Heights lecture was presented without any problems. The fiery minister packed the YMCA gym with over two thousand people. The lecture was a calm presentation that focused on his Kean College affair, his love of Farrakhan, and how Jews were out to destroy the Nation and kill him. What the speaker did not realize was that a few weeks later it would be a Black Muslim and possibly an NOI conspiracy, not the Jews, who would attempt to take his life.

On May 29, 1994, Khallid was scheduled to speak at the University of California's Riverside campus. The lecture, sponsored by the Black Student Union, advertised Khallid as the next Malcolm X. But unknown to the sponsors and Khallid, there were individuals who wanted Khallid to die like Malcolm had some thirty years earlier. Minutes before the scheduled event, while Khallid was greeting friends and admirers, a disgruntled member of the Nation released a barrage of gunfire, wounding Khallid and several of his bodyguards. In seconds Muhammad's supporters burst out in a mad sprint to attack anyone who looked like the assailant.

Similar to Malcolm's murder scene in Harlem, the crowd captured a member of the Nation of Islam who had formerly been a minister. James X Bess, also known as Abdul Hakim Muhammad, a zealous follower of Farrakhan, was nearly beaten to death when the crowd captured him with his 9 mm pistol. In an interesting twist, had it not been for the white police officers who rescued Bess from the irate crowd, he might have been beaten to death. Immediately, the Nation of Islam attempted to distance itself from the attack by branding James X Bess a crazy man who acted alone. Also, the NOI denied Bess was a member of the Chicago-based organization. Nonetheless, speculation surfaced that the Muslim triggerman was part of an elaborate conspiracy to assassinate Khallid Muhammad.

The conspiracy theory focused on the fact that James X Bess had very little previous contact with Khallid Muhammad, thereby negating the argument that James X wished to settle a personal feud. According to Khallid, he had very little knowledge of the man before the shooting, but he suggested that Bess was very close to powerful ministers in the Nation. Police investigators discovered several weapons in Bess's escape car. Khallid alleged that further information suggested that Bess did not act alone.

The injuries suffered by Muhammad and the three bodyguards were serious but not critical. He remained in a California hospital for one week for treatment that included surgery, recuperation, and therapy. However, although Khallid rebounded physically, mentally he was depressed. As he and many of his close friends stated, he was hurt and saddened at the Nation's lethargic attitude toward the murder attempt, and he was shocked and disappointed that Farrakhan, his mentor, did not pay him a visit in the hospital.

Critics of Khallid argued that turbulence and violence consistently followed Khallid. For instance, when he had served as the Los Angeles minister, the temple's FOI was involved in a violent scrimmage with a local street gang. In Chicago, as the supreme captain, he got involved with a south-side street gang that shot up Farrakhan's Final Call Building. In Atlanta rumors circulated that he was involved in an illegal money scam with the local mob. Defenders of Farrakhan maintained that Khallid was a liability to the organization and that his negative behavior outweighed his aggressive and positive campaigning for the Black Muslims. According to these advocates, that is why Farrakhan did not pay great attention to Khallid when he was shot. Minister Farrakhan was tired of the problems that seemed to follow Khallid.

But again, another story was broadcast by Khallid and several national newspapers. The reports claimed that Minister Conrad Muhammad's and Khallid's relationship had degenerated into a series of heated exchanges involving profanity, threats, and an atmosphere of potential violence. Shortly after the California incident Muhammad traveled to New York to give a lecture in Harlem. Speaking to a large audience, Khallid said, "Niggers, some wearing bow ties, tried to get me, but I am a hard Nigga to die."[11] He said they should not play with him because there would not be a second chance. Many of the listeners were members of Minister Conrad Muhammad's Harlem Temple Number Seven. Khallid knew that his comments would get back to Conrad and any others who might have had a hand in the murder attempt. In bravado fashion he put them on notice that he was willing to respond violently to protect himself.

The rumor mill within the Nation was working overtime. Speculation about Farrakhan and Khallid was a hot but judicious topic among the Muslim faithful. Whether or not individuals within the Nation plotted to assassinate Khallid, it was obvious that a rift had separated him and Louis Farrakhan.

Ultimately, Farrakhan banned Khallid from all Black Muslim temples, stores, and events. Khallid, on the other hand, embraced an extreme form of Islam based on armed resistance and struggle. His new Islam became punctuated by machine guns, armored vehicles, and predictions of a global white and black war. Apparently, the two leaders were not ready to heal their differences. As long as the two failed to reconcile their differences, the threat of violence within the Nation increased. Unfortunately, the Cain and Abel syndrome had resurfaced within the Nation.

· · ·

In 1996 Khallid Muhammad joined the New Black Panther Party. By 1998 he had become the Panthers' national chairman and its most recognized spokesperson. In this capacity he led three controversial youth marches in Harlem that were known as the Million Youth March. In 1998 he led an entourage of heavily armed members of the New Black Panther Party to Jasper, Texas, site of the white racist dragging death of James Byrd Jr., a black resident of the southern community. In February 2001, following a series of meetings in New York City, Khallid Muhammad fell gravely ill at his home in Atlanta, Georgia, and died seventeen days later. On February 24 his supporters at the Mt. Olivet Baptist Church in Harlem eulogized Muhammad. Panther members took their fallen leader on one last tour of Harlem by carrying his casket through the streets and ending their march in the front of the Apollo Theater on 125th Street, where Muhammad was placed in a hearse and driven to his final resting place.

9

The Story behind the Million Man March

On October 16, 1995, Farrakhan led over one million black men to Washington, D.C., for prayer, atonement, and the creation of a new sense of responsibility to their families, communities, nations, and foremost, themselves. The one-day event signified the largest all-black demonstration in American history. Minister Farrakhan, the mastermind, persuaded several of America's most influential and powerful leaders, Jesse Jackson, Al Sharpton, Maya Angelou, and Rosa Parks, to name a few, to address the crowd with inspirational presentations that encouraged positive and progressive action. The day ended with a gleaming Farrakhan speaking on the issues of equality and justice for the African American. The Million Man March was a success for Farrakhan and his Nation; however, both in the planning of the event and in the aftermath, confusion, antagonism, and financial mismanagement corrupted the Million Man March, transforming its image from having been a totally successful historical spectacle into a mass gathering filled with many lingering questions.

In 1994 Minister Farrakhan announced at the annual Savior's Day convention that Elijah Muhammad, through a divine vision, had ordered him to organize and lead an all-black-male mass rally in Washington, D.C. Farrakhan remembers that Muhammad had thought the 1963 march on Washington, organized by A. Phillip Randolph of the Brotherhood of Sleeping Car Porters Union and led by Martin Luther King Jr. of the Southern Christian Leadership Conference, was filled with "entertainment, frolicking, and groping" of female marchers.[1] Farrakhan said that Elijah Muhammad maintained that "one day the Muslims would have a serious March on Washington."[2] The march that the minister envisioned evolved out of the series of all-male meetings that were being held throughout the country. These all-black-men's meetings featured Farrakhan as the lecturer preaching on racial solidarity, black self-help principles, male bonding, family values, and atonement to God for past sins. The series of meetings had been quite successful, packing theaters, auditoriums, churches, and stadiums. In fact, in places like Boston, Chicago, Miami, and Atlanta, Farrakhan's appeal brought hundreds of thousands to the events.

Although the Million Man March proposal expressed excitement, it created several potential problems for the Nation. Throughout its history the Nation had classified itself as a social-religious organization that valued its position as apolitical. Except for a few human rights rallies during the 1960s, the Nation did not have the experience necessary to plan and organize a major civil rights rally. Farrakhan, realizing the dilemma, instructed his top lieutenants to seek assistance in planning and promoting the Million Man March.

The Nation's Million Man March had the potential to make Farrakhan a legitimate power broker in the United States. As Black Muslims sensed the great possibilities of the march, individuals outside the Nation also smelled the roses of a successful event. The greatest opportunist was civil rights veteran and former executive director of the National Association for the Advancement of Colored People, Dr. Benjamin Chavis. He currently found himself an embarrassed national leader who had been fired from a $175,000-a-year job with the association for plunging it into a debt of $1 million, which brought the NAACP to the brink of bankruptcy. He had also used $325,000 of the association's money to pay a woman who had threatened him with a sexual discrimination lawsuit because of their sexual affair. Chavis, understandably unsure of his future, sought out his friend Farrakhan for support, aid, and comfort.

The Farrakhan-Chavis alliance originated during Chavis's sixteen-month tenure as the head of the NAACP. During this period Chavis organized the National African American Leadership Summit, which brought several major black political, economic, academic, and religious leaders together to discuss the problems of and solutions for black Americans. Individuals like Conrad West, Roger Wilkins, Al Sharpton, Betty Shabazz, Dorothy Height, and Mary Frances Berry were invited to attend the summit meetings. However, in June 1994 the greatest commotion centered on Chavis's inviting Farrakhan to attend the NAALS conference. Several white, Jewish, and black civil rights activists condemned the association's inclusion of Farrakhan. They maintained that Farrakhan's acceptance into the association's meetings tarnished the objectives of the organizations. However, Farrakhan, the master of the black political rhetoric, answered his critics as follows:

By keeping the radicals and extremists out of the tent, you cannot affect their radicalism or their extremism. Nor can they affect your lethargy or bourgeois attitude. By bringing everybody under the tent, it raises the discomfort level of all those present, because we are all comfortable with those who think and feel as we do. . . . We have a chance to dialog with many in our community that we never would have dialoged with before. . . . If I am an anti-Semite, [Harvard Professor] Cornel West is not an anti-Semite and Roger Wilkins [George Washington University Professor and grandson of Roy Wilkins, Executive Secretary of the association between 1955 and 1977] is not an anti-Semite. Those who have traditionally been members of the NAACP are not haters of Jews or Whites. Sharing ideas and concepts with men like this can effect change in us as we effect change in them. I don't think that we can change them for the worse."[3]

Chavis, excited by the possibility of Farrakhan's acceptance into the fold, diligently campaigned with his colleagues about the importance of Farrakhan and the Nation of Islam to America's black youth. As he told one critic, "Farrakhan has proven that he can reach the youth. Apparently, we can't. We can learn something from the Minister and the Nation."[4] Ultimately, Farrakhan joined the summit. He did not make the moderates more militant, nor did they change his mind on the state of black America. If anything, Farrakhan proved that he was not a "weird and crazy polemic" but was reasonable, graceful, and approachable. Farrakhan was forever thankful to Chavis for the opportunity to join the table of black leaders. Therefore, when Chavis heard of the Million Man March, he decided to call in a favor.

As an ousted black leader without an organization, finances, or a platform, Chavis needed Farrakhan's assistance. Approaching the Black Muslim leader was an easy and logical direction for the former civil rights leader. If he could persuade his Muslim buddy that his skills as a civil rights advocate, former militant member of the Wilmington 10 (a black group who had a shoot-out with local Ku Klux Klan members in North Carolina, for which Chavis spent several years in jail), and United

Methodist Church minister were needed for the Million Man March, he could possibly resurrect his civil rights career. His quick approval and endorsement of the march influenced Farrakhan to appoint him coconvener of the Million Man March and executive director of the National African American Leadership Summit, Inc., a civil rights front organization financed by the Nation of Islam. The NAALS was intended by Farrakhan and Chavis to be the political leg of the Nation, that is, an organization that would promote the aims of the Muslims but exclude their religious ideology.

The Reverend Chavis's initial duty was to tour the black communities in the United States to drum up support for the march while organizing chapters of the NAALS. In January 1995 Dr. Eric Abercrumbie, director of the Afro-American Cultural Center at the University of Cincinnati, invited Rev. Chavis to address the university's annual Black Man's Think Tank Conference. Joining the stage with Dr. Maulana Karenga, who was the first to theorize the notion of Afrocentrism, Chavis officially announced his position with the Million Man March organization and his quest to have twenty thousand men from Cincinnati join the march.

During this period I created an organization designed to supply transportation to Washington, the site of the march. The buses were to transport men from Cincinnati, Dayton, Columbus, and Wheeling, West Virginia. However, although the organization was active with advertisements on television, on radio, in newspapers, and on billboards, we were locked out of advertising in the Nation's *Final Call* newspaper. At this juncture I decided to approach Benjamin Chavis.

My relationship with Chavis and the Cincinnati supporters of the Million Man March began during the Black Man's Think Tank, for which I organized Muslims, as well as male students and community activists, to provide security for Chavis. For three days the men diligently escorted Chavis to all of his functions, providing a twenty-four-hour bodyguard service during his stay at the downtown Hyatt Hotel. During this time I told Chavis that my organization had arranged for passage to Washington that included an overnight hotel stay but that I was having a very difficult time getting through to the National Center to negotiate a travel package that would officially include the Nation of Islam. I said it appeared that the Nation only wanted to work through a company called Windows to the World, which was owned by Minister Farrakhan's eldest son, Louis, and his wife, Lisa. Rev. Chavis responded that he was aware of the problems in getting through to the Nation but that he would guarantee our inclusion in the travel package. However, Chavis's guarantee was based on a sidebar deal with my company, Destinations of the Diaspora.

Rev. Chavis thought that neither Farrakhan nor his son-in-law, Leonard Farrakhan, the chief of staff of the organization, nor any of the top administrators knew anything about staging a civil rights march. In addition, the civil rights advocate recognized that the Nation was perceived by many as a militant organization. That is why, according to Chavis, they needed him. However, the Nation had been slow to grant him financial support for his activities. Every few days he would either have to call or visit Farrakhan in his Hyde Park mansion in Chicago, requesting money to handle his personal business and to run the haphazard NAALS operation in Washington. One of the major reasons he needed funds was because his firing from the NAACP had left him broke. He had a mortgage on a $350,000 home, payments on a Jaguar, and a wife and several children to feed. But, interestingly, he maintained to the outside world that he was debt free—owed nothing on his credit cards, had no student loan to repay, and owed no debts to any individual. I, half jokingly, said, "You're still living better than 80 percent of all Americans." Nonetheless, Chavis saw himself in a financial bind, and he wanted my company to promote the Million Man March through NAALS so that he could receive a percentage of the revenue. Since I was apparently blocked out of the travel network by the Nation's monopoly, I agreed that 20 percent of the profit be given to Chavis for the use of his name in the promotion of the Destinations of the Diaspora travel package.

During Louis Farrakhan's tenure, the Nation of Islam held a monopoly on all business arrangements. Although the Nation's message promoted the ideal of black business development, in practice most Black Muslims were not supported by the central office. The National Center did not offer financial, legal, or general business advice for potential entrepreneurs, for example, the bean pie business that the Nation is known for. In fact, during the last twenty years several young Muslim businessmen have attempted to develop bean pie enterprises through the Nation. Instead of supporting the young businessmen, the Nation destroyed them by labeling them hypocrites, enemies of Elijah Muhammad, and just bad Muslims. This was done to protect Farrakhan's assistant, Akbar Muhammad, who until recently owned the Nation's bean pie operation.

Another example occurred during the February 1994 Savior's Day event in Chicago. At that time my travel agency had begun to run advertisements in a publication owned by H. Khalif Khalifah, a member of the Nation of Islam, who operated United Brothers and Sisters Publications. The advertisements were promoting travel and hotel accommodations for the Nation's convention in Accra, Ghana. I was severely threatened by Akbar Muhammad and the Nation in several ways. First, in front of more than five thousand Muslim officers Akbar Muhammad stated that even though he had trained me as a minister, I was now undermining the Nation's efforts by advertising travel plans to "our international Savior's Day in Ghana." Next, he issued orders to the FOI that when I entered the arena, they were to escort me immediately to the stage. The FOI followed orders. As I walked into the University of Illinois Pavilion, selected FOI guards handed me over to Minister Donnel Muhammad, who then escorted me to the stage to see Minister Akbar. The elder Muslim then roughly scolded me and said that he was going to tell the international audience about my wickedness. Then he called Alken Tours, a Brooklyn-based company that was handling the travel arrangements for my company, and threatened them with violence and Muslim retaliation. Fortunately, Alken Tours, a West Indian–owned company, did not succumb to Akbar's tactics. Alken's Brooklyn manager told the Muslim that Mr. White and Alken Tours had a long and steady record of doing business together, adding that they would not undermine another Caribbean business at the insistence of the Nation. Thus, when the Nation's monopoly was threatened, the national leadership created a hostile environment with the potential for violence by Muslims against me because I was a young Muslim entrepreneur. Therefore, when Chavis offered to assist me in getting past the Nation's policy of capitalist protectionism for its own inner circle, I agreed to his terms.

The Reverend Chavis negotiated a sidebar not only with me but also with William Land, pastor of Freemen's United Methodist Church in Cincinnati. Chavis made Land the president of the local chapter of NAALS, the first local community formed in Chavis's new organization. The deal was for Chavis to receive a percentage of the registration fees and chapter dues in exchange for a stake as a future power broker in

NAALS and the Nation of Islam. In reality Chavis never had the power to keep his promises. In addition, his historical track record illustrated a pattern of broken agreements and irresponsible acts. However, the Cincinnati supporters of Chavis believed and hoped that the NAALS president would be different from the reports the NAACP had given about him.

Ultimately, time brought the real Chavis to the forefront. He told a cheering crowd at the Freemen Avenue Church that he was a close assistant to Louis Farrakhan, that as Farrakhan's representative he was touring the country speaking on the upcoming Washington rally, and that he was currently en route to Dr. Louis Sullivan's African-American Summit meeting in Senegal, West Africa, to spread the same message. At this point Chavis stated that, "We [the NAALS and the NOI] support black businesses. On behalf of the Nation and NAALS, I am going to allow Cincinnati to arrange for my travel to Africa."[5] After the meeting Chavis asked me to finalize travel plans via Air Afrique from New York City to Dakar. I complied and responded that he would be able to pick up the ticket the next day in Manhattan, where he was scheduled to speak. That Monday Chavis purchased the $765.00 ticket with an American Express Card; however, he informed the travel agent in New York that he must change the date of his return. The agent told Chavis that he would not be able to guarantee a return trip on the new date and that he might have to be on a standby status. Chavis played the odds that he would get back to the United States on his schedule.

Chavis made it to Dakar as planned, but his return was filled with confusion. The New York agent told him the plane was full and that it would be one week before he could return to the States via Air Afrique or Air France. However, they could arrange for him to get to France. Deciding on this option, Chavis landed in Paris. Now without funds Chavis could not afford to purchase another ticket, and his American Express and VISA credit cards were maxed out. Scared, confused, and without a friend, Chavis called me collect, pleading for me to arrange for his return ticket to the United States. I instructed Chavis to calm down and to be patient, saying that Air France would honor the ticket back to New York. Chavis then whined that he was to be a part of a White House delegation and that he must be there. I then asked Chavis why he couldn't get help from Minister Farrakhan, saying that surely the minister would send him the money for a special flight back to America. In response Chavis moaned that Leonard Farrakhan and the minister would not return his phone calls and that they were already late on their stipend to him. He had no one to call on except the brotherhood of NAALS in Cincinnati. Believing him and feeling a bit sad for the former civil rights leader, I arranged for a wire service ticket on the Concorde from Paris to New York City. Chavis, using the names of God, Allah, and Muhammad, promised to repay my agency the $3,000 for the ticket, plus the $300 in service fees immediately on his return to the States. Chavis made his White House meeting, continued to lecture for the Million Man March, but never repaid the money. In fact, on the few occasions that I was able to reach Chavis, he told me to contact Minister Farrakhan, Leonard Farrakhan, or Kamah Muhammad, the national secretary of the Nation of Islam. On several occasions Kamah Muhammad recognized that this was a debt of the Nation and the Million Man March because Chavis had represented the Nation and agreed to repay the money. But, like Chavis, the leadership of the Muslims reneged on their promise to repay my small black struggling travel agency in Cincinnati.

In the aftermath of this international excursion Chavis invited me and several of my employees to meet with Farrakhan and the Million Man March planning committee in Chicago. The session, to be held at Farrakhan's residence, was to be an opportunity to present my company's proposal for travel plans to the group. The massive home, built by Elijah Muhammad and referred to by the Muslim faithful as the Palace, was filled with twenty-five major social, economic, and political black leaders, including Dr. Nathan Hare, Craig Hodges (former Chicago Bulls professional basketball player), Haki Matabuta, and several other national advocates and black power brokers.

The May meeting was one of several conferences sponsored by the Nation to include a cross-section of the black leadership community in the decision-making process of the Million Man March. Minister Farrakhan opened the session with his vision of the march, but it was Leonard Farrakhan who dominated the meeting. It soon became obvious that Chief of Staff Leonard Farrakhan's statements were just manipulative jargon to influence us to support the march on the Nation's terms. When individuals commented or advised on issues such as the cost of the event, the tone or message to be used in advertising, the selling of Million Man March materials, or the general logistics, Leonard bluntly reminded them that the Nation had called the march. We soon realized that the Nation wished only to give the appearance that the black community was involved in planning the event and that Farrakhan was being democratic in taking advice from blacks of different political and religious beliefs. Both cases were false.

From the very inception of the Million Man March meetings, the Nation acknowledged that it was in charge and that individuals and groups would not play a major role in decision making. Specifically, Farrakhan and his supporters would not tolerate any questions regarding the cost of the event, its specific agenda, or who would be invited to speak. At the same time Chavis, under the direction of Farrakhan, was working diligently to hold a national NAALS Conference in Houston, Texas.

The Houston convention was designed to showcase Chavis as a progressive civil rights leader and organizer who could work with the militant Nation of Islam. However, the NAALS Conference was riddled with confusion and disorganization from the start. First, the money needed to set up the conference was lacking. According to Chavis, the Nation was lethargic in sending promised financial support to him and NAALS. Second, NAALS needed a cross-section of national black leaders to attend or at least endorse the meeting to help legitimize the new organization. However, the only national leader to attend was his boss, Louis Farrakhan. Finally, NAALS and the NOI boasted that thousands of African Americans were planning to attend. The final count of NAALS delegates and spectators showed that less than one hundred attended. By all accounts the NAALS/NOI meeting was a failure.

The poor showing at this conference caused concern among several Muslim leaders and march supporters who feared that the Million Man March would be another embarrassing failure for Farrakhan. In fact, many of the national leaders who spoke on October 16, such as Jesse Jackson, did not endorse the march or agree to address the crowd until seven days before the event. The larger black community and the national media did not get excited until a few days before the march. However, either because of divine intervention or just plain luck, word of the march captured the imagination of the black community at the midnight hour. In a mass exodus reminiscent of Pap Singleton's black migration movement of the nineteenth century from the American South to Oklahoma, African American males boarded planes, buses, automobiles, trains, and some even walked hundreds of miles to attend the greatest black march demonstration in American history.

Although Farrakhan thought these men came because of his leadership and appeal for religious atonement, they came rather because of the growth of black solidarity and the absence of black leaders. Unfortunately, African Americans lacked race advocates such as A. Phillip Randolph, Thurgood Marshall, Ralph Abernathy, and Martin Luther King Jr. to aggressively challenge American racism in the 1990s. Nonetheless, like the 250,000 marchers who in 1963 heard Dr. King electrify the world with his "I Have a Dream" speech, one million men listened for over ten hours to the words of Benjamin Chavis (NAALS), Imam Malick Sylla (Dakar, Senegal), Professor Naim Akbar (Florida State University), Bishop George Stallings (African American Catholic Congregation), Senator Adelbert Bryan (Virgin Islands), Dr. Betty Shabazz (widow of Malcolm X), and, of course, Louis Farrakhan. But unlike King's address, which even today can be recited by school children, very few can remember Farrakhan's lecture theme. By most accounts it was the worst speech he had ever delivered to a black audience. It lacked focus, a thesis, any real analysis of the state of black America—it even lacked personal enthusiasm.

For over two hours Farrakhan rambled on about the founding fathers, black liberation, and the formation of the "Negro mind." His use of numerology confused listeners, and he deviated time and again from the stated theme on the importance of atonement and the calling of the Million Man March. His problem was that he attempted to turn this event into a Nation of Islam prayer meeting. As one marcher stated, "He conducted a one million man prayer meeting or religious tent revivals [sic] even to the point of taking up a collection." At times it appeared that Farrakhan was posturing for an audience outside the rim of the American community, perhaps for potential international supporters who might be impressed with his command of a massive audience.

But it did not seem to matter to whites, blacks, or even many Jews if Farrakhan was attempting to impress foreign colleagues or not. By all accounts the march was a success. In Cincinnati for example, scores of former Farrakhan critics admitted that they had misjudged the Muslim leader and that they were impressed with the October 16 affair. Many leaders, such as Henry Louis Gates Jr. of Harvard University, remarked that Farrakhan had America eating out of his hand. But, as noted by famed religious scholar C. Eric Lincoln, Farrakhan squandered the moment.

For some strange reason Farrakhan went into a self-imposed isolation after the march. For several weeks he confined himself to his Phoenix mansion, refusing to speak to the press or to take care of his Muslim business. He ultimately blamed his retreat on depression caused by the negative comments he received in the media, especially the American press, concerning the Million Man March. But most press accounts were quite positive regarding Farrakhan's march. Some speculate that Farrakhan was not depressed by the white media but rather by African American businessmen and companies who had begun filing lawsuits against the Nation for services rendered but not paid by the organization.

According to several FOI members I interviewed who were part of the collection of many at the march, the NOI received literally millions of dollars from the audience. One FOI recalled loading garbage bags of money into the trunks of automobiles and trucks. Believing that the NOI made a tremendous amount of money, many blacks began to pressure Farrakhan for money owed. Several companies had provided the NOI with services ranging from laying the marble floor in the Salaam Restaurant to supplying school equipment and employee uniforms. Thus, when these business owners heard stories about the FOI collecting vast amounts of money and saw them on television toting coffin-shaped receptacles filled with cash, they naturally expected payment. But Farrakhan did not want to pay the black business owners. Feeling the heat from his creditors, Farrakhan created a diversion that first focused on his alleged depression and later on travels to Asia, Africa, and the Caribbean.

To divert the press from this potentially embarrassing story—after all, the owners might tell the press about debts owed them—Farrakhan embarked on one of the most controversial trips of any African American leader in history. Taking an entourage of over twenty-eight people, he traveled to Iran, Libya, Iraq, Sudan, Nigeria, and Cuba and met with the respected presidents of each of these nations. He spoke publicly of the evils and hypocrisy in the United States and of the solidarity that the Nation and the larger black community shared with the nations that hated the United States. Farrakhan announced during this tour that he supported their efforts to destroy the United States. He said he was "depressed because it appeared that America did not appreciate his efforts and that many people were criticizing him." However, Al Sharpton had once told Farrakhan that as long as he was only doing the Nation's business, the larger community did not have the right to question his internal policies, but once he said he was the leader of black America, then he should expect to be challenged not only by the media but by the masses.

Farrakhan, noted for being stubborn and self-centered, did not believe that anyone, especially a black American, should question his leadership. But to secure his untouchable position, he visited the most controversial leaders and nations that he could locate. By traveling to what the State Department described as rogue countries, Farrakhan realized he would garner attention and build a bulwark between himself and those African American business people who wanted the Nation to fulfill its financial obligations.

In a move to guarantee controversy the Muslim leader used extreme language to repudiate, criticize, and reprimand the United States in the international community. In Iraq he stated that America was evil in attempting to starve the Iraqi people into extermination; in Iran he broadcast to millions of the nation's citizens that God would destroy America by the hands of Muslims; in the Sudan he claimed that America had no right to talk about alleged slavery in the African nation when America had sanctioned the institution for hundreds of years. In addition, Farrakhan argued that America headed a conspiracy to destroy the great Islamic government of the Sudan; in Nigeria, supporting a brutal dictatorship, he scolded the United States for calling the Nigerian government corrupt and asked, "Who is more corrupt than America?" In Cuba he reaffirmed the argument that the United States had tried to destabilize the island nation since the early 1960s. However, Farrakhan's most steaming diatribe came in Libya, when he verbally accepted a $1 billion pledge from Qadhafi to mobilize blacks, Arabs, Muslims, and Native Americans to influence America's foreign policy and to exert pressure on the ultimate outcome of the presidential elections. In referring to the Libyan president as his friend and Muslim brother, Farrakhan endorsed Qadhafi's views that Farrakhan and the Nation could become Qadhafi's agent within the fortress called the United States. Although the minister visited other nations, such as Jamaica, Ghana, and Trinidad and Tobago, his visits to America's proclaimed enemies received the attention that he believed the Nation wanted and needed.

When Farrakhan returned to the United States, he was met by a chorus of reporters, scores of black critics, and hostility from the United States Senate, Justice Department, and State Department. New York representative Pete King, a constant critic of Farrakhan, maintained that the Muslim should register as a foreign agent. The Justice Department also advised him to register as a foreign agent if he continued his policy as an advocate for the Libyan government. Black reporter Clarence Page reprimanded Farrakhan for not speaking out against slavery in the Sudan and for ignoring Libya's role in supporting the peculiar institution.

On February 25, three days after his arrival in the United States, Farrakhan addressed twelve thousand of the Black Muslims' faithful members and supporters at the University of Illinois Chicago Pavilion. Posing and strutting before the crowd, he challenged the American government to bring him before the Senate to testify. Resplendent in his custom-tailored suit, he boasted that he was born for this day, a time to confront the greatest and most wicked country in the world: "How dare you ask me to register as an agent? Bring me before Congress and I will call the rolls of the members of Congress who are honorary members of the Israeli Knesset. We will then see who are the real agents for another nation. Every year, you [American government] give Israel $4 to $6 billion of the taxpayers' money and you haven't asked the people nothing. Who are you an agent of?"[6]

Defending his World Friendship Tour, Farrakhan threatened that the American government had better allow him to receive the $1 billion from Libya because if it did not it would earn the rage of Louis Farrakhan. He notified the federal government that if the money was kept from the Nation of Islam, he would travel throughout America stirring up blacks, whites, Arabs, Native Americans, and Muslims into a hysteria that would promote mass unrest and confusion. In addition, he argued that he would take the government to court and sue for his monetary gift. As expected, Farrakhan's threats and promises never materialized. The Nation did not receive the money, and there has not been a rainbow coalition of rallies against the government on behalf of the Nation.

In the aftermath of the march and the World Friendship Tour the Nation was pressured by the black community to provide an audit of the revenues and the expenditures of the march. Farrakhan had announced prior to the event that the Nation would provide a monetary account of the Million Man March. According to Farrakhan, he wanted to show that the Nation was honest. However, the internal audit performed by Kumah Muhammad and Leonard Farrakhan was received with suspicion and charges of organizational mismanagement, corruption, and fraud. Prior to the march the Nation's local temples and study groups, together with Chavis's NAALS, had raised millions of dollars to put on the march. During the activity millions of dollars were collected. In several meetings of organizers, held primarily at Farrakhan's residence, it was estimated that the march could be done for approximately $750,000 or less. However, the audit maintained that the Nation and NAALS had an outstanding balance of $67,000. Chavis, Farrakhan's agent, had used his position as the director of NAALS to ask chapter members and support groups to give $1,000 to the Million Man March. Many now speculated that if the Nation was in debt, or had not turned a profit, it was not because of expenditures related to the march but because Farrakhan, his family, and his closest aides had embezzled or mismanaged the Nation's money.

The *Washington Post National Weekly Edition* published two lengthy articles in September 1996 titled, "A Dream Past Due: The Nation of Islam's Mission Is Mired in a 10-Year Heap of Unpaid Bills" and "Who's Guarding the Guards?" The journalist traced Farrakhan's first corporate purchase under the name of the Final Call corporation of a funeral parlor on Seventy-ninth Street in Chicago to the acquisition of three separate residences, two in Chicago and one in Phoenix; the buying of office buildings; a Georgian farm; the Mosque Maryam (the grand mosque of the NOI); a secondary school in Chicago; and the building of the Salaam Restaurant and Bakery. The author also traced the forming of several businesses such as the NOI Security Firm, Clean-N-Fresh Skin Products, the *Final Call* newspaper, and the FCN Publishing Company. He reported that all these businesses and corporate entities were riddled with debt and that all were owned and controlled by the Farrakhan family, which is directly contrary to Farrakhan's statement that he owns none of the Final Call businesses or religious structures.

The major problem is that the Nation pressures its members to give at least 60 percent of their incomes to finance the dreams of Farrakhan. The Muslims believe that they are giving charitable gifts to a religious body. Under this doctrine Muslims, starting in 1981, gave millions of dollars to build a new mosque, restaurant, bakery, bookstore, auditorium, hair salon, classrooms, and a soup kitchen. Underclass individuals, who make up 95 percent of the Nation's body earning less than $12,000 annually, found themselves giving a minimum of $2,000 per family. That is $1,000 per adult. In addition, these same individuals were encouraged to present at least 20 percent of their income to the Nation through various charitable funds like the Number 2 Poor Treasury, whose revenues go directly to Farrakhan, the NOI Building Fund, and the Five Year Economic Program. However, this does not include the other funds for Farrakhan's Savior's Day (gifts, often times $1,000 per person), financial support of the Georgia farmland, and excessive rallies that are held at least three times a year to raise additional monies. In addition, members must give additional financial support for the local temple or study group.

Many of the Nation's financial problems started in 1985 with the announcement of an economic program titled People Organized and Working for Economic Rebirth (POWER). Financed with a $5 million loan from Qadhafi, the Black Muslim leader envisioned that it would become a $1 billion personal care enterprise. However, before the program could get off the ground, Farrakhan used the Qadhafi loan to purchase personal homes for himself and his children that amounted to more than $2 million. The remainder of the Libyan loan went into travel, entertainment, and lavish living that culminated in excess of over $800,000 alone in 1986–1987. As the Muslims were living high on the hog, private contractors and government tax departments labored diligently to force the Nation to honor delinquent debts. For example, a company that installed tile and built a perimeter wall around the $400,000 Phoenix mansion occupied by one of Farrakhan's daughters filed a lien against the Nation for failure to pay $6,000 for services rendered. The sadness of the mismanagement is even more pronounced when the Nation had to struggle to raise $45,000 in back taxes in 1995 to keep its Final Call Building on Seventy-ninth Street in Chicago. The travesty is that Farrakhan and the Nation amassed millions of dollars that they have literally thrown away on individualized arrogance.

Unfortunately, Farrakhan's Nation continued to destroy itself financially throughout the 1980s. With the remainder of the Qadhafi loan the Nation purchased the Nation of Islam original flagship mosque from the followers of his chief rival, Warith Deen Muhammad, for $2.1 million. Shortly after the closing the Black Muslims took out a $1.6 million mortgage against the mosque and the Hyde Park mansion. Now the Nation had to pay $37,000 a month on each of the loans. In 1988 the Nation started extensive renovations on the Stony Island mosque. The huge structure had so many interior problems that NOI members openly questioned the wisdom of buying back such an old building. From the very beginning the Nation had problems paying for the renovations. Between 1989 and 1990 seven companies filed suit against the Nation, claiming that the organization owed them $34,293. One particular black company, Airtite Incorporated, which had installed acoustical ceilings in the mosque and school, sent several letters to Farrakhan and other NOI officials, according to its president, George Irvin. On several occasions the Nation promised that the bills would be paid, but these promises were not kept. Irvin stated that he went to the mosque to request his payment of $12,000, but, as happened to other creditors and business-men, he was intimidated by the FOI and left the premises without the payment.

The 1990s proved no better for the Nation. In 1991 the organization paid off two $800,000 loans but turned right around and borrowed $3.2 million from Seaway National Bank, Chicago's largest African Ameri-can–owned financial institution. Given that Farrakhan was already deeply in debt, the black bank apparently was showing racial solidarity and benign but blind faith toward the Nation. As soon as the contract was signed between Seaway and the Nation, Farrakhan announced to ten thousand followers at the February 1991 Savior's Day that the three-year economic plan had been reinstated. He intended to buy again the farm-land in Terrell County, Georgia, that was once owned by the Nation prior to 1975 and the leadership of Warith Muhammad. In November 1994 the Nation made a $500,000 down payment to purchase 1,556 acres, less than half of the original farm that Elijah Muhammad owned. The Nation agreed it would make payments on the $1 million still owed on the farm. It is interesting that misleading articles in the *Final Call* newspaper stated that the purchase of the property came from the three-year eco-nomic development plan donations.

In 1994 Farrakhan continued his free spending and bad-credit habit. He secretly used money from the Number 2 Poor Treasury to sign a mortgage for seventy-seven acres of country property in New Buffalo, Michigan, a two-hour drive from the Chicago headquarters. The prop-erty, which cost $500,000, was to be used to build Minister Farrakhan a mansion that included a tennis court, Olympic-sized swimming pool, a fitness running track, a cabana, three cabins, and a heliport. According to contractors, the estimated cost of the new development, excluding the heliport, would be in the area of $800,000. What is so confusing and wrong in this blatant squandering by the Farrakhans of at least $1.4 mil-lion of the Nation's money on this lavish retreat is that the Nation was going bankrupt; and all the while poor believers and supporters were being told to give their last few pennies to the organization.

One example of this economic plight was the rising unpaid bills of the mosque and the new Salaam Restaurant. The Nation first promoted the development of the Salaam Restaurant during the early 1980s. Farrakhan had asked his followers to give at least $1,000 per person to the project. By 1985 the majority of the registered Muslims had completed their financial obligation for the new structure. Meanwhile, the Nation's executive officers were mismanaging the Libyan loan. Rusted construction support pillars that stood on a barren plot from 1984 to 1994 were the only evidence that a structure was going up. Unfortunately, details of the official reasons for the long delay in construction are not known. Minister Farrakhan never gave an account to the members of the expenditures and revenues raised for the project. No expected operational date was ever given. But it was clear that the Nation did not have the money to complete the structure in a timely manner. Between 1987 and 1996 at least eight major black companies and several white businesses, including the local telephone service of Chicago, filed suits against the Nation, alleging that they were owed collectively $850,000. In addition, the Illinois Department of Revenue and the Cook County Office of Taxes had filed liens against the organization totaling $100,000 for nonpayment of Retailers' Occupation Taxes and county taxes. However, seemingly blind to these problems, Farrakhan was telling his followers to dig deep into their pockets to help generate a kingdom of God on earth. The only kingdom that was growing was the one owned and controlled by Farrakhan.

To operate and develop such an elaborate scheme of fraud and deception requires a supporting cast. The leading character was Leonard C. Searcy, who married Farrakhan's daughter, Donna, in 1983 and then changed his name to Leonard Farrakhan. Leonard Searcy arrived on the Farrakhan scene around 1982. Most of the Muslim brotherhood found it odd that Leonard—overweight, unattractive, and a non-Muslim—was allowed to date, let alone marry, Donna, who looked like a model from the Miss Universe Contest. However, it was soon learned that Leonard had something that the underclass brothers lacked: he owned three Popeyes Famous Chicken enterprises and a company named LCS Enterprises, Inc. (which had gone bankrupt). The point was that Searcy could acquire major purchases and run them—even if they failed. Unfortunately, the problems that Searcy demonstrated in his own dealings were eventually duplicated within the enterprises of the Nation. According to court documents, LCS Enterprises folded because Searcy failed to pay his employees, suppliers, several lending institutions, and the IRS.

After becoming Farrakhan's son-in-law, Searcy, or Leonard Farrakhan, moved into the leadership structure with blinding speed. By 1986 Farrakhan had appointed Leonard a director of the *Final Call* newspaper, a director of Muhammad's Holy Temple of Islam, a director of Final Call, Inc. (the organization's business arm), the chief executive officer of the Nation's Chicago Security Guard Service, and, of course, Farrakhan's chief of staff. But Leonard's most infamous business role in the Nation started in 1986, when he was appointed POWER's business manager. Again, like his new father-in-law, Leonard paid little attention to detail concerning the company's legal issues. Because Leonard did not pay POWER's franchise tax to the State of Illinois, POWER, Inc., was dissolved by Illinois in early 1987. Then, under the leadership of Leonard, the former POWER, Inc., developed into two new enterprises—Nationway Ventures International, Ltd., and DiNar Products. Both were to take Clean-N-Fresh orders for the defunct POWER program. By 1987 it became evident that the Nation's Clean-N-Fresh cosmetic line was primarily owned by Leonard and Donna and not by the Nation's faithful.

Changing the names of the toiletries companies did not improve the business habits of poor service, bad community relations, and nonpayment to creditors. Since 1988 the two companies, located in a small disorganized and disjointed office at 2021 South Wabash Avenue in Chicago, have been served with several lawsuits and tax liens totaling over $225,000.

POWER, Nationway, and DiNar's most frustrated creditor had been the Internal Revenue Service. In 1993 the IRS filed a $138,240 lien against the three companies and notified Nationway that it planned to seize all its assets. However, a few days before the IRS action, the cunning Leonard Farrakhan turned over Nationway's assets to a Chicago company named the Assignment for the Benefit of Creditors Trustee, Inc. This company soon sold Nationway's assets for $8,635 to a new company named Nationway Ventures International Groups, Inc. The owner of the new company, coincidentally also located at 2021 South Wabash Avenue, was Franklin D. Searcy, the brother of Leonard Searcy Farrakhan. The new Nationway continued the practices of the former companies by selling Clean-N-Fresh products and racking up unpaid bills. Since 1995 three suppliers have filed suit claiming that collectively they are owed $15,673. One thing is certain—the business ventures of the Nation were a family affair.

Another of the Nation's failed businesses was the NOI Security Agency, Inc. It had gained national attention when an unarmed Fruit of Islam member patrolling the notorious crime-infested District of Columbia's Mayfair Mansion's housing project, often called "Little Beirut," kicked a shotgun out of a drug dealer's hand. Almost immediately, the Mayfair homes became a safe place to live. For the first time in several years, kids could play in the courtyard without running for cover to escape drive-by shootings, the elderly walked freely, and women and girls could leave their apartments without fear of being assaulted or even raped. The incident of the well-dressed man in a bow tie capturing and beating drug dealers caught the attention of the media, the American community, and most important, the federal government. Individuals like former District of Columbia mayor Sharon Platt Kelly, U.S. Housing Secretary Jack Kemp, and First Lady Barbara Bush praised the Nation's guards for a service that neither the police nor the federal government had been able to provide. Minister Farrakhan rejoiced over the incident and took credit for the service by stating that "the will, dedication and the grace of Allah enable us to turn our communities around without guns."[7] Within a few months the FOI guard service formed a corporation that controlled four smaller security companies that were scattered throughout the United States. The corporation was an instant success. It was well respected by Muslims and non-Muslims, by black militants and white conservatives. In four years the corporation won over $20 million in public contracts in ten major cities. Finally, it looked as if the Nation was going to make good on its promise of black economic development. But in a matter of a few years after the Mayfair experience, the security companies became riddled with debt, mismanagement, and blatant corruption.

The largest of the companies, NOI Security Agency, Inc., was primarily owned and controlled by Abdul Sharrieff Muhammad, supreme captain of the Fruit of Islam, and Mustapha Farrakhan, the minister's son and assistant supreme captain. This company had offices in Illinois, California, Pennsylvania, and the District of Columbia. But in 1995 it filed for bankruptcy. According to court records, the organization was unable to pay its creditors, could not contribute to the worker's compensation fund, and owed the IRS over $600,000 dating back to 1992. The company was ultimately forced to fire hundreds of bodyguards. However, while the company was going bankrupt, the owners enjoyed a lavish lifestyle. They purchased luxury vehicles such as Lexuses and Mercedes Benzes, traveled first-class on airlines, vacationed in luxury suites at some of the best hotels in the United States and wore full-length mink coats during winter months in the Northeast and Midwest.

The U.S. Department of Housing and Urban Development, which had initially given grants to the Nation's security groups for their outstanding work in curbing crime in several of the country's problem public housing projects, decided that there were too many problems within the Nation's security teams to continue to grant them $20 million contracts. HUD first terminated the Nation's security team in Baltimore; later it fired other security chapters in Chicago, Washington, New York, and Philadelphia.

Another area of concern was that hundreds of security workers began filing complaints with local and federal agencies over unpaid wages. Residents of public housing also voiced their complaints about the Nation's security. Contrary to many others who praised the Nation for patrolling dangerous areas, they reported that the security squad leaders were more concerned with driving Jaguars and BMWs, flirting with young girls, selling *Final Call* newspapers, pestering people about the evils of eating pork, and recruiting for the Nation of Islam. One young resident of Clifton Terrace in Baltimore remarked that they had "hired guards—not preachers, teachers, social workers or newspaper sellers."[8]

Although the NOI Security Agency filed for bankruptcy, it somehow continued to gain private contracts under new corporate names. For example, in New York the company became known as the X-Men Security Agency, and in Chicago it was New Life Self Development. Although the companies were controlled by Farrakhan's son and the supreme captain, it appeared that the real brains of the operation was the familiar Leonard Searcy Farrakhan, CEO of the Chicago branch. By 1996 the CEO controlled the Nation's entire group of security firms. Unfortunately, the trio of Leonard Farrakhan, Mustapha Farrakhan, and Abdul S. Muhammad had brought the Nation an accumulated debt of over $5 million.

The security companies' services ranged from being extraordinarily good to overwhelmingly bad, but in both extremes they operated in a sea of corruption and abuse. The leaders apparently saw the opportunity to make millions of dollars in the black community through government grants, instead of recognizing an opportunity to reform themselves and the black community through honesty, hard work, and community service. Unfortunately, just as the Nation's security firms got sidetracked, so did the dream of a productive farm enterprise.

Under the leadership of Elijah Muhammad, his Muslim followers were taught to "take their mouths out of the White man's kitchens";[9] that is, they must develop a black society able to produce its own food. By 1975 the Nation owned five thousand acres of farmland in Georgia, one thousand acres in Michigan, and nine thousand acres in Alabama. These working farms produced corn, string beans, apples, tomatoes, okra, soybeans, and various grains and raised chickens, cows, and sheep. In 1994 the Nation under Louis Farrakhan attempted to duplicate Elijah's feat by purchasing fifteen hundred acres for $1.5 million from Tracy and Charles Bridges of Terrell County, Georgia.

The sale of the property by the Bridges to the Nation was a godsend, not to the Muslims but to the Bridges' estate. The farmland was a waste of territory. The vegetable farm was located in a dry climate better suited for cotton and wheat. Contrary to advertisements placed in the Nation's paper that vegetables were being sent to the Nation of Islam people all over the country, very little was provided for the Muslims, let alone the larger black community. The United States Department of Agriculture reported that the majority of the property was forest and that the owners—Muhammad's Holy Temple of Islam—had neither irrigated nor purchased equipment for stable farming. It was impossible for the farm to produce enough vegetation to feed the larger black community. In fact, contrary to the Nation's picture of a productive farm with silos, dairy barns, watermelon patches, and a cannery, reality showed a dented old trailer home, rusted farm equipment, an abandoned eighteen-wheeler, and a nonworking old pickup truck at the end of a dirt road.

Therefore, with the Nation's skyrocketing debt and the mounting criticism based not on Farrakhan's religion or his views on Jews and whites but on his personal and financial affairs, it was not surprising that he became very depressed after the Million Man March. He needed to hide—he longed for a comfort zone that would deflect criticism away from him and the Nation. What better way to do this than by creating a controversy that involved the Nation, black Americans, Arabs, Persians, Jews, West Indians, and the American political structure?

Farrakhan's World Friendship Tour paid off. Even though he did not get the promised $1 billion, he crippled his adversaries. Although he lost the Million Man March in the domestic market, his activities outside the States, especially in the Middle East and Africa, were viewed as remarkable and enhanced his international image as the leader of black America. It must be remembered that Farrakhan viewed himself as a global citizen who had the power—imagined or not—to influence international laws and activities. The United States's refusal to allow the Libyans to give Farrakhan the $1 billion gift surprised neither Farrakhan nor Qadhafi.

The $5 million that the Libyan government gave Farrakhan was eventually repaid; however, the State Department, on the advice of the Reagan administration, placed the money in an escrow account. The money will only be given to the Libyans when they change their political policy on international terrorism. Knowing this, both Muslim leaders understood that the Nation had a very slim chance of ever receiving the promised money. Nonetheless, in a half-hearted attempt Farrakhan threatened lawsuits and civil uprisings to get the money. He ordered his new surrogate, Benjamin Chavis Muhammad, to work with Marion "Rex" Harris, a southern black self-made millionaire, to get the money.

Harris had made his fortune in the dry cleaning business. Also, he directs several special interest groups, such as the International and Domestic Development Corporation, a Fayetteville, North Carolina, company that exports medical and food supplies; Custom Molders, Inc., which makes plastic-injection molded parts like razor blade handles; Rexon Coal Company of Stearns, Kentucky; and the All-American Food Service-NC, Inc. Farrakhan and Chavis Muhammad viewed the senior businessman as a partner who had experience in international business. For example, in 1996 Harris applied under United Nation's regulations to supply medical aid and food to Iraq. Although Harris had been successful in developing domestic businesses and generating productive governmental and corporate business contacts internationally, he had little experience with the Nation's political objectives. Harris maintained that he trusted Farrakhan and that he was not motivated by the potential 7 percent or $70 million he could earn from his future partnership with the Black Muslims.

Since the initial discussions between Harris and the Muslims, nothing substantial has been done to receive the Libyan funds. It remains to be seen if U.S. prohibitions will be waived, allowing the Nation of Islam to accept the money. But if prohibitions are waived, it will then be up to the Libyans to fulfill their promise of such a large gift.

In 1992 the Libyans offered to give the American Red Cross $1 million. The organization, at that time headed by Elizabeth Dole, the wife of Robert Dole, former Republican senator and presidential candidate, said it was willing to accept the gift. Because the Red Cross is a neutral and apolitical organization, its receipt of such a gift would be no problem. However, Libya never delivered on the offer.

Internal strife and tension may have also prevented Libya from giving Farrakhan the money. By 1996 the country was facing high unemployment and civil and military unrest. During the same year, Libya depleted its foreign assets to finance its 1993–1995 deficits. Sanctions imposed by the United States also restricted the nation's short-term credit. Realizing the economic problems of his country, Qadhafi urged Muslims in the Middle East to help finance the gift, stating that ". . . the American black [was] not the sole responsibility of the Libyans."[10]

In August of 1996, almost a year after the Million Man March, the Nation attempted to capitalize on the success of the march by sponsoring a national black political rally headed by Benjamin Chavis Muhammad. The event, scheduled to be held in the Trans World Dome in St. Louis, according to Chavis Muhammad, expected to attract over thirty thousand people to decide on a black political agenda. The NOI and NAALS believed they were responsible for registering over one million new voters to the political system. Therefore, they concluded that several thousands of the Million Man March supporters would flock to the NAALS/NOI political convention, but Chavis Muhammad and Farrakhan miscalculated the African American response. Apparently rejecting Farrakhan and Chavis Muhammad and questioning their political motivation, the black community stayed away. In a massive auditorium that could easily accommodate over sixty thousand people, fewer than two thousand African Americans showed up. In fact, a few hours before Farrakhan was to give the keynote address, the FOI had to comb the city of St. Louis to muster three thousand people to hear the Muslim leader. However, the Nation attempted to organize one last major rally before the end of the year to illustrate the continued strength of Farrakhan and the spirit of the Million Man March.

One year after the march, the Nation organized the World Day of Atonement to celebrate the first anniversary of the Million Man March. The affair, held across the street from the United Nations in New York City, attracted 150,000 black New Yorkers who listened patiently to Farrakhan's three-hour lecture. Whereas the Million Man March had presented a diversity of African American leaders, however, only a few black advocates joined Farrakhan for the Day of Atonement. Besides Muslim ministers and supporters of the Nation such as Benjamin Chavis Muhammad and the Reverend James Bevel of Chicago, the only well-known personalities to appear onstage with Farrakhan were the Reverend Al Sharpton and former first lady of South Africa, Winnie Mandela. These two major non-Muslims not only allowed themselves to be part of a spectacle that most black leaders boycotted; they were the center of a minor controversy. First, the Reverend Mr. Sharpton, who had demonstrated his willingness to confront white, black, and Jewish leaders who held different opinions from his, challenged Farrakhan to invite his former friend Khallid Muhammad to address the crowd. Sharpton pointedly asked Minister Farrakhan, "How can we have atonement when the Nation has not made any overture of atonement with Khallid?"[11] The New York civil rights leader forced Farrakhan, however reluctantly, to ask Khallid Muhammad to speak.

The second issue involved Winnie Mandela. The South African leader stood before the crowd but did not utter a word. James Muhammad, editor of the *Final Call* stated, "She could not speak on orders of the South African Government."[12] As she stood silently, another person read her address that was bluntly apolitical and conservative. However, a year later, at the Million Woman March in Philadelphia, Mrs. Mandela addressed more than five hundred thousand black women without an interpreter. As for Farrakhan's New York City event, the South African government has denied that Mandela was instructed not to speak to the audience.

Farrakhan's World Atonement event not only lacked the appeal of the Million Man March; its focus deviated from being problack to being pro-Libyan. In a desperate attempt to connect the Libyan struggle against the

United States to problems that blacks suffer because of racism and discrimination, the minister told his audience that America practices evil against the North African nation just as it is destroying the black community. He also argued that Libya, Iraq, and Cuba were suffering from the bigotry and racism of the American government, which controls the United Nations. Although Farrakhan's analysis may have been academically correct, he misunderstood the political nature of most African Americans. Black Americans, like the larger white community, historically have aligned themselves with America's international policies, especially if doing so means increasing and expanding black influence and power in the United States. But again, the World Atonement Day was designed to convince Qadhafi that Farrakhan was the leader of black America and that African Americans supported the policies of the Libyan government. The World Islamic Peoples Leadership Conference held in Chicago on July 6, 1997, further illustrated Farrakhan's interest in developing a closer relationship with the Libyan leader.

After the Million Man March Mu'ammar Qadhafi, chairman of the World Islamic Peoples Leadership Organization, based in Tripoli, Libya, named Farrakhan as his vice chairman. The Libyan urged the American Muslim leader to take advantage of his current popularity and hold the annual World Islamic Peoples Leadership Conference in the United States. However, unlike the Million Man March or the World Atonement Day that sought to attract African Americans, the World Islamic Peoples Leadership Conference was designed primarily for Arab and Persian Muslims in North America. Even though there were Muslims who represented Europe, Asia, and Africa, Farrakhan and Qadhafi sought the support of the most influential and educated group of Muslims in the world—the North Americans.

The conference, financed by the Libyans, invited and attracted approximately five hundred Muslim advocates, scholars, and political leaders. In a three-day affair they held workshops on health, education, religion, and economics. Farrakhan was continuously praised by guests as a great Islamic leader. In fact, the politically dominant Qadhafi crowd bestowed on Farrakhan the title of sheik, a title used to indicate a spiritual and academic Islamic leader. However, there was an uneasy undertone during this conference that went against the traditional values and history of the Nation of Islam.

First, the affair overwhelmingly sought to make Arabs and Persians a

184 | Inside the Nation of Islam

part of the gathering. Although there are more Muslims in Africa than in the Middle East, only a few African Muslim leaders attended the conference. The Africans who did attend were not major figures in Islamic affairs on their continent. The few African Muslim scholars and advocates who came to the meeting were primarily from Ghana. Knowing the close relationship that Farrakhan had with President Rawlings of Ghana, who had allowed the Nation to open its African international office and to hold its first International Savior's Day there in 1995, it was not surprising that Islam in Africa was represented overwhelmingly by Muslims from Ghana. A universal representation of Islam would have included leaders of the various tariqas or Islamic brotherhood societies located in Senegal, Mali, The Gambia, and Algeria. Just as the diversity of Islam in Africa was not represented, neither was the larger black American Muslim community. Outside the Nation of Islam, few Black Muslims attended the affair. Members of the American Muslim Mission, the largest black Islamic group in the United States, were not invited to the meeting nor were the many splinter Nation of Islam groups or the several smaller African American Islamic groups, such as the Moorish Science Temple Organization. It seemed as if Farrakhan deliberately excluded black American and black African Muslims.

Another issue that clashed with the Nation's theology was Farrakhan's demotion of its two greatest leaders, Fard Muhammad and Elijah Muhammad, from being divinities of the Quran to being merely great Muslim leaders. Throughout the history of the Nation its members, including Farrakhan, considered Master Fard Muhammad as Allah and Elijah Muhammad as the last Messenger and Christ of God. In fact, prior to 1994 Farrakhan named Elijah as the Messiah and Fard as the Great Mahdi who would judge America and the world. However, at the conference Farrakhan's Nation placed Prophet Muhammad Ibn Abdullah as the last and greatest of God's messengers, affirming to the audience that only through the Sunna or teachings of Prophet Muhammad of Saudi Arabia could the world know true Islam.

Farrakhan's reversal was motivated by Qadhafi's and the Nation's need for support among traditional Islamic leaders and groups. Orthodox Muslims, as they are called, had much greater education, wealth, and international influence than did Farrakhan's all-black nation. Both Qadhafi and Farrakhan desperately needed these individuals and organizations to make an impact on Western society and politics. However, before the Nation could attract these traditionalists, Farrakhan had to make theological concessions.

In 1990 Farrakhan sought the support of Sayyid Muhammad Syeed, the leader of the Islamic Society of North America (ISNA) based in Canada. Imam Syeed flatly told Farrakhan that if he wished to align with the ISNA, the most powerful and influential Islamic body in North America, he must repudiate the teaching that Fard Muhammad was God and Elijah Muhammad the last messenger. Farrakhan agreed, stating that the Sunna of Prophet Muhammad is the only truth of Islam. However, a few weeks after the discussion Farrakhan went back to the Nation's concept of divinity. But in his invitation to Syeed and several other Arab and Persian Muslims, Farrakhan promised that he would openly speak of the Muhammad of the Quran as the last prophet of God. An example of Farrakhan's open concession was his address to the Islamic International Conference on July 6, 1997: "Never in my wildest imagination could I have dreamed that becoming a student of Islam under the Honorable Elijah Muhammad, who taught me the Quran and showed me the glorious life of the Prophet Muhammad Ibn Abdullah, Peace be Upon Him, who laid the foundation upon which we stand and only his Sunnah, only his way, only his practice will lead us to success in establishing Islam in America and reviving the spirit of Islam in the Muslim world."[13] Throughout the 1980s, however, Farrakhan had preached that the "Arab way of Islam is not [the NOI] way. The Messenger taught us, the Nation, that we don't have to pray or worship like you. You, Arab, prostrate [yourself] because you have an evil nature. The black man is good by nature, he is a God. Thus, you're trying to be what we are by nature—righteous."[14]

The Million Man March opened up both a can of worms and a world of opportunities for Farrakhan. It defined his moment in American history. Scholars of history, political science, and religion cannot ignore the great feat that Louis Farrakhan accomplished in spearheading over one million black men to the District of Columbia. After the one-day event the Muslim leader became the ultimate black leader of the United States. Blacks, Jews, and whites who criticized the leadership of the march were forced to recognize Farrakhan's organizational talents, political astuteness, and appeal among the black community. But within a few weeks the controversial leader tossed away what he had gained to align himself with international Muslims and political extremists. The domestic popularity he had earned depreciated quickly among the same people who were forced to accept him as a legitimate and responsible power broker. But although he lost favor with most Americans, he earned praise and much-needed financial assistance from his international militant comrades.

These issues that flowed from the Million Man March created a strange paradox for Farrakhan. Many openly questioned the sincerity of the Black Muslim leader—his concern for the black community, his relationship with the nations in the Persian Gulf, his motivation for redevelopment of the Nation of Islam, and his religious-political ideology and motivation. Unfortunately, no one knows the real Farrakhan. Perhaps he has transformed, as many believe. The problem is—what has he become? His followers say a prophet, Jesus, even a Christ. Critics say, a Hitler, a Jim Jones, a disciple of evil. The objective viewer sees an even more confused man, unsure if he wants to be a preacher, politician, race advocate, family man, or corporate magnate. At this point I do not think that even Farrakhan knows what or who he is. The old saying that "a rolling stone gathers no moss" applies to Farrakhan, who has run politically from pillar to post. His movement has been based on his personal appeal. Because he has never taken the time to identify himself and the objective of the Nation of Islam, he has failed to gather sustained support from the black community. The membership of the group has fallen, financially the institution has become bankrupt, and internally the practices are corrupt and disjointed. Traditional Islam will not save the Nation; only Farrakhan can. He must rededicate himself to the underclass and build real programs that can benefit the black community—programs and institutions not based on ethnicity, race, gender, or national origin but on respect, integrity, and a passion for building a better and more egalitarian world.

10

Farrakhan's World Tours

Louis Farrakhan had created an image of himself as an international power broker in world affairs. Since 1984 the Nation of Islam had conducted several world tours in which Farrakhan met with international political and religious leaders. These elaborate tours took the minister to hundreds of nations and territorial colonies. The world tours, as they were called by the Nation, spanned every continent except for the North Pole and Antarctica. However, most of the Muslim leader's destinations have been to the Middle East, West Africa, and the Caribbean.

The Nation of Islam promotes Farrakhan as a global religious advocate who commands the attention of kings, presidents, dictators, and religious leaders. The American public, black and white, tend to believe this view. But close scrutiny reveals that Farrakhan's international fame is more myth than fact. Except for a few leaders like Qadhafi of Libya, very few world leaders take Farrakhan seriously. Thus, he is not an international black icon but a world traveler with a thirst for power, fame, and fortune.

Farrakhan's aspiration for global travel originated in the historical fabric of the Nation of Islam. From its creation in the 1930s, the Black Muslim movement established a cultural theory that included African, Arabic, and Asian peoples. It taught that the Nation of Islam represented dark people—black, brown, and red—of the world. Because the Nation represented all the international dark race, Black Muslims cannot be controlled by selected governments; thus boundaries are meaningless. Fard Muhammad, the original leader of the Nation of Islam, illustrated this view in several of his eccentric and elaborate question-and-answer formats. For example, if he asked, "Who is the original man?" the devoted Muslim answered, "The original man is the Asiatic black Man, the maker, the owner, the cream of the planet earth, God of the universe."[1] The answer to the question "What is the population of the original man on the planet earth?" is "The population of the original nation in the wilderness of North America is 17,000,000 with the 2,000,000 Indians makes it 19,000,000. All over the planet earth there are 4,400,000,000."[2] Fard Muhammad asserts that the Nation of Islam comprises the black, brown, and red nations of the world.

Fard Muhammad's theology of global activism expanded during Elijah Muhammad's tenure. The new leader openly taught that nonwhites, including the Japanese, whom Americans hated during World War II, were brothers to African Americans. Solidarity was pivotal to Elijah's race and religious theories. The unification of the dark races was necessary for the overthrow of white supremacy according to Muhammad. However, his views began to change during the 1950s from rhetoric to conventional programs. The impetus for Black Muslims to think more seriously about Third World countries was the rapid governmental changes in colonized nations. The Nation of Islam observed black and brown countries revolting and ridding themselves of European domination. The Nation considered itself a participant in the struggle for liberation. Therefore, the Black Muslims saw an alliance with these nations as logical and progressive moves.

Nations in Africa and the Caribbean such as Ghana, Nigeria, Egypt, Jamaica, Trinidad, and Tobago searched and found cultural roots that led them to struggle for political and social liberation. Leaders and theorists like Kwame Nkrumah and Franz Fanon lectured and published scores of manuscripts that reflected the newly found sense of African/black global solidarity and political action. The Black Muslims highlighted the importance of racial solidarity and branded all whites and European societies the greatest problem for Third World nations. Thus, Black Muslims, in their quest for liberation, aligned themselves with Asians, Arabs, Indians, Native Americans, and Africans as brothers and sisters in the struggle against white domination.

To illustrate the Nation's solidarity with dark governments, the *Muhammad Speaks* newspaper increased its coverage of international events and started a column titled "Middle Eastern News." By the 1970s the Nation extended its commitment by establishing economic and educational links in Latin America and the Middle East. Between 1970 and 1975 the Nation traded with Japan, Turkey, Argentina, Panama, and Brazil, importing such items as fish, shoes, clothes, and bananas. During this period the Nation also established relationships with Jamaica, Cuba, Costa Rica, Saudi Arabia, and Ghana. One of the leading figures who assisted in promoting the Nation's overseas exploits was Louis Farrakhan.

In 1965 Louis Farrakhan became the national spokesperson for the Nation of Islam and Elijah Muhammad. In this position he traveled the world, speaking on the unity of blacks, the importance of the Nation of Islam in world affairs, and the evils of white Americans and Europeans. By the time Elijah Muhammad died in 1975, Farrakhan had traveled extensively throughout Latin America. As the Nation grew internationally, the Nation's internal structure weakened. Between 1975 and 1978 Wallace Muhammad, the leader of the movement, restructured the Nation into a decentralized traditional Islamic organization. Ultimately, Farrakhan left the group to build a new Nation of Islam.

During the late 1970s and early 1980s, Farrakhan's new venture, the Final Call, Inc., was a small struggling group that had fewer than five thousand members. The minister, preaching black solidarity, racial pride, antiwhite thought, and hatred for America, needed financial support to promote the organization's many proposed programs. In response to these concerns Farrakhan embarked on three programs for financial profit: a domestic scheme that centered on massive rallies held approximately every three months; the formation of the *Final Call* newspaper, the centerpiece of the organization's propaganda scheme; and the development of programs that located, borrowed, and made money from foreign investors.

In late 1980 the international movement of the Nation started to bloom within the organization's inner circle with a scheme for purchasing fish from Japanese fisheries. Akbar Muhammad masterminded this program and at the time was executive administrative assistant to Minister Farrakhan. Akbar, a brilliant technician and strategist, had worked with Farrakhan since 1965 and previously served as an aide to Malcolm X and Wallace Muhammad. His experience propelled the new Nation of Islam/Final Call into international markets.

Between 1975 and 1978 Akbar Muhammad/Larry X Prescott labored as Wallace Muhammad's assistant as the Nation transformed to traditional Islam. In that capacity Akbar traveled throughout the world, meeting Islamic and political leaders in an effort to change the Nation's image as a black nationalist religious group to that of an orthodox Islamic group concerned with spiritual uplift. Akbar proved a reliable and competent adviser for Wallace, under whom the Nation adopted Sunni doctrines and principles. However, in his heart Akbar was a black nationalist. Ultimately, he left Wallace to join Farrakhan's new adventures. His defection was a severe blow for Wallace and a great find for Farrakhan. Akbar brought to Farrakhan all of his contacts, experiences, and concepts that he had developed in Wallace's World Community of Al-Islam, the new name for Elijah's Nation of Islam.

As Farrakhan's assistant, Akbar sought to reestablish the Black Muslims' fish enterprise. Blue Seas Whiting Fish Program, as it was called, was designed to be an extension of Elijah Muhammad's fish enterprise that between 1970 and 1975 had annually imported millions of pounds of fish from Argentina. Under Muhammad the program became one of many initiatives that brought employment to Black Muslim followers. Farrakhan's idea was similar but with a twist. The Muslim faithful were told of the "great wealth" they could make selling Blue Seas Whiting Fish. The fish would come in several forms and flavors that would appeal to the most discriminating fish eater. Farrakhan stated at the Final Call Building in Chicago, "We have fish that tastes like shrimp, lobster and catfish. How can you not make money from this?"[3] Farrakhan and Akbar made several trips to Japan to fine-tune the agreement. Members of the Nation of Islam were told that the Japanese, their brothers, were willing to work with them in international trade.

The negotiations between the Nation and the Japanese culminated with the Blue Seas corporation. The company, controlled by Leonard Farrakhan, the son-in-law of the minister and the chief of staff of the Nation of Islam, sought to manipulate Black Muslims into purchasing and selling the fish. Leonard, attempting to use a pyramid structure like Amway, promised that Muslims could become wealthy, even millionaires, if they sold Blue Seas Whiting Fish. The promised whiting that tasted like shrimp, lobster, and catfish never materialized, and neither did the promised wealth. As one Muslim put it, "Farrakhan's talk of the coin in the mouth of the fish was hogwash. The only coin that was associated with Blue Seas was the one I used to purchase the fish. And that coin is in the hands of Brother Minister Farrakhan."[4] The only beneficiary of the relationship between the Nation and the Japanese was Louis Farrakhan. The Japanese corporations did not make money; the Nation did not make money; the believers who sold the fish did not make money. However, Farrakhan received a brand-new car as a gift from the

Japanese and an enhanced image as a respected power broker in international affairs, especially in the field of business development.

This fish program continued for several years as a failure that saddled the organization with debt and the eventual bankruptcy of Blue Seas Whiting Fish. However, the failure did not slow Farrakhan's pursuit of an international market. Even before the fish enterprise he had set his sights on Libya. Colonel Mu'ammar Abu al-Qadhafi, who had been a friend of the Nation of Islam from the days of Elijah Muhammad, was contacted by Akbar to reestablish relations.

In 1972 the oil-rich North African state lent Elijah Muhammad and the Nation $5 million. The loan came at a time when the Nation was struggling to pay its vast employment system, mortgages, taxes, and general operational debt. Qadhafi agreed to give the organization an interest-free loan for political influence with the Nation and a voice in the domestic affairs of black Americans. Muhammad, who had a reputation as a stubborn leader, quickly let the Libyan leader know that he was not going to concede his Nation for a "bag of silver and gold." Qadhafi responded that he wanted the money repaid within a year. Muhammad countered that he would pay them back when he got the money. Although Qadhafi was rudely entertained by Muhammad, he continued to labor with the group until a different leader emerged.

In 1979 Qadhafi's new leader had emerged. As the Japanese deal was sputtering, Farrakhan and Akbar contacted the Libyan government in an attempt to reestablish communications between the Nation and the Libyans. Farrakhan's objective was to raise needed financial support and to create a magnetic, revolutionary, and progressive international personality.

At the February 1982 Savior's Day convention Farrakhan announced that the Nation needed financial support for the construction of a national mosque and a convention center that would house a restaurant, cafe, bakery, fish store, classrooms, computer centers, barbershops, beauty salons, and a five-thousand-seat auditorium. In the same year the minister boasted of another project called People Organized Working for Economic Rebirth (POWER), for which the Nation needed initial funding. Both projects illustrated the organization's lack of business sense and its quest to quickly raise substantial amounts of money by exploiting its own members and international friends.

The misuse of the Muslim followers became evident in the planning of the National Center complex. The organization solicited and raised millions of dollars from its members; however, little if any of the money was used for the structure. Instead, Farrakhan distributed the contributions to purchase mansions formerly owned by his mentor, Elijah Muhammad. Therefore, the Nation had no money for the promised National Center. Farrakhan's solution was to build POWER as a cosmetic firm that worked on a pyramid business scheme. To accomplish this he hired a black-owned marketing company from New Jersey, the Wellington Group. The Wellington organization, like the Nation of Islam, knew nothing about business development or marketing. As a result the Nation invested over $3 million in a marketing company that had no experience with what the Nation expected and needed. Attempting to recover from this error, Farrakhan went to Johnson Enterprises of Chicago for possible investment in POWER. Initially, the Johnson corporation supported Farrakhan and made arrangements to get involved with the Nation's cosmetic firm. But Farrakhan blew the deal. Within days of signing the agreement the minister delivered a controversial lecture that accused Jews of practicing a gutter or dirty religion. The Johnson firm quickly withdrew its support and canceled the agreement. The company did not want to be associated with Farrakhan's anti-Jewish statements and beliefs. At this point the minister was really in a bind. The only person he could go to for support was Qadhafi, who needed a way to influence the people of the United States. Farrakhan was the tool, so the Libyan leader gave the American Black Muslim leader $5 million.

In 1984 Farrakhan invited the militant Arab leader to address the annual Savior's Day convention via satellite. Qadhafi seized the moment and urged the Black Muslim delegation to rebel against "American imperialism" by quitting its military and picking up arms against the United States government. The North African even stated to a glowing Farrakhan and cheering audience, "I will supply you with guns if you need them."⁵ Qadhafi, speaking to a black American audience for the first time, was pleased with the feelings of solidarity and praise he received from the Nation. In response Qadhafi labeled Farrakhan the black leader of African American people and his personal friend and ally. In subsequent years Farrakhan would speak before Libya's parliament and at many public government rallies in Tripoli, the Libyan capital. Farrakhan's manipulation of Qadhafi caused the North African to view him as a serious black leader in the United States and in the world.

Farrakhan's image grew among his followers as a world leader. His prestige was magnified even more in January 1984, when he joined Jesse Jackson and twenty other black advocates on a trip to Syria to retrieve Lt. Robert Goodman, an Air Force pilot who had been shot down while flying a bombing mission over Lebanon. Lt. Goodman was being held by the Syrian government. Jackson, the leader on the trip, met with President Hafez al-Assad in Damascus, where the pilot had been detained. Farrakhan's role on the trip was only briefly mentioned in the American press. Nevertheless, the Muslim clergy played a very important part in the negotiations. Farrakhan's fluency in Arabic was quite impressive to Goodman's captors. In all of the meetings between Jackson and the Syrian government Farrakhan opened and closed the negotiations with an Arabic prayer from the Quran.[6]

Farrakhan's status among the faithful Nation of Islam membership again increased. However, it was uncertain how the Syrian government treated him after the Goodman ordeal. It was undeniable that Farrakhan's overall image as a black Islamic figure in the large Arab and Persian community encouraged Syria to view him as a potential religious and cultural ally in the United States. In the same year Farrakhan received an invitation from Colonel Qadhafi to attend his international Mathabah Conference.[7]

The Mataba Conference is described in Qadhafi's *Green Book*, which proposes a theory of domestic and international world revolution against capitalist and racist governments.[8] The week-long conference brought together an assortment of leaders, such as Nelson Mandela and Kwame Toure (formerly Stokely Carmichael), and groups such as the Palestine Liberation Army and the African Socialist League. Farrakhan and the Nation of Islam were in good company.

The Nation of Islam was one of the smaller organizations at the meeting. Yet Farrakhan traveled with a twenty-member entourage that included such major NOI leaders as Akbar Muhammad; Alim Muhammad, minister of health; Wali Muhammad, editor of the *Final Call*; Tynetta Muhammad, one of the seven wives of Elijah Muhammad; Wakila Muhammad, Native American member of the NOI; Mustapha Farrakhan, son of Farrakhan; and Shariff Muhammad, supreme captain of the Fruit of

Islam; and, of course, Farrakhan's wife, children, grandchildren, personal aides, bodyguards, and cooks. For one of the smallest units there, the Nation of Islam had by far one of the largest delegations.

Farrakhan held several meetings with the Libyan strongman at the president's residence, where he ultimately negotiated for another $5-million loan. More significant were the pictures that were taken of him with Qadhafi that were plastered on the front page of several editions of the *Final Call.* On this stage Farrakhan had the opportunity to meet and impress many Third World leaders, which enhanced his portrait as the premier black leader in the United States. In 1988 the Nation was again invited to the conference; this time Farrakhan took an even larger group, which included Khallid Muhammad and thirty black American students, intellectuals, and entrepreneurs. Qadhafi opened many doors for Farrakhan, especially in the Middle East and Africa. The American Black Muslim leader took full advantage of these opportunities.

Near the end of the 1980s Farrakhan started to forge a dialogue with several African states. Taking advantage of Ronald Reagan's and George Bush's overwhelming support for Israel and their poor relationship with African nations, Farrakhan eschewed the language of Marcus Garvey, W. E. B. Du Bois, Malcolm X, and Elijah Muhammad by calling for unity between black Americans and black Africans. During this period many Africans, especially blacks in South Africa who were fighting apartheid, listened intently to the ideas of Farrakhan. The young government of The Gambia, including its thirty-two-year-old president, was also impressed with Louis Farrakhan. And Ghana, which had promoted Pan-Africanism with black Americans since the revolutionary days of Kwame Nkrumah in the early 1960s, was receptive to Farrakhan's message. As Farrakhan became more comfortable with Africa, the Nation attempted to become more entrenched in the domestic affairs of African governments.

In 1982 the Nation organized one of several world tours that took Farrakhan to various African nations. During the tour, directed by Akbar Muhammad, the Nation considered itself a legitimate global Islamic group. However, while Akbar and Farrakhan sought to establish this view, they had to battle their own racist nationalistic reputation, which followed them on excursions. En route to Nigeria Farrakhan tried to sneak into England. Before Farrakhan landed on the island, the British government stated that he would not be permitted to enter their nation.

Akbar, who organized the trip, set up the itinerary to have the Nation's twenty-member entourage land in Heathrow, London's international airport, and fly out of Manchester, whose international airport was approximately three hundred miles north of London. Akbar had arranged for Farrakhan to have a brief lecture and press conference in Liverpool. The city of Liverpool had the second-largest black population in England. Akbar believed that blacks in the Liverpool and Manchester areas would rally behind Farrakhan's black nationalist theory. The British, aware of Farrakhan's reputation and operational style, negated Akbar's plan. English police detained Farrakhan, his wife, son, and several others at a holding area at Heathrow until a connecting flight was ready to transport Farrakhan's group out of the United Kingdom.

The British government and the British Jewish community rejected Farrakhan and his organization. In addition, the majority of the black Brits neither knew nor cared about the Black Muslim group. Farrakhan's only entrance into black England was through Khallid Muhammad, who lectured and assisted in establishing a small study group of twenty-five in London. In 1977 there were three small study groups in London with a total of seventy-six members. Incidentally, the British group brought thirty of its followers to the Nation's Savior's Day lecture in 1993 and a small group in 1994. The minuscule size of the Nation in England reflects the Black Muslim's ignorance of British society. Farrakhan knows nothing of the unique problems that blacks have in England or the specific issues that plague different quarters of the nation. For example, the problems blacks face in London are sometimes quite different from the racial issues in Liverpool or Wales.

The minister's next stop was Nigeria. The Nation again showed its disrespect and its lack of knowledge of world affairs when it attempted to hold a mass rally in the capital city of Lagos. The Muslim organizers assumed that they could hold a major lecture with typical American antigovernment and racial rhetoric. However, when Farrakhan was to address the audience, Nigeria's military personnel showed up, chased people away, and escorted the Muslim leader and his entourage off the stage and forced them to fly out of the nation. Farrakhan argued that America's Central Intelligence Agency (CIA) forced Nigeria to shut down the meeting. However, evidence supports the idea that the Nigerian government viewed Farrakhan as a loose cannon. Because Farrakhan had a history of attacking the administrative policies of countries he visited, the Nigerians were not willing to take a chance with his rhetoric. But strangely enough, in February 1997 the dictator of Nigeria addressed twenty thousand of Farrakhan's members via satellite in Chicago. This may have been in response to the minister's cry of lifting United States and United Nations sanctions against the West African state. The next stop was Ghana.

Throughout the history of Farrakhan's strange international policy, Ghana had consistently been a friendly place for him. In fact, on many of Farrakhan's travels in Africa, President Rawlings allowed him to use government air and ground transportation. In response Farrakhan made Ghana the headquarters of the Nation in Africa with a promise to build schools, hospitals, and a major mosque. To date the Nation's only properties in Ghana are the residence of Akbar Muhammad and a small storefront bookstore called the Nation of Islam Mission in the capital city of Accra. Incidentally, when I interviewed the American ambassador to Ghana, he was amused when I said Akbar was the representative of the Nation of Islam for Africa stating, "I thought I had a big job in Ghana."[9] The relationship between the Nation of Islam and Ghana is really between the two leaders. The majority of the people see no value in having the Black Muslims in their nation. In the weeks leading up to the Nation's 1995 international convention in Accra, Ghana's leading newspapers voiced opposition to the Black Muslim event. Scores of editorials condemned Rallings's invitation to Farrakhan and questioned the benefits that the Muslim would bring to the West African state.

In 1994 the Nation of Islam held its first International Savior's Day convention. The meeting was filled with African American entertainers, such as Jermaine Jackson, Isaac Hayes, and members of the rap group Public Enemy. In addition, approximately seven hundred American Black Muslims traveled with Farrakhan to the convention. On Sunday, the day of the convention, only a few hundred Ghanaians showed up at the stadium. In a field across the street from the stadium stood thousands of young people watching two soccer matches. Akbar, realizing the potential embarrassment, asked Flavor Flav, the lead rapper/singer of Public Enemy, to go to the soccer field and encourage the crowd to attend Farrakhan's lecture. Flavor Flav, toting a large kitchen clock around his neck and moving erratically, told the teenagers to, "come listen to Farrakhan 'cause he's a badd nigger." Many came, not because of the Nation but because of the "crazy black American rap star with gold teeth." Like the Pied Piper Flav led hundreds of people from the games to listen to Louis Farrakhan at the stadium.

The reporters for the *Final Call* wrote that the event was an overwhelming success. They ignored the negative response to the event by the Ghanaian people. The next day, the Ghanaian press asked, "What now, Mr. Farrakhan?"[10] The article mentioned that the convention brought few tourism dollars or investment resources to the country. If anything, it brought to the small struggling state criticism from the United States and Great Britain, its two most important trading partners. However, Farrakhan continued to maintain that the Nation of Islam, under his leadership, commanded international respect, and that was why Ghana granted the Nation an invitation to hold the convention.

Farrakhan's review of the success of the Ghana meeting was overstated. The only real significance of the event was based on his close relationship with President Rawlings. However, since the convention, Rawlings's relationship with Farrakhan has cooled tremendously. The lukewarm relationship that now exists can be attributed to Kofi Annan's appointment in 1997 as the secretary general of the United Nations. Annan, a Ghanaian, was supported and endorsed by the United States government. The Americans threatened that if Annan was not elected, they would withhold their billion-dollar payment to the United Nations. President Clinton's support of Annan inadvertently brought Ghana and the United States politically closer, creating a wedge between the Nation of Islam and Ghana. One year after the Accra convention, Farrakhan announced that Akbar Muhammad would move his Accra office to an undisclosed site in Africa. Farrakhan promised that a member other than Akbar Muhammad would handle Nation of Islam business in Ghana. However, the replacement person was a myth to hide the fact of the tainted relationship between Rawlings and Farrakhan.

In the 1990s Farrakhan showed interest in Gambia. Gambia, led by one of the world's youngest administrations, seemed to accept Farrakhan's message of African pride, independence, and building a relationship with black Americans. On two occasions the Nation's largest entourage visited the African nation. During these brief visits Farrakhan held talks with President Yahya J. J. Jammeh. However, like Ghana, the people of Gambia paid little attention to Farrakhan's words of solidarity and promises of economic and educational support. In February 1997, when Farrakhan asked Jammeh for permission to attend Gambia's inauguration ceremony, the president's office replied, "We have no room for your 20-member traveling group."[11] Apparently, like Ghanaians, Gambians were unwilling to get too close to the controversial American Muslim leader.

Minister Farrakhan also attempted to infiltrate the Sudan. The Islamic government of the Sudan is closely connected to Farrakhan's friend Colonel Qadhafi. According to the United Nations and the U.S. State Department, Sudan consistently trained and harbored international terrorists. Also, the Sudan has one of the world's worst human rights records against its own citizens. Farrakhan's activities in the northern African state were more connected to Libya; he had no concern for terrorists and human rights violations. Libya financially supported the Muslim government of Khartoum. Qadhafi, like the leaders of Iran, encouraged Islamic nations to enforce the Quran's strict laws. These actions in the Sudan had fueled a civil war between the Muslim government and the Christian rebels. Promoting zealous Islamic law, Libya allowed the Sudanese government to terrorize, enslave, and brutalize opponents of their doctrine.

Between 1996 and 1997 Farrakhan made three trips to Khartoum for unspecified reasons. When he returned to the United States, the American press, especially black reporters, asked him why he had refused to reprimand the government of the Sudan for its participation in the current slave trade. Farrakhan angrily responded, "There is no slavery in the Sudan. But prove me a liar and go there and see for yourself and come back and tell the world what you have found."[12] Well, reporters for the *Baltimore Sun* did so. They spent several weeks there, visited slave camps, and even purchased a slave boy. They then published their report. Akbar Muhammad and Farrakhan branded them liars, part of an elaborate Jewish conspiracy to stop the Nation from having a relationship with Islamic governments. But again, outside the presidential office of the Sudan, no one really paid attention to Farrakhan. He is known by the Muslim leadership, white and black Nubian Christians in the South who regard him as an enemy. The Nubians do not understand why Farrakhan embraces Arabs, who are responsible for their enslavement, instead of supporting the fight of black Africans who share a heritage with African Americans. However, the harshest response to the minister's actions on the continent came from President Nelson Mandela of South Africa.

Minister Farrakhan toured the African continent after his successful

Million Man March on Washington. Nelson Mandela, the former leader of the revolutionary African National Congress and current president of the newly formed multicultural nation, was not impressed with Farrakhan. Mandela was disturbed that Farrakhan entered South Africa with a twenty-two-member entourage and an aristocratic lifestyle that would have made any twentieth-century king jealous. The minister rode around South Africa in a white stretch limousine that was plated with fourteen-karat gold. In addition, the group resided in an elaborate hotel complex, a retreat that was usually reserved for very wealthy white South Africans and Europeans. During his stay Farrakhan had the fortune, or perhaps misfortune, of talking with President Mandela. Mandela severely reprimanded the minister for statements he had made calling Jews and whites devils, evil, and genetically inferior. Even though his government suffered from apartheid, stated Mandela, racism, discrimination, and racial baiting would not be tolerated in South Africa. Farrakhan, not accustomed to being lectured and reprimanded, stated gingerly that he supported the racial views of Mandela. Although Farrakhan met with Mandela, the larger black South African community did not take him seriously as a great leader. The only reason some blacks noticed him was because of the brouhaha surrounding the meeting between the two leaders. Many whites did not want Farrakhan to meet the president, but blacks, not really knowing Farrakhan, believed that because Mandela had met with white racists, it was natural for him to meet with a black racist as well.

Farrakhan traveled through Africa trying to win friends and to promote his image as a great black diplomat. However, it was apparent that in Africa and the Middle East his relationships were with the governments and not with the people. However, in the Caribbean his impact on local citizens seemed a bit more influential.

The minister often used his cultural heritage as a child of Caribbean parents to connect with the West Indians. Using this approach, he made inroads in establishing relations with Cuba, Jamaica, Panama, Bermuda, Trinidad, and Tobago. But generally, Farrakhan's popularity in these nations was extremely limited, especially in Bermuda.

Bermuda, the small British colony often called the Jewel of the Caribbean, had been targeted by the Nation throughout the 1980s. With its overall solid economy and its high rate of educated black people, the island inhabitants have luxuries that neighboring islands cannot afford.

The first major attempt by Farrakhan to establish a presence in Bermuda came in 1985, when a small group of local black politicians invited him to Hamilton, the capital city. However, most Bermudans at the time cared little for Farrakhan's message. His rhetoric did not fit into the political dialogue of the island. Nonetheless, the Nation had been able to create a small study group of about thirty members. Attempts by Farrakhan to visit the island, however, had met with resistance. The Bermudan Parliament voted in 1986 to indefinitely ban the minister from their country.

The Nation met with greater success in Trinidad and Tobago. The islands' history recorded an Islamic presence that spanned at least two hundred years, so it was not surprising that the two-island dominion had the largest Muslim population in the Caribbean. In 1980 the island census reported 115,000 Muslims lived in Trinidad and Tobago. In 1997 more than twenty thousand people along with local officials welcomed Farrakhan's visit to Port of Spain, the capital city.

By far, Trinidad and Tobago offered Farrakhan the greatest of Caribbean possibilities. He had built a sizable mosque with a membership of about 150 people. Also, according to the Nation's rumor mill, Farrakhan had developed plans to construct a multimillion-dollar home and complex in Port of Spain. Although Trinidad and Tobago offered the largest Muslim community and the highest expectations for Farrakhan, however, his cultural and political love was for Jamaica.

Jamaica, the island that gave birth to the black nationalist roots of Marcus Garvey, Bob Marley, Haile Selassie, and the Rastafarian movement, had been very open to the ideas of the Black Muslims. Since the early 1970s the Nation had forged relationships with its government and people. During the Marley administration of the 1970s and 1980s Farrakhan had grown close to the leadership. Like Castro, who had also become a friend of Jamaica, Farrakhan found avenues for inserting his influence into the nation. However, when Sieaga, a man who was very conservative and pro-American, became the prime minister, the Nation lost a bit of its influence. Nonetheless, the radical youth of the island continued to embrace the NOI's ideology. Still, although Farrakhan once enjoyed a great deal of popularity on the island, he failed to establish a permanent base of support. It appeared the Jamaicans respected his oratorical abilities but not the organization of the Nation of Islam. The citizens and government apparently wished only to embrace Farrakhan on scheduled visits but rejected overtures for the establishment of a mosque on the island.

In the summer of 1996 Farrakhan traveled to Cuba. On his three-day visit he toured the island and met with President Fidel Castro. Again, the Cuban people did not take notice of the visit. Castro was polite only because of his fond memory of Malcolm X and the manner in which black Harlem had embraced him on his visits to the United States in the 1950s, 1960s, and 1996. Interestingly, Farrakhan maintained that the reason for his twenty-member team's visit to Cuba was to study its educational system and its health department. The minister did not have any educators and had only one physician on the trip.

In the mid-1990s Farrakhan also visited such nations as Iran, Malaysia, North Korea, Egypt, Palestine, Uganda, Brazil, and Israel. His relationships with these countries have been primarily one-sided. The minister has attempted to create a portrait of himself as a man of international power, prestige, and influence. Unfortunately, the only ones he has deceived into believing his notion were the Muslim faithful and himself. The foreign leaders who have claimed him as a brother, friend, and ally are only using him and the Nation of Islam for their own purposes. The people of these nations often do not even know about Farrakhan. Farrakhan's great influence outside the United States was really a figment of his own imagination.

11

A New Nation

The Millennium

On October 16, 1997, Minister Farrakhan and the Nation of Islam called for a World Day of Atonement. In a gallant attempt he encouraged African Americans not to attend work or school but to stay home and fast, pray, and reflect on their personal future and goals and the larger objectives of the black community. In several cities in the United States Local NOI temples sponsored outdoor rallies to promote the new holiday.

Unfortunately for the Nation very few blacks paid attention to Farrakhan's call. In Harlem, once called the black cultural capital of the world by Langston Hughes and the place that laid the political-religious foundation for Malcolm X and Louis Farrakhan, fewer than two hundred people attended the Nation's rally to listen to Minister Benjamin Chavis Muhammad. In St. Louis, the home of Akbar Muhammad, close friend and international representative of the Nation, a sparse crowd of five hundred people gathered at the St. Louis Arch to listen to antiwhite and pro-Farrakhan rhetoric. In Los Angeles, one of the strongest Muslim enclaves under Elijah Muhammad, fewer than 150 supported the Nation's spectacle; and in Philadelphia, a city that hosted over five hundred thousand black women for the Million Woman March, Minister Rodney Muhammad could muster only fifty, including Muslims, to meet at the Liberty Bell for the Day of Atonement. Sparse crowds like these were recorded all over the country, except for Chicago.

Farrakhan went all out in Chicago to gather a crowd for the Day of Atonement and evening lecture. His presentation, delivered to a live audience of hundreds, created a festive atmosphere, suggesting that the event was a success and that black Americans supported the minister's holy holiday. The videotaped affair already was marketed domestically and internationally as a great victory for the Honorable Louis Farrakhan.

However, the aftermath of the Day of Atonement illustrated that there were several major dents in the armor of Louis Farrakhan. One, he was not the dynamic and feared leader that once commanded the attention of the media of even a few years ago. Two, outside the Nation very few blacks considered him divine or believed that the Nation of Islam held the answers to the problems of black America. Three, after the Million Man March the black community lost their trust in Farrakhan, especially in the area of finance. Only members of the Nation believed that a meager $250,000 was collected in donations during the march. Four, internal strife threatened to destroy the Nation. Insiders were questioning Farrakhan's decision to elevate Benjamin Chavis Muhammad to the paid position of the minister's special assistant and minister of the powerful East Coast region of the Nation. Five, ostracizing Khallid Muhammad from the Nation of Islam was unpopular with the membership. Six, the open and constant relationship with Libya made it appear to many in the Nation that Farrakhan had become Qadhafi's special assistant and agent in the United States. And last, the apparent theological shift of Farrakhan from a militant black religious nationalist to that of a radical Arab American Shiite Muslim concerned many members. Although Farrakhan and the Nation may have benign reasons for these actions, their followers, critics, and observers are watching these changes with interest.

But another academic notion has become more evident about Farrakhan's and the Nation's future in the United States. It appears that the Nation has become decentralized and lean. The central office of the Nation has terminated its legal commitment to study groups and temples. The study groups have become independent religious groups that are economically, politically, and legally on their own—Farrakhan does not share responsibility for the problems and concerns of the affiliated organizations. Also, the Nation has designed a program that will ultimately make the local temples and study groups obsolete. In the last several years Farrakhan has increased satellite usage in spreading his message. In these satellite presentations the minister is able to communicate with millions of people in a short period. The Nation's books, tapes, and other Muslim materials are sold through the Chicago office.

Donations from viewers are sent directly to Chicago, not through the local temples. The satellite audience is not encouraged to attend local Muslim meetings. The names of local ministers and the addresses of temples have become obsolete in spreading Farrakhan's message. With this new stratagem Farrakhan has reshaped himself into an American Islam televangelist. Farrakhan's new message tells people to function like Muslims and to support Farrakhan but that it is not necessary to attend or join local temples and study groups. In reality, membership in the Nation is not important. There is speculation that Farrakhan will have a television show much like Pat Robertson's *700 Club*, which preaches a radically conservative brand of Christianity. The emphasis is on supporting the gospel of Minister Farrakhan, not the organization called the Nation of Islam.

However, while Farrakhan is streamlining the Nation, a militant element waits in the wings, eager to shift the focus back to the black nationalist days of Elijah Muhammad. The leader of this element is Khallid Muhammad. Minister Khallid represents the anger, hurt, and despair of the militant wing of the Nation and the larger black community. This man, like the young Malcolm X and the young Farrakhan, is confrontational and unwilling to negotiate or compromise. His unyielding position on black nationalism makes him a hero to the youth and the militants who originally joined the Nation for its problack and antiwhite agenda. When and if Khallid Muhammad decides to build a new coalition outside of the Final Call Nation of Islam, he will very likely command a waiting audience that will number in the thousands. Farrakhan realizes that Khallid is a legitimate threat to his operation, which is why he has failed to openly denounce and excommunicate him from the Nation of Islam.

There are other lesser threats to Farrakhan. His top leaders are very concerned and unhappy with the direction of the movement. Akbar Muhammad, who is largely responsible for the early success of the organization, questions the role that the Farrakhan family, especially Leonard Farrakhan, has taken to dominate major aspects of the Nation. Abdul Alim Muhammad, a physician, the minister of health, and former spokesperson for the Nation, is, according to many of his aides, uncertain about the minister's relationship with Benjamin Chavis Muhammad. Minister Conrad Muhammad, who represents the intellectual young moderates and was once Farrakhan's youth minister at the University of Pennsylvania, has expressed uncertainty because of his removal as the minister of the Harlem mosque and the minister's apparent new religious theology.

Elijah Muhammad's sons Rasul and Ishmael (born to Tynetta, who has replaced Clara, Elijah's legitimate wife, as the new matriarch of the Nation) promote and lead the conservative branch of the government. However, in recent years they have caused traditionalists to view them with suspicion and alarm. One reason for concern was their quick advancement under Farrakhan: Ishmael to the ministership of the Nation's flagship temple, Mosque Maryam in Chicago; and Rasul, former leader of the powerful Detroit Temple Number One, to the Miami temple and to the position of Farrakhan's Caribbean and Latin American representative. These two men are also viewed with contempt because they married white Mexicans.

Jabril Muhammad, once called Bernard Cushmeer, author of the Nation's religious monograph, *This Is the One*, is a longtime power broker and friend of Farrakhan. The membership credits him with bringing the minister back to Elijah Muhammad. Although he has been quiet on Farrakhan's new direction, Jibril could possibly become an element of tension if Farrakhan deviates too far from Elijah Muhammad's ideology. Unfortunately for Farrakhan there are major leaders within the structure who are quietly grumbling and who are unsure of the directions of the leader. The possibilities are great that if the inner structure of the movement is not handled judiciously, Farrakhan's Nation could erupt quickly and violently. If this happens, there are several Nation of Islam minor organizations ready and willing to take the place of the Final Call.

First among these is Farrakhan's chief rival, Warith Deen Muhammad. Abandoning the black militancy of his father, Elijah Muhammad, Warith Muhammad has silently built the largest Black Muslim community in the United States. His American Mission Movement has achieved domestic and international respect and admiration from political and religious leaders and organizations. Although his views differ from those of the earlier Farrakhan, they are similar to the current more moderate Farrakhan. Warith Muhammad could gain from the destruction of the Nation of Islam. Individuals who want to embrace a global and traditionalist brand of Islam may choose to follow him because of Farrakhan's eccentric and paradoxical theology in following Fard and Elijah Muhammad but at the same time embracing the global concept of

Islam. In essence, Warith Deen Muhammad's track record of hating the theology and promising to bury his father's teachings is better than Farrakhan's bumpy ride of embracing two diametrically opposed religious ideas.

Then there is Silas Muhammad, who heads an organization named the Original Nation of Islam. Silas, who was a business manager of the Nation of Islam during the tenure of Elijah Muhammad, resigned from the American Muslim Mission (World Community of Al-Islam) in 1977. Dedicated to the ideas of Elijah Muhammad, he recreated the Nation of Islam with some biblical revisions. Although his organization is much smaller than Farrakhan's and Silas is a far less accomplished speaker, he has built a small but solid black economic foundation. In major cities like Chicago, Atlanta, and Philadelphia Silas's Nation has created scores of jobs in the development of stores, cafes, barbershops, low-cost apartments, and bookstores. In real construction and business ventures Silas has outshone Farrakhan over the last twenty years. However, what appeals to potential Farrakhan deserters are Silas's consistent views that whites are devils, that the fall of America is coming, and that Elijah Muhammad was a messenger or prophet.

The most recent group to develop, and perhaps the boldest in confronting the teachings of Farrakhan, is the United Nation of Islam. This group is headed by Solomon Muhammad, who claims that he is Allah and urges all true followers of the Messenger to return to God by joining his Nation. Headquartered in Kansas, Solomon has created and developed a masterful business plan that includes apartment buildings, service stations, grocery stores, dry cleaning businesses, and several other enterprises. Although developed by him, these businesses are owned by his followers. Already Solomon has recruited former members of Elijah's Nation of Islam, such as Abass Rassoull, former national secretary of Elijah Muhammad, and John Muhammad, the brother of Elijah Muhammad. Except for the view that Solomon is God and that Elijah is alive, the United Nation of Islam follows the same tenets as the original Nation of Islam. Solomon has the personality, the polemical style, and enough passion for the old teachings to attract members from the Final Call.

The future for Farrakhan's Nation is grim. His views are controversial, the organization is structurally and financially weak, its theology is unclear—changing from day to day and audience to audience—and its politics are shaped by Farrakhan's personal friend Qadhafi. If things do

Farrakhan supporters maintain that his revisionist theology was rooted in his "new" understanding of Islam. The counter argument rests in Farrakhan's personal history. In 1964 the then Minister Louis X held contempt for Malcolm's review that he finally understood Islam after making his pilgrimage to Mecca. Minister Farrakhan stated in 1982 at the Final Call Building in Chicago, "Malcolm had been to the Holy Land before, he had seen White Muslims. But, look at Malcolm. . . . When he lost his base in the Nation he attempted to act like he was void of any understanding of orthodox Islam. He just did this to smear the Honorable Elijah Muhammad's name and his work."[1] As Malcolm had traveled to the Middle East during his tenure in the Nation, Minister Farrakhan made several voyages to the region throughout the 1980s and, in the early 1990s he made his pilgrimage to Islam's holiest city, Mecca. Therefore, like Malcolm he saw Muslims of every race, nationality, and color. He witnessed the unification of all Muslims under one creed. But why did he not report his observations to the body of believers? Did he not see and realize that the way to Allah is through the traditional worship of Islam? The answers are quite similar to Farrakhan's indictment of Malcolm: he needed financial support from international Arab and Persian groups. The new conversion of Farrakhan is based on the survival of the Nation of Islam.

The 1999 and 2000 Savior's Day event was cosponsored by President Qadhafi of Libya. Mr. Qadhafi, a devout Muslim, had been attempting to get Middle Eastern and African states to financially support the Nation of Islam. However, most nations, although they may enjoy the minister's fiery polemics against the American government and Jews, hedge on granting monetary assistance to Farrakhan's Nation because of the organization's extreme Islamic doctrines. Like his accusation of Malcolm, Minister Farrakhan has made himself available to change his theology to gain shillings from alleged foreign allies. The issue is about financial stability of Farrakhan and his organization.

But what about his near-death experience? Again, strident Farrakhanites focus on the fact that the death angel caused the minister to accept traditional Islam. It may be true that his battle with prostate cancer changed the Muslim cleric. Unfortunately, the bout with cancer raises several questions.

The minister's episode of illness recalls the Honorable Elijah Muhammad's final battle with bronchial asthma and diabetes. In the Savior's

Day address of 1981 Farrakhan depicted the last days of the Messenger as a roller-coaster ride between death and life. He said that the Messenger often times "appeared to be on the brink of death in the morning, however, by the evening, he was teaching as if nothing had occurred." The Messenger's recovery was a miracle, according to Minister Farrakhan.[2] Therefore, it was a shock to the minister, as he stated, when it was announced that Elijah Muhammad had died.

Jabril Muhammad has a similar story of Louis Farrakhan made in February 1999. In a *Final Call* newspaper article, "A Miracle in Our Midst," the Nation's theologian revealed that Farrakhan was so weak in the days leading up to the convention that many thought he was going to die. Minister Jabril Muhammad writes:

What follows are many of my impressions, not of his speech, but of a man, my brother, whom I have known for 44 years, as he is engaged in one of the greatest struggles of his life. My brother is struggling to overcome the forces of death.

He has been gravely ill since near the beginning of January. He was suffering when he came to Phoenix on January 9th to address the Black publishers. . . . He became progressively worse on leaving Phoenix for Chicago on the 19th. Over the next three weeks he went further down. . . . His trainer, Brother Rodney, cried over the Minister's weakened state.[3]

However, a miracle occurs. According to Jabril, Farrakhan is rejuvenated: "[Farrakhan experienced] a sudden burst of energy, the Minister dictated all of the speeches he intended to make in Chicago. He did it in a little over three hours. It was awesome. Not long after he again went into a slump."[4] For the next couple of days the minister was weak. Khadjah Farrakhan, the minister's wife, allegedly told her husband, "I saw death on you."[5] However, when Farrakhan delivered the Savior's Day lecture, he presented a picture of youth and vigor. In response to his recovery several leading ministers, such as Dr. Alim Muhammad, said that they were looking at a miracle.[6]

Increasingly, Farrakhan's sickness, recovery, and actions sounded like his mentor's bout with his illness. The next issue that raised eyebrows was the minister's admission to Howard University Hospital in the District of Columbia for emergency surgery. Dr. Alim Muhammad, Leonard

Farrakhan, and several of the minister's top aides stated that he was rushed by plane from his Michigan City, Indiana, estate to the Nation's capital. It seems that if the minister was as close to death as reported by the Nation's staff, they or the family would have taken him to one of the numerous world-class medical centers in Chicago or in the Midwest, such as Detroit, Indianapolis, Cleveland, Columbus, Cincinnati, or Ann Arbor. But to fly two hours to the Howard University Hospital is, to say the least, eccentric. But if the physicians declared that their dying patient had to meet them in the Washington area, logic would have dictated that Farrakhan's surgery or care be done at Baltimore's Johns Hopkins Medical Center, a world-renowned medical facility.

Again, the story is quite similar to the Messenger's final struggle against death in 1975. The story line is that Elijah Muhammad was in his villa in Mexico when sickness overtook him. His advisers and family flew him from Central America to Mercy Hospital in Chicago for emergency medical treatment. Literally dying from long-term illnesses, the Messenger bypassed several outstanding facilities to receive care at Mercy. Perhaps this is just a coincidence, but the similarities in both cases cause one to wonder about the activities of all involved in the treatment of Louis Farrakhan. Or, God forbid, was the severity of the illness as grim as reported by Leonard Farrakhan and Dr. Alim Muhammad?

Farrakhan never provided black Americans or the NOI with an explanation for the events surrounding his prostate cancer nor for his new sense of religion and spirituality. In the early 1980s Farrakhan boldly proclaimed to his constituents that he was indeed a follower of Fard Muhammad and Elijah Muhammad. He stated that he was like the biblical Peter, who denied the Christ. But he thanked "Allah, Fard Muhammad and his Christ, Elijah Muhammad, for bringing me back," stating, "If I turned my back on Allah and Fard Muhammad again, the FOI . . . should brand me as a hypocrite."[7] The fiery oratory influenced many former NOI Muslims and African Americans to join forces with the national representative of the Honorable Elijah Muhammad and Louis Farrakhan. In the 1999 and 2000 Savior's Day events the minister presented a clear picture that the theology of Fard and Elijah Muhammad is dead. The "Apologia" of 1999 and the hugging, kissing, and crying on Warith Muhammad may have been acceptable to Islamic critics and the Warith Muhammad family, but it did nothing for thousands of suffering Muslims who gave their time, energy, resources, and sometimes their lives for Minister Farrakhan's crusade against the United States government, Jews, and whites in the scheme of uplifting Elijah Muhammad's message, ideology, and social structure. The people who sojourned with Louis Farrakhan down this apparently dark and discarded road deserve an explanation and an apology. He never openly discussed the possibilities to the thousands of supporters that he may have been wrong on the interpretation of the Nation's theology and his understanding of the Quran. Farrakhan's silence presented a picture that he willfully manipulated the Nation's theology for personal gratification.

The importance is that thousands of sincere Black Muslims followed, believed, and revered Minister Farrakhan as the true heir of Elijah Muhammad's throne. These poor righteous followers uplifted, cared, and protected Louis Farrakhan when the majority of the American Muslim community, black Americans, and foreign Muslims did not want to associate with him. It was these believers who purchased groceries for Farrakhan when he was hungry, who purchased shoes for him when he had no money, who put their lives on the line when it was rumored that some in the Muslim community wanted to kill him. The believers, followers, and supporters who knew Farrakhan when he was only a shell of himself, when he could not make his car payments, deserve a bit more respect and love. They expect clear answers and reasons for the actions from the man who cried that he was Elijah Muhammad's messenger. Men like Leotis Muhammad, a dedicated member of Farrakhan's Nation, whom the minister recognized by naming the organization's fleet of trucks after him and who gave his life for the words and deeds of Minister Farrakhan. Wali Muhammad, the brilliant editor of the *Final Call* newspaper, who gave up a promising career as a journalist to join the Nation and transform the Nation's organ from a cheap tabloid to a recognized world-class international paper and who also gave his life for Farrakhan's Nation. They went to their deaths believing in Fard, Elijah, and Louis Farrakhan. Their families, friends, and even their spirits must know if they died in vain. They must know that the man they trusted with their hearts, souls, and lives was honest in his review of the Bible and Quran. The believers, living and dead, must hear Louis Farrakhan's reasons for his actions.

If Minister Farrakhan believes that he has found "true" Islam, then he must acknowledge his past errors in declaring Shahada, the verbal belief that "there is no God but Allah, and Muhammad is his prophet." In 1990, in Dakar, Senegal, I came fully to terms with the fact that the doctrine I had followed was divisive and destructive to the overall development of African American society. The blatant and consistent attack on groups because of their religious, political, racial, ethnic, and sexual orientation did not cohere with the overall spirit of Islam. Thus, as a person of conscience I purged myself of such beliefs and activities. As the greatest religious leader of black American society, Farrakhan must do the same—but at a greater level. He is arguably the most influential black leader in the United States. No other leader can consistently attract ten and twenty thousand people to hear a religious sermon. No other individual, black or white, could have pulled off the Million Man March. Therefore, a man and advocate of this magnitude must be an example to his followers. The point is that when a person of leadership makes a mistake that has influenced the masses of people toward a certain perspective, that leader is bound by honor, conscience, and decency to right the wrongs of his or her actions. Unfortunately, Minister Farrakhan refuses to openly denounce the Nation's theology and to explain the reasons to his following. Instead, he favors the road of speaking in biblical and Quranic parables and of telling his followers that they would understand his direction and mission if they had studied. A minister stated to me at the Savior's Day 2000 conference, "Most of the brothers study what they are told."[8] The Muslims were not told to study suras or scriptures that pointed to the elimination of Fard's and Elijah's message. However, there is a reason for Farrakhan's double-talk of Islamic dogma. The answers are based on the fact that the Nation's theology has made him popular, wealthy, and influential.

The Nation's theology is central to Farrakhan. It is his essence, manner, and stability. To discard it would place him on the podium as just another black preacher, regardless of whether he be a Muslim, Baptist, Hebrew, or televangelist. The minister wants to be special. He likes the idea of being unique, controversial, and "bad." Farrakhan and his advisers enjoy heightening tensions and polarizing groups while maintaining their perception as a vanguard for liberation.

In twenty-three years Louis Farrakhan created an organization that gave hope, pride, and a religious ideology to African Americans. During that time he developed a controversial group that attacked individuals and groups because of their ethnic and cultural background or because of their sexual preference. This in turn promoted a strange element of ethnic pride and hope among his followers. That is, they viewed themselves as superior to Jews, white Americans, Arabs, and homosexuals simply because they, the Muslims, were black. Ultimately, this warped sense of black nationalism placed the Nation of Islam in the same ideological league as the Ku Klux Klan, the John Birch Society, extreme Zionists, and skinheads, who all claim superiority because of race, nationality, culture, religion, and ethnicity.

Minister Farrakhan has had the opportunity to right the wrongs of his perspective on several occasions over the last twenty years. Surely, he would not have been popular with several members in the Nation and the larger African American community if he chose to aggressively change his behavior. Unfortunately, many whites and Jews may view such a change with suspicion. He would not be making atonement for them, anyway, but for himself. I tend to believe that Minister Farrakhan, a brilliant man, considered such an action. But as smart as he is, Farrakhan is a victim of America. He is subject to the lore and greed that America offers. The power, influence, money, and image of being invincible are greater than the rewards of being apologetic and humble. In a 1994 lecture in Columbus, Ohio, Minister Farrakhan gave a pin's eye view of his thoughts on being strong or being right. Referring to his colleague and friend Benjamin Chavis and his problems with the National Association for the Advancement of Colored People, Farrakhan said, "Chavis was wrong . . . but, I would have denied it. I would not have given that woman a single cent."[9] Again, Farrakhan apparently valued the look of strength over the moral issue of what is right.

Of course, one can claim that Minister Farrakhan's move to traditional Islam signals a purging of the bigotry that has tarnished his leadership. But why does he not stop the prejudice featured regularly in the Nation's *Final Call* newspaper? The organization could become the greatest tool for Farrakhan's atonement and social change. It has the power to radically transform the minister from his being, as he claims, a "misquoted and misunderstood" leader to becoming indeed the most influential black leader of our era.[10]

Unfortunately, such a course of action seems unlikely. So what does it mean? What is the course of Louis Farrakhan? The path of logic he follows is simple: Why stop a good thing? Indeed. Farrakhan's celebrity has netted him luxuries that few in the world can imagine. In nations such as Libya, Iraq, Iran, Nigeria, Ghana, and Trinidad, he is treated like a king.

In the United States followers of the Nation view him as a modern prophet. Such strength and power are very difficult to relinquish.

It appears, then, that Farrakhan is not going to change his position radically, so where does this leave the Nation and its followers? As long as there is racism and bigotry in the United States the Nation will always have an audience. Certain groups, the underclass, the uneducated, the victims of blatant white racism, and the hopeless will join the Nation. They will shout approval when the Nation's leaders say, "Jews are blood-suckers of the poor." "The Pope is hiding the truth of Christ from you." "The White man is the devil." But will the organization feed these people practical skills and an education that will enhance their lives?

The answer is a dismal no. Unfortunately, people will join or be a part of the Nation because of bitter feelings toward white society. After a few months in the Nation, where they will be exploited, they will leave, angry not only with the white community but also with black leaders, organizations, religion, and especially Islam. This is far from what the Honorable Elijah Muhammad taught. I remember speaking to Abdul Akbar Muhammad in the early 1990s about this issue. And at that time, during the height of Louis Farrakhan's popularity, we were concerned for the Muslims who left the Nation of Islam. We were concerned not just because they left Farrakhan and Elijah Muhammad's teaching but be-cause they also left the totality of Islam. Many of these people went back to drinking, smoking, whoring, and illegal drugs. As we agreed, it was fine if they chose to leave the Nation, but to depart from the discipline of Islam was another story. Apparently, stated Akbar, we are not supplying enough spiritual support and understanding.[11]

It is unlikely that the Nation will evolve into anything more than what it already is: a nonspiritual religious organization. As I mentioned in a previous chapter, individuals do not typically join the Nation for a religious experience. In most accounts they become Black Muslims be-cause of their anger at white hypocrisy and racism. The young urban blacks who are constantly the target of police harassment, unconcerned school teachers, insensitive Christian ministers, and employers who are unwilling to trust them as laborers are attracted to the Nation's con-cepts. As many gang organizations, like Crips, Bloods, and Folks, who attended the Million Man March testified, "Brother Farrakhan is my leader; he speaks for me." However, do Farrakhan and the Nation really speak for this group?

Between 1987 and 1993 Minister Farrakhan and that Nation of Islam labored diligently to reach out to the black street gangs in several major cities. Farrakhan, calling these groups "boy's clubs or organizations" set out to forge a peace between such groups as the Crips and Bloods of Los Angeles. In addition, he brought several gang leaders to his Hyde Park mansion to discuss their objectives and plans for the black community. At the time Farrakhan perceived these groups as being victimized by state and federal law enforcement agencies unfairly. A relationship with these young groups to the Nation would have been a great move for the Nation. Although many of the gang leaders appreciated Farrakhan's overtures, they did not unite under the Nation's flag or religious ideology. Thus, the gangs would not be used by Farrakhan. The minister, a showman and supreme opportunist, lost his "humanitarian" interest in gangs.

Another incident that questions the Nation's sincerity was the Mike Tyson affair. Farrakhan, an active boxing fan, attempted to replay a page from Malcolm X's life when Malcolm had recruited and influenced Cassius Clay, later known as Muhammad Ali, to join the Nation of Islam in 1964. Louis Farrakhan, realizing the popularity that Muhammad Ali brought to the Nation and to Elijah Muhammad, perhaps viewed heavyweight champion Mike Tyson in the same manner. However, instead of traveling and personally associating with the boxer, the minister sent his son, Mustapha.

Mustapha, assistant captain of the Fruit of Islam and personal bodyguard to his father, forged a relationship with Tyson during the late 1980s. On occasion Mustapha visited the boxer at his home and training camps. It was rumored in the Nation that the younger Farrakhan was "working to bring Tyson into the fold."[12] The relationship grew to the point that both men considered the other as a friend and confidant. The bond that developed between Mustapha and Tyson allowed Minister Farrakhan to aggressively defend the fighter when he was accused and later convicted of the rape of Desiree Washington, a contestant of the Ms. Black America beauty contest. Minister Farrakhan, speaking before a Cleveland audience, said, "What type of woman was she? What type of woman would go to a man's room at 2:00 in the morning? She knew that they were not going to look at television. She knew what a hotel room looked like. And, now, she has the arrogance to cry rape."[13] The minister even argued that there was a conspiracy to get Tyson. He was too arrogant, too black, too outspoken, according to Minister Farrakhan.

When the Indiana court convicted Tyson for the rape of Washington, Mustapha continued the relationship. In fact, he and his father visited the boxer as he served his sentence at the Indiana State Penitentiary. During this period it was rumored and later reported by the media that Tyson had converted to Islam. However, his conversion was not to the Nation of Islam but to traditional Islam. He had become a Sunni Muslim. It appears that after Tyson's acceptance of traditional Islam, Farrakhan and the Nation of Islam gradually separated themselves from the boxer.

Farrakhan's Nation also attempted, in vain, to recruit Riddick Bowe, the heavyweight boxer who succeeded Tyson as the world champion. Bowe, like Tyson, was considered one of the great fighters of the era. He had the skills, talent, charisma, and potential to be a dominant fighter. Bowe could be the Muhammad Ali of the 1990s. In fact, Farrakhan started the relationship with Bowe when Tyson was incarcerated. During the early 1990s Bowe's trainer and manager, Rock Newman, appeared at several of Farrakhan's lectures, including the Million Man March. The friendship between the Farrakhans and Newman grew to the point that the minister and his family were invited to Bowe's heavyweight championship fight with Evander Holyfield in Las Vegas on November 6, 1993. The minister's presence, along with his entourage of ten people, was noted by fight fans in attendance. However, Farrakhan's stature at the event quickly diminished when people took notice of a parachutist's attempt to land in the ring. One of the exciting acts of the event was witnessing Farrakhan's bodyguards scurrying to protect Farrakhan from the white parachutist.

Apparently, Bowe's camp was very fond of Farrakhan. Rock Newman, a great boxing manager but far less than a civil rights activist, went on New York's *Imus in the Morning* radio talk show to discuss such topics as civil rights, racism in boxing, fight promoter Don King, Riddick Bowe, and Louis Farrakhan. Newman boasted that "Farrakhan is a great leader for Black and White America."[14] He acknowledged that Minister Farrakhan was a friend and that he represented a very large segment of black Americans. Unfortunately, Newman did not know that his relationship with Minister Farrakhan would alter when Riddick Bowe changed his career path. In late 1996 when Bowe decided to retire from boxing to join the United States Marines, the Nation retreated from Newman and Bowe. Newman and Bowe no longer had anything to offer the Nation.

Louis Farrakhan has made his mark in twentieth-century American history. He developed as a surrogate minister to Malcolm and as a student of Elijah Muhammad to become the head of the Nation of Islam. After the death of Elijah Muhammad, the restructuring of the Nation of Islam, and Farrakhan's resignation from Wallace Muhammad's World Community of Al-Islam, Farrakhan was spiritually and financially broke. Now, at the beginning of the twenty-first century Louis Farrakhan is spiritually sound, following the consciousness of his soul, and a millionaire. What possibly can the Nation of Islam or his followers give him? Or, what does Farrakhan need from them? The answer is very little.

As Minister Farrakhan used to say to officers and laborers who questioned him about the finances or the direction of his leadership, "I sacrificed for you, nobody gave me a thing."[15] The minister really believes that because he is the one who mortgaged his home for the Final Call Building in Chicago and exerted his time and energy to rebuild and lead the Nation, he is not obligated to the followers of the Nation of Islam. Farrakhan's independent thought runs contrary to his views during the formative years of the Final Call, in the early 1980s. Minister Farrakhan, issuing statements that he represented the Honorable Elijah Muhammad, would not change or deviate from the Messenger's program and theology. Maintaining that Elijah Muhammad told him "not to change the teachings while he is gone," the Minister instructed the Fruit of Islam in 1982 "to take my life if I become a hypocrite to the Messenger," adding, "You have the right to kill me if I deviate from the Messenger."[16]

However, by the late 1980s Farrakhan's humility and appreciation for the Muslim body would change. Unfortunately, he came to believe that had it not been for him, there would be no Nation of Islam and that believers could do nothing for him. If Farrakhan held this view in the 1980s, we surely can imagine what his ideals are in the new century. As a modern-day prophet, Farrakhan believes that he "raised the people to a higher standard of life, the people did not raise me." As Minister Farrakhan has stated many times, "I was raised by Allah (God) and Elijah Muhammad."[17]

If this is true, then what are Farrakhan's plans for the Nation of Islam? It appears that Farrakhan's plans for the Nation have not been completed. He rebuilt the Nation of Islam. Of course, Farrakhan did not achieve the same physical level of Elijah Muhammad's movement, which had a membership of at least 250,000 and a very large business structure. Still, he has made the Nation an international organization with satellite temples in the Caribbean, Africa, Europe, and Central America. He has become the most popular Black Muslim since Malcolm X. Last, he has commanded the attention of the federal government like no other African American in history. In essence, for Louis Farrakhan, he has captured success. There is nothing more he can do but shed his ideology of polarization, an option that is, unfortunately, out of the question for the Muslim leader.

In fairness, however, he is not doing any more than what many other Americans have done when they have achieved success, wealth, and popularity. Why change? Minister Farrakhan may ask. Did robber barons of the nineteenth century change? Did powerful politicians like Richard M. Nixon change? Did George Bush Sr. change? Of course not. If great political and corporate leaders in the United States who used questionable tactics to get their way did not alter their views and ways in their senior years, why expect Louis Farrakhan to be any different?

As an American, Farrakhan is bound to follow the traditions of his culture, even to his grave. We cannot forget that Farrakhan and his Nation always promoted the virtues of Americanism. The tools or virtues of success in the United States are hard work, thrift, belief in God, an unapologetic attitude, and the appearance of individual strength.

As Minister Farrakhan continues to undergo criticism and review by scholars, journalists, theologians, and the general American community, he will again embark on projects that will cause black Americans to question his judgment and motivation. On October 16, 2000, Minister Farrakhan staged a Million Family March in the nation's capital. Surrogate organizers, Minister Benjamin Chavis Muhammad, the national director of the march, and Sister Claudette Muhammad, a member of the Nation of Islam's National Board of Laborers, attempted to rally support for Farrakhan's "multiracial family march," which was designed to promote "family atonement."[18] Unfortunately, many aspects of the MFM followed the same negative activities of the 1995 Million Man March. Like the former march, the spectacle took on the atmosphere of a flea market; that is, Nation of Islam vendors hawked everything from Farrakhan pencils to Million Family March flags. Also, like the historic

MMM, participants paid $3.99 per minute to pay the $11.00 registration fee by telephone and others gave the Nation of Islam $1,000 to be vendors. Of course, according to Minister Farrakhan, the only purpose of the various registration fees and the selling of souvenirs was to defray the cost of the event. In keeping true to the spirit of the MMM, the minister asked in the Nation's *Final Call* newspaper for individuals to donate thousands of dollars as contributors for the Million Family March.[19] The major point is that the minister must stop the monetary and business schemes that are always stated to liberate African Americans but are used to line the pockets of Farrakhan's family and members of the upper echelon of the Nation of Islam. Activities like the MFM and Leonard Farrakhan's new venture, One Nation Communication Services, a business that sells communication devices such as cellular phones, phone cards, and long-distance services, and the Nation of Islam's secured Visa card that is offered to supporters must truly enhance the quality of life for the people the Nation is supposed to serve. In addition, Farrakhan asked in his three-and-a-half-hour MFM lecture that each American family send him $100 by October 16, 2001, for the development of a fund that will challenge and motivate corporate America to invest in poor communities in the United States. He added that the billion-dollar fund would change the relationship between poor people and corporate America.[20] The disturbing issue is that the poor, hopeful, and sincere believers of Elijah Muhammad's message will support the movement wholeheartedly. They will give their time, energy, and love to endorse an effort that they believe is spiritually and divinely inspired. But, in the end, like the Million Man March, they will have more questions than answers. As for Louis Farrakhan, he will have secured a major stage— this one for the new millennium—and an enormous payday.

Like it or not, this is the Farrakhan way.

Notes

1. Early American Islam: The Building Blocks for the Nation of Islam

1. Chukwunyere Kamalu, *Foundations of African Thought*, 21.

2. Vibert White, "The Lynene Brotherhood of Senegal and the Nation of Islam in the United States: Religious Fights for Equality," *Journal of Caribbean Studies* 8, no. 3 (winter 1991/spring 1992): 187.

3. Ibid., 187, 189.

4. Aminah Beverly McCloud, *African American Islam* (New York: Routledge, 1995), 93.

5. White, "Lynene Brotherhood," 192.

6. Mohammed Alexander Russell Webb, *Islam in America: A Brief Statement of Mohammedanism and an Outline of the American Islamic Propaganda* (New York: Oriental Publishing Co., 1893), 5.

7. Ibid.

8. Members of the Moorish Science Temple repeat this statement as one of the last communiqués that Noble Drew Ali had with his followers. Most agree, however, that Drew constantly criticized the inhumane manner under which blacks were forced to live in the ghettos of northern industrialized cities.

9. Adib Rashad (James Miller), *Elijah Muhammad and the Ideological Foundation of the Nation of Islam*, 53.

10. Ibid. The Moorish Science Temple Movement and the Nation of Islam under the leadership of Master Fard Muhammad and Elijah Muhammad referred to African Americans as the lost tribe of Israel. During the 1950s the Nation of Islam, through its most outspoken leader, Malcolm X, taught that the lost tribe of Israel was actually members of the tribe of Shabazz, the family of Prophet Muhammad, the founder of Islam.

11. Levi Dowling, *The Aquarian Gospel of Jesus the Christ: The Philosophical and Practical Basis of the Religion of the Aquarian Age of the World* (Marina Del Rey, Calif.: DeVoress, 1864), 58–74.

12. Rashad, *Elijah Muhammad*, 56.

13. C. Eric Lincoln, *Black Muslims in America*, rev. ed. (Boston: Beacon, 1973), 28–29.

14. Charles Flint Kellogg, *NAACP, a History of the National Association for the Advancement of Colored People:1909–1920*; Walter White, *Rope and Faggot: A Biography of Judge Lynch*, 263–69.

15. Ibid.

16. Lincoln, *Black Muslims in America*, 36.

17. Allan H. Spear, *Black Chicago*.

18. William Tuttle Jr., *Race Riot: Chicago in the Red Summer of 1919*, 118.

19. Richard Brent Turner, *Islam in the African-American Experience*, 100.

20. The New Negro and the Negro Renaissance refer to the period between 1915 and 1945 when blacks experienced a sense of cultural and political identity within their own racial group. At this time black writers, artists, teachers, and orators took on a newfound sense of activism that challenged the notion of equality in a segregated America. See Nathan Irvin Huggins, *Harlem Renaissance*.

21. John H. Clarke, *Marcus Garvey and the Vision of Africa*, 96–97.

22. Randall K. Burkett, *Garveyism as a Religious Movement*, 8.

23. Malu Halasa, *Elijah Muhammad: Religious Leader*, 41.

24. Lemuel Hassan, interview by author, Cincinnati, September 23, 1994. Hassan was one of Elijah Muhammad's early ministers. When Malcolm Little, later to be known as Malcolm X, was released from prison in August 1952, he was instructed to work under Lemuel Hassan as an assistant minister. Hassan taught Malcolm X the history, laws, lessons, and structure of the Nation of Islam under the leadership of Master Fard Muhammad and the Honorable Elijah Muhammad.

25. Robert Weisbrot, *Father Divine: The Utopian Evangelist of the Depression Era Who Became an American Legend*, 145–47, 157, 161.

26. On sex and marriage see Robert Weisbrot, *Father Divine*, 214–15.

2. Allah Meets His Messenger

1. Field Report, National Association for the Advancement of Colored People, Library of Congress, Washington, D.C., 1931.

2. Harry A. Ploski and James Williams, *The Negro Almanac: A Reference Work on the Afro-American*, 557.

3. For a detailed discussion on the significance of Jane Addams and Robert La Follette in the Progressive Era, see David Kennedy, ed., *Progressivism: The Critical Issues*.

4. John Hope Franklin and Alfred A. Moss Jr., *From Slavery to Freedom: A History of Negro Americans*, 328.

5. Richard Barksdale and Kenneth Kinnamon, *Black Writers of America: A Comprehensive Anthology*, 493.

6. Wallace Muhammad, lecture, Mosque Number Two, March 3, 1975, Chicago.

7. Discussion with Dr. Helen Edmonds, civil rights and constitutional scholar, and Earl B. Dickerson, civil rights lawyer and former member of the Legal Defense and Educational Fund under the leadership of Charles Houston and Thurgood Marshall. Also, former members of the National Lawyers Guild. Dickerson handled the famous Chicago Restrictive Covenant case for the

Hansberry family of Hyde Park, Chicago, April 11, 1986, at the home of Etta Barnett, the wife of Claude Barnett, founder of the National Negro Press.

8. Halasa, *Elijah Muhammad*, 23–24.

9. John Muhammad, speaking of his mother, Clara, interview by author, Chicago, 1982. Minister John Muhammad is the biological brother of the Honorable Elijah Muhammad. John Muhammad, like Louis Farrakhan, differed with Wallace Muhammad's interpretation of his father's message and left the World Community of Al-Islam to resurrect the Nation of Islam as designed by Master Fard Muhammad and Elijah Muhammad. Currently, John Muhammad heads a smaller but influential rival Nation of Islam in Detroit, Michigan. He maintained that Farrakhan is not teaching the proper ideology of the founders of the Nation of Islam and that Farrakhan was not chosen to become the successor of Elijah Muhammad.

10. Halasa, *Elijah Muhammad*, 28.

11. See Derrick A. Bell Jr., *Race, Racism, and American Law.* Professor Bell offers an outstanding discussion on the *Plessy* case and its ramifications for black life during the twentieth century.

12. Vibert White, "Pullman Porters and Redcaps of Ohio," Exhibit, Cincinnati Historical Society, Cincinnati, 1989–91. The exhibit was recognized by the Brotherhood of Sleeping Car Porters Union, Inc., National African American Museum, and the Smithsonian Institution as the most thorough exhibit ever completed on Pullman porters and redcaps. See also *NIP Magazine*, January 1989–April 1989 (Cincinnati), for articles on my exhibit at the Cincinnati Historical Society.

13. Abdullah Muhammad, one of the sons of Elijah Muhammad, interview by author, Chicago, February 1983. Abdullah, although not the son of Clara Muhammad, had a very close relationship with his father during the patriarch's later years as the leader of the Nation of Islam.

14. Master Fard Muhammad, the founder of the Nation of Islam, used a variety of names. He was also known as Fard Muhammad, W. F. Muhammad, Wallace Muhammad, Mr. Fard, Professor Fard, and Farrad Muhammad. According to the teachings of the Nation of Islam, Fard Muhammad held many names to hide from whites and blacks who sought his death. Also, Elijah Muhammad argued that Fard is the name of the greatest of the Gods. Elijah Muhammad wrote: "'Fard' is a name meaning an independent One and One Who is not on the same level with the average Gods (Allah). It is a name independent to itself which actually means One whom we must obey, or else he destroys us. . . . The reason we call him the Supreme Being is because He is Supreme over all beings and or is wiser than all. The Holy Qur'an teaches: He is wiser than them, meaning all the Gods before and all who are now present." See Abdul Akbar Muhammad (Larry X), "Brief History of the Nation of Islam," audiotape of lectures. Abass Rassoull, *The Theology of Time: The Honorable Elijah Muhammad, the Messenger of Allah.*

15. Warith Deen Muhammad, lecture, University of Cincinnati, February 28, 1995.

16. Louis Farrakhan, "Has America Entered Divine Judgment?" (lecture delivered at the Savior's Day convention, Conrad Hilton Hotel, Chicago, February 24, 1982).

17. Fard Muhammad had a little difficulty deciding on the proper name for Elijah Poole. Before he settled on the surname Muhammad, Fard had given Elijah the names Karriem, Muckmud, Muckmood, and Sharrif.

18. Moorish Science Temple legend has it that Elijah Muhammad was an active follower of Noble Drew Ali. The Moors also take credit for Fard Muhammad. Many believe that Noble Drew Ali was reincarnated as Fard Muhammad. Other stories surfaced that Fard Muhammad was one of Ali's greatest officers and that before Ali disappeared, he ordered Fard to continue the teachings of Islam through a new movement. Additional stories report that Elijah Poole was also in Marcus Garvey's Universal Negro Improvement Association. For further discussions see Lincoln, *Black Muslims in America*; Peter Goldman, *The Death and Life of Malcolm X* (New York: Harper and Row, 1973); Abdul Akbar Muhammad, "Brief History."

19. Abass Rassoull, "America Is in the Throes of Divine Attacks," in *Theology of Time*, 464–66.

20. Abdul Akbar Muhammad, "History of the Nation of Islam" (lecture delivered at the Final Call Building, Chicago, February 16, 1982).

21. Wallace D. Muhammad, *As the Light Shineth from the East*, 10–11.

22. Erdmann D. Beynon, "The Voodoo Cult among Negro Migrants in Detroit," 903.

23. "Zebra Killings," *San Francisco Examiner*, 1970.

24. Jay Robert Nash, *World Encyclopedia of 20th Century Murder* (New York: Paragon House, 1992), 618; *New York Times Index 1974: Book of Record*, vol. 2 (New York: New York Times Company, 1974), 2182.

25. John Sansing, "You Killed My Babies and Shot My Woman," *Washingtonian*; *Washington Post*, January 19, 1973, 1; *New York Times*, January 20, 1973, 62.

26. Arthur J. Magida, *Prophet of Rage: A Life of Louis Farrakhan and His Nation* (New York: Basic Books, 1996), 43.

27. Ibid., 47.

28. Ibid., 47–48.

29. Fard Muhammad hid his real identification not only from members of the Nation of Islam but also from enforcement authorities. Often when booked on illegal charges, he varied stories of his personal background, heritage, and culture. Fard's stories ranged from his being the offspring of a Polynesian woman and an English father to his being Hawaiian, Mexican, a New Zealander, Persian, Arab, a black American, and white. Nation of Islam members refer to Fard as Allah (God); however, they accept his being of earthly parents—a jet-black man and a white woman. See Elijah Muhammad, *Our Savior Has Arrived*; Elijah Muham-

mad, *Message to the Blackman in America*; Bernard Cushmeer, *This Is the One: Messenger Elijah Muhammad, We Need Not Look for Another*; Elijah Muhammad, *The Supreme Wisdom: Solution to the So-Called Negroes' Problem.*

30. Elijah Muhammad, *Supreme Wisdom*, 15.

31. Ibid.

32. Turner, *Islam*, 167.

33. "Nation of Islam Offers Hearst $100,000 to Prove Charge," *Muhammad Speaks*, August 16, 1963, 1; Abdul Akbar Muhammad, interview by author, Chicago, 1984.

34. Abdul Akbar Muhammad, interview by author, Chicago, 1982.

35. Louis Farrakhan, "The Rebirth of the Nation of Islam" (lecture delivered at the Savior's Day convention, Conrad Hilton Hotel, Chicago, February 26, 1981).

36. The Honorable Elijah Muhammad had ordered NOI members not to comment publicly on the assassination of the president. Malcolm's statement was in reply to a journalist's question about what he thought of the president's murder. Malcolm made the remarks after a December 3, 1963, lecture titled "God's Judgment on America." Abdul Akbar Muhammad, "Brief History of the Nation of Islam."

37. Malcolm X, "God's Judgment on America," lecture, New York City, 1963.

38. Elijah Muhammad Jr., lecture to Fruit of Islam, Nation of Islam Mosque, Boston, November 1962.

39. Karl Evanzz, *The Judas Factor: The Plot to Kill Malcolm X* (New York: Thunder's Month Press, 1992), 224.

40. *New York Times*, February 14, 1964; Malcolm X, "Last Message," Ford Auditorium, Detroit, 1964.

41. *Muhammad Speaks*, March 13, 1964, 2.

42. Wallace D. Muhammad, *As the Light Shineth.*

3. Malcolm: Mentor, Rival, Enemy

1. Louis Farrakhan, Final Call Administration Building, Chicago, Illinois. Article, July 1984. Stephen X Hobbs, "Miracle Man of the Muslims," *Sepia* (1978).

2. Alvin Farrakhan, interview by author, University of Islam, Chicago, February 1990. Louis Farrakhan, Final Call Administration Building, Chicago, interview, July 1984.

3. Alvin Farrakhan, interview by author, University of Islam, Chicago, February 1990.

4. Ibid.

5. Al Saladin, interview by author, Chicago, September 1980.

6. The Nation of Islam's theology teaches that the original man is the black man and that the white man is the devil, the author of all evil. Fard Muhammad and Elijah Muhammad preached this idea in response to white racism. An illustration of Yakub's theory reads "Yakub was six years old when he started his work. He was six years old and he was on time because he was going to make a

people live 6,000 years. . . . So 6,000 years ago we had a black God whose name was Yakub. When he grew up, Yakub began teaching the people, and he went out to start grafting the man he had decided he would make to rule others." The white race came out of this grafting. In reference to white racism Muhammad stated: "He [the white race] was made a hater of you and Me in the first place. He can't go change out of that today, because anything that is made by nature of what it is doing and practicing, is of that work that it is doing." See Rassoull, *Theology of Time*; Elijah Muhammad, *Supreme Wisdom*; Elijah Muhammad, *Message to the Blackman in America*.

7. "Biographical History of Minister Louis Farrakhan"; Abdul Akbar Muhammad, "Brief History."

8. Abdul Akbar Muhammad, "Brief History."

9. Lemuel Hassan, interview by author, Cincinnati, 1996. Minister Hassan was one of the major leaders under the direction of Elijah Muhammad from the 1940s to the 1960s. He is credited with being the principal mentor of Malcolm X when Malcolm was released from prison. By the late 1950s Hassan and Malcolm had become bitter rivals. Hassan accused Malcolm X of utilizing and exploiting the Nation for personal power and fame. See Bruce Perry, *Malcolm: The Life of a Man Who Changed Black America*.

10. Malcolm stated that he had never experienced the kind of love and respect that Muslims gave to him and to each other. It was remarkable that blacks could treat each other in the honorable way that they (Muslims) did. In his autobiography Malcolm wrote:

The Muslims, the individuals and the families alike. The men were quietly, tastefully dressed. The women wore ankle-length gowns, no makeup, and scarves covered their heads. The neat children were mannerly not only to adults but to other children as well. I had never dreamed of anything like that atmosphere among black people who had learned to be proud they were black, who had learned to love other black people instead of being jealous and suspicious. I thrilled to how we Muslim men used both hands to grasp a black brother's both hands, voicing and smiling our happiness to meet him again. The Muslim sisters, both married and single, were given an honor and respect that I'd never seen black men give to their women, and it felt wonderful to me. The salutations which we all exchanged were warm, filled with mutual respect and dignity: "Brothers" . . . "Sisters" . . . "Ma'am" . . . "Sir." Even children speaking to these children used these terms. Beautiful! (Malcolm X and Alex Haley, *The Autobiography of Malcolm X*, 105)

11. Minister Hassan claimed that Malcolm was an opportunist and a liar. His ambition was always to become the top minister in the Nation of Islam. Malcolm used associated ministers and other officials in the Nation to advance himself by making others look bad while glorifying his own exploits. For example, Hassan

stated that Malcolm claimed to be the only assistant minister in Temple Number One but that in reality there were seven assistant ministers and that Malcolm was not even the best teacher among them. Lemuel Hassan, interview by author, Cincinnati, April 17, 1994. See also Perry, *Malcolm.*

12. Al Saladin, interview by author, Iowa City, Iowa, September 19, 1986. Saladin's membership in the Nation of Islam spans more than thirty-five years of service. As a member of Mosque Number Seven in New York City he was a strict follower of Malcolm. After Malcolm's resignation he joined the black nationalist leader to form the Islamic Mosque Incorporated and the Organization of Afro-American Leadership. After the assassination of the leader he joined several militant groups before returning to the Nation in the early 1970s. In 1975 Elijah Muhammad died, and Saladin again left the Nation. In 1978 he joined Louis Farrakhan's new Nation of Islam, Final Call Incorporated. Currently, Saladin is an exiled member of the Nation of Islam.

13. Louis Farrakhan, "The Honorable Elijah Muhammad and Malcolm X" (lecture delivered at the Savior's Day convention, Chicago, February 1993). The lecture was advertised as Farrakhan's story about the killing of Malcolm X. However, it was merely a broad revisited analysis of the Nation's position on Malcolm X: that he was a hypocrite and an unfaithful follower of Elijah Muhammad. Farrakhan's lecture was also a response to Spike Lee's film *Malcolm X*, which had recently been released.

14. Magida, *Prophet of Rage*, 60. Magida's book is a valuable work that traces the life of Louis Farrakhan as the leader in the Nation of Islam. It is one of the two great literary works on the organization. The other and foremost model for Nation of Islam scholars is C. Eric Lincoln's *Black Muslims in America.*

15. Magida, *Prophet of Rage*, 60.

16. Lemuel Hassan, interview by author, Cincinnati, September 15, 1995.

17. Ibid.

18. As an assistant minister and later minister in the NOI in the late 1950s and early 1960s, Farrakhan's lectures seldom presented any aura of militancy. His lectures reflected the theology of the Nation that whites are devils who are remarkably productive and progressive. See Elijah Muhammad, *Message to the Blackman in America*, 63, 100–122; Elijah Muhammad, "The Theology of Time," lecture series; Louis Farrakhan, *The Meaning of the FOI*, 13–15.

19. Louis Farrakhan, "Believers' Meeting," Chicago, February 1991.

20. Steven Barboza, *American Jihad: Islam after Malcolm X* (New York: Doubleday, 1994), 88.

21. "White Man's Heaven Is a Black Man's Hell" was first released by the Nation of Islam in 1958 and was distributed throughout the 1960s by the Nation of Islam. Also, the Nation made sure that it was placed in jukeboxes in establishments owned by the organization. Major black music dealers and producers ignored or boycotted the distribution of the work. In 1981 Louis Farrakhan released the song on an album. Along with the fifteen-minute song, the album featured a

lecture given in Atlanta on "Black Music and Distribution." The lecture was part of the "Jake the Rapper" conference. In 1988 Farrakhan again released a record titled "Let Us Unite," a calypso composition designed to forge black Christian and Muslim solidarity and the Nation's political structure with Jesse Jackson's Rainbow Coalition.

22. *Orgena* and *The Trial* were usually featured on the same bill. The uniqueness of Louis's plays in the Nation is that Elijah Muhammad branded the arts and other forms of entertainment as "sport for white folk." Therefore, members of the Nation were forbidden to participate in such endeavors; however, Louis was an exception. Louis's productions helped to make him a popular power broker and a future rival to Malcolm X.

23. *Brown v. Board of Education*, 347 US 483 (1954). The Supreme Court ruled that separate educational systems were inherently unequal. In 1955 *Brown II* addressed the issue of implementation of the original decree. The Supreme Court ruled that states must use "all deliberate speed" to enforce the first verdict. The interpretation meant that southern states could not take their time to enforce integration in education.

4. Personal Testimony

1. Louis Farrakhan, question and answer session after lecture at Bethune-Cookman College, Daytona Beach, Fla., February 1977.

5. Seventy-Ninth and Emerald

1. Lincoln, *Black Muslims in America*, 192.
2. Abdul Akbar Muhammad, "Brief History of the Nation of Islam."

6. Conflict, Religion, and the Ministry

1. W. E. B. Du Bois, "Striving of the Negro People," 197.

7. Farrakhan Speaks: Conventions, Rallies, and Savior's Day

1. Wali Muhammad, interview by author, Chicago, January 23, 1983.
2. Louis Farrakhan, "Islam When All Else Fails," lecture, Final Call Building, Chicago, March 11, 1984.
3. Ibid.
4. White to Louis Farrakhan, letter, April 12, 1984.
5. Louis Farrakhan, lecture, Final Call Building, Chicago, June 24, 1984.
6. Louis Farrakhan, "The Upliftment of the Black Man," lecture, Final Call Building, Chicago, February 2, 1986.
7. Louis Farrakhan, "Save the Black Family," lecture, Final Call Building, Chicago, December 1990.
8. Carmine Radio Talk Show. A caller stated that he was a rabbi in the Cincinnati area. Radio 550 WCKY, October 15, 1995.

9. Louis Farrakhan, press conference, Mosque Maryam, National Center for the Nation of Islam, Chicago, January 17, 1995.

10. Louis Farrakhan, "Free Qubilah," lecture, Apollo Theater, Harlem, May 6, 1995.

11. Louis Farrakhan, Fruit of Islam meeting, Final Call Building, Chicago, October 16, 1982.

12. Khallid Abdul Muhammad, "Secret Relationship: Blacks and Jews," lecture, Kean College, November 1993.

13. "ADL Praises African-American Leaders for Condemning Anti-Semitism," Anti-Defamation League press release, January 21, 1994.

14. Louis Farrakhan, transcript of press conference, February 3, 1994.

8. Cain and Abel: Division in the Brotherhood

1. White to Farrakhan, April 7, 1987, personal files of author.

2. Abdul Wali Muhammad, discussion with several East Coast and Midwestern NOI officials, Gary, Ind., February 26, 1983.

3. Akbar Muhammad, interview by author, Chicago, October 1985.

4. White to Farrakhan, July 23, 1984, personal files of author.

5. Khallid Muhammad, interview by author, Cincinnati, Ohio, June 17, 1994.

6. Malik Asante (aka Robert Gordon), interview by author, St. Petersburg, Fla., August 13, 1997.

7. Akbar Muhammad, interview by author, Bloomsbury, Pa., February 1989.

8. Khallid Muhammad, David Muhammad, Steven X Coats, Howard Muhammad, Callie Muhammad, Malik Asante, and Keren Muhammad, telephone conference, Columbus, Ohio, March 1987.

9. Abu Koss, telephone interview by author, October 12, 1995. Abu Koss was the national representative of Silis Muhammad and the Lost-Found Nation of Islam. He described the relationship between Louis Farrakhan and Silis Muhammad as being "very tense." On October 23, 1995, Abu Koss faxed me a copy of a letter from Minister Farrakhan to Minister Muhammad concerning the latter's participation at the Nation of Islam's Million Man March. Abu Koss's life as a Black Muslim was as controversial as the two Nations. While Abu Koss was dying of AIDS in the Elizabeth General Hospital in Elizabeth City, N.J., Silis Muhammad dispatched several ministers to him on November 23, 1996, to charge him with homosexuality and to oust him from the Lost-Found Nation of Islam. Later that day he died as a "fallen and disgraced" Muslim. The ministers only referred to Abu Koss by his "slave name," Eddie Mason. See also Peter Noel, "Allah's Prodigal Son: Living and Dying with AIDS in the Nation of Islam," *Village Voice* (New York), the Queer Issue, July 1, 1997, 48. <http://web.lexis-nexis.com/universe/document?_ansset=GeHauKO-EVYRMsSEVYRUUBRA>, accessed November 9, 2000.

10. Steven A. Holmes, "Farrakhan Repudiates Speech for Tone, Not Anti-Semitism," *New York Times*, February 3, 1994.

11. Khallid Muhammad, lecture, Harlem, January 9, 1995.

9. The Story behind the Million Man March

1. Louis Farrakhan, Savior's Day lecture, Chicago, February 7, 1994.
2. Ibid.
3. Louis Farrakhan, Congressional Black Caucus meeting, Washington, D.C., September 16, 1993.
4. Benjamin Chavis, lecture, Mosque Maryam, Chicago, October 24, 1993.
5. Benjamin Chavis, lecture, National African-American Leadership Summit Rally, Freeman Avenue Church, Cincinnati, May 1, 1995.
6. Louis Farrakhan, Savior's Day lecture, Chicago, February 25, 1996.
7. Louis Farrakhan, lecture, mosque Maryam, Chicago, April 29, 1988.
8. Peter Hermann, "New Questions Arise about NOI."
9. Elijah Muhammad, *How to Eat to Live,* Book 1, 15–16.
10. Mu'ammar Qadhafi, lecture, World's People Leadership Conference, Benghazi, Libya, 1995.
11. Rev. Al Sharpton, interview by author, Springfield, Ill., November 18, 1996.
12. "Farrakhan Fires Up 'Million Man' Anniversary Rally," *U.S. News Story Page,* CNN Interactive, October 16, 1996. <http://www.cnn.com/us/9610/16/mmm.farrakhan/index.html#winnie>, accessed March 12, 1997.
13. Louis Farrakhan, lecture at Islamic International Conference, Nation of Islam and Libyan Government, McCormick Center, Chicago, July 6, 1997.
14. Louis Farrakhan, lecture, Indianapolis, July 22, 1982.

10. Farrakhan's World Tours

1. *Student Enrollment—Rules of Islam.* Chicago: Department of Supreme Wisdom, 1976.
2. Ibid.
3. Louis Farrakhan, lecture, Fruit of Islam meeting, Final Call Building, Chicago, March 1984.
4. Unidentified FOI member, Chicago, February 1986.
5. President Mu'ammar Qadhafi, speech, Savior's Day convention, Chicago Armory, February 26, 1984.
6. Louis Farrakhan, lecture to registered Muslims, Final Call Administrative Building. Chicago, 1984.
7. Tripoli, Libya, 1984. International Conference of Liberation Organizations from around the world. Groups converge on Libya to discuss programs and policies to promote a global agenda for change. Qadhafi refers to the group as his "Green Army," a political and military strike force that will be chartered in every nation in the world. The Green Army will be under his direct orders only. In this regard Farrakhan is considered one of Qadhafi's leading world lieutenants.

8. *The Green Book*, written by Col. Qadhafi, details an elaborate theory of how different racial and cultural groups have been misused. For example, he states that blacks are accustomed to living in tropical areas. The climate makes them slow-moving and passive; thus it is unnatural for them to live and function in a highly complex, industrialized nation.

9. Kenneth Lee Brown, American ambassador to Ghana, appt. July 14, 1992–July 19, 1995, interview by author, March 15, 1994.

10. *Ghanaian Times*, Accra, Ghana, October 17, 1994.

11. Aminah Sonko, minister of youth and recreation, interview by author, Banjul, Gambia, March 21, 1997.

12. Jeff Jacoby, "Farrakhan and the Slave Traders," *Boston Globe*, April 1, 1997; "Close-up: Reporters Buy Slaves Freedom," *Baltimore Sun*, June 18, 1996.

Epilogue. Where Do We Go from Here?

1. Louis Farrakhan, Friday study group class, Final Call Building, Chicago, April 1982.

2. Louis Farrakhan, Savior's Day lecture, Chicago, February 22, 1981.

3. Jabril Muhammad, "A Miracle in Our Midst," *Final Call* 18, no. 19, March 3, 1999.

4. Ibid.

5. Jabril Muhammad, "A Miracle in Our Midst," *Final Call* online, March 3, 1999. <http://www.finalcall.com/columns/sd99-mlfspks.html>.

6. Ibid.

7. Louis Farrakhan, Savior's Day lecture, Chicago, February 22, 1981.

8. Minister Roland Muhammad, interview by author, Cleveland, April 10, 1998. This information was also conveyed at the Savior's Day convention, 2000.

9. Louis Farrakhan, "Are Black Organizations Really Our Own?" lecture, Greater Convention Center, Columbus, Ohio, August 27, 1994.

10. Louis Farrakhan, "Stop the Killing," lecture, Jacob Javitz Center, New York City, December 18, 1993.

11. Abdul Akbar Muhammad, interview, New York City, October 20, 1992.

12. During Mike Tyson's imprisonment, Minister Farrakhan delivered several lectures defending the boxer. The Nation's ministers responded that Tyson was studying Islam and that he would be in "the ranks of the FOI" soon. The Nation under Farrakhan's leadership was already successful in recruiting championship boxers. In 1993 heavyweight World Boxing Organization champion Michael X Brent joined the Nation after his stunning one-round knockout of undefeated white boxer Tommy Morrison.

In addition, other celebrities, such as former football star and actor Jim Brown, gospel singer Cece Winan, and hip-hop rap singers Ice Tea and Ice Cube, were openly supporting the Nation of Islam. Some entertainers, such as the rap groups Public Enemy and Niggas With Attitude, crossed the line to become members in Farrakhan's Nation of Islam.

13. Louis Farrakhan, "Are Black Organizations Really Our Own?" Lecture, Columbus, Ohio, August 27, 1994.

14. *Imus in the Morning* radio talk show, interview with Rock Newman, WXYT, 1270 am Radio, New York City, March 7, 1995.

15. Louis Farrakhan, Fruit of Islam meeting, Chicago, February 1986.

16. Louis Farrakhan, Fruit of Islam meeting, Final Call Building, Chicago, December 1982.

17. Louis Farrakhan, Savior's Day lecture, Gary, Indiana, February 27, 1983.

18. A Million Family March was first mentioned on October 16, 1996, during the Nation's "new holiday" celebrations in New York City: the Day of Atonement. In 1998 Minister Benjamin Chavis Muhammad was named national director for the Million Family March, and under his direction the Nation of Islam published the *Million Family March: The National Agenda*, which details the objectives of the MFM movement.

19. An advertisement, "Become a Friend of Farrakhan and the Nation of Islam," appeared in the weekly *Final Call* newspaper from March to October 2000. It asked readers to send money to the Nation to defray the cost of the MFM. *Final Call* 19, no. 34, June 27, 2000, 31.

20. See Lou Granhke, "Farrakhan Creates Political Fund for Poor," *Chicago Sun-Times*, October 24, 2000, news section, 14.

Bibliography

"Achievements of Elijah Muhammad." *Christian Century* 92 (March 26, 1962): 301–2.

"ADL Research Report: The Anti-Semitism of Black Demagogues and Extremists." Anti-Defamation League Fact Finding Report. New York, 1991.

Akbar, Na'im. Interview by author. St. Petersburg, Fla., 1983.

Ansari, Zafar Ishaq. "Aspects of the Black Muslim Theology." *Studica Islamica* 53 (1981): 137–76.

Arnold, Johann Christoph. "A Meeting with Louis Farrakhan." *The Plough*, no. 49 (autumn 1996): 28–30.

Aziz, Samima. Interviews by author. Chicago; Cincinnati; St. Louis, Mo.; New York; Egypt; Ghana, 1982–91.

Bakewell, J. D. X. "Brotherhood Crusade." *Black Scholar* 7 (March 1975): 22–25.

Baldwin, James. *The Fire Next Time.* New York: Dell, 1962.

Barboza, Steven. *American Jihad: Islam after Malcolm X.* New York: Doubleday, 1994.

Barksdale, Richard, and Kenneth Kinnamon. *Black Writers of America: A Comprehensive Anthology.* New York: Macmillan, 1972.

Barnett, Etta, Earl B. Dickerson, and Helen Edmonds. Interview by author. Chicago, April 11, 1986.

Bell, Derrick A. *Race, Racism, and American Law.* Boston: Little, Brown, 1984.

Berger, M. "Black Muslims." *Horizon* 6 (winter 1964): 48–65.

"Bermuda Bans Farrakhan as Risky Visitor." *Chicago Tribune*, December 20, 1985.

"Bermuda Divided on Farrakhan Visit." *Chicago Tribune*, December 19, 1985.

Bey, Phillip. "Noble Drew Ali and the American Negro." Presentation to the Association for the Study of African-American Life and History. Philadelphia, September 17, 1978.

Beynon, Erdmann D. "The Voodoo Cult among Negro Migrants in Detroit." *American Journal of Sociology* 43 (May 1938): 894–907.

"Biographical History of Minister Louis Farrakhan." *Savior's Day Souvenir Journal.* Chicago: Final Call, 1981.

"Black Capitalism Muslim Style." *Fortune* 81 (1970): 44.

Black, Edwin. "Would You Buy a Toothpaste from this Man?" *Chicago Reader*, April 11, 1986, 1–36.

"Black Muslims: Why Do They Look Towards Mecca." *Senior Scholastic*, April 21, 1978, 11.

Boggs, X. J. "Beyond Malcolm X." *Monthly Review*, December 29, 1977, 30–48.

Borg, Gary. "Farrakhan Has 'Wonderful' Meeting with Iraq's Hussein." *Chicago Tribune*, February 16, 1996.

———. "Nigerian Democracy Movement Decries Farrakhan's Remarks." *Chicago Tribune*, February 9, 1996.

Boyd, Herb. "Farrakhan: The War of Armageddon Is upon Us!" *Black World* (1996). <http://www.tbwt.com/views/feat/feat1490.asp>, accessed February 1997.

Breitman, George. *Malcolm X: On Afro-American History*. Exp. ed. New York: Pathfinder, 1970.

———, ed. *Malcolm X: By Any Means Necessary*. New York: Pathfinder, 1970.

———, ed. *Malcolm X Speaks: Selected Speeches and Statements*. New York: Grove, 1965.

"British Officials Bar Entry of Farrakhan." *Chicago Tribune*, January 18, 1986.

Browne, J. Zamgba. "Farrakhan Brings Home $1,000,000,000: A Pledge, Promise, or Plan." *New York Amsterdam News*, February 3, 1996.

Burkett, Randall K. *Garveyism as a Religious Movement*. Metuchen, N.J.: Scarecrow, 1978.

Cedras, Jennifer. "Muhammad Speaks: Condemning the Damnable." *The Plain Dealer* (Cleveland, Ohio). Editorial and Forum. February 8, 1994.

"Chavis' Minister Standing Revoked." United Press International, June 11, 1997. <http://web.lexis-nexis.com/universe/document?_ansset=GeHauKO-EVYRMsSEVYRUUBRA>, accessed November 9, 2000.

Clarke, John H. *Marcus Garvey and the Vision of Africa*. New York: Vintage, 1974.

———, ed. *Malcolm X, the Man and His Times*. Toronto: Macmillan, 1969.

Clines, Frances X. "The March on Washington." *New York Times*, October 17, 1995.

Cone, James H. *Black Theology and Black Power*. New York: Seabury, 1969.

"Conversion of the Black Muslims." *Time*, March 14, 1977, 59.

Cooper, Abraham, and Harold Brackman. "After the March: Farrakhan's Truths Distort History, Frustrate Dialogue." *Miami Herald*, October 23, 1995.

Copage, E. "Farrakhan on the Road." *Life*, August 1984, 51–54.

Cripe, C. A. "Religious Freedom in Prison." *Federal Probation*, March 1977.

Curry, George E. "Farrakhan, Jesse and Jews: Unity in the Community: Can Ben Chavis Pull It Off?" *Emerge*, September 1994, 7.

———. "Farrakhan Reveals Loan from Libya." *Chicago Tribune*, May 3, 1985.

Curtis, Richard. *The Life of Malcolm X*. Philadelphia: McRae Smith, 1971.

Cushmeer, Bernard. *This Is the One: Messenger Elijah Muhammad, We Need Not Look for Another*. Phoenix: Truth Publications, 1971.

"Daughters of Civil Rights Struggle Heroes Unite to Defend Shabazz." *Jet* 87, no. 14 (February 13, 1995): 12–14.

Dawkins, Wayne. "Dawkins: What's Farrakhan's Stand on Black Slavery in Africa?" *Courier-Post*, Camden, N.J. February 29, 1996. <http://web.lexis-nexis. com/universe/document?_ansset=GeHauKO-EWERMsSEWERUUARAZC-AAVEAA-WRAREDBYD>, accessed November 7, 2000.

Dawsey, Darrell. "Keeping the Pledge: A Year after the Million Man March." *Emerge*, October 1996, 46–50.

"Divided Islam." *Economist*, March 19, 1977, 43.

Dowling, Levi. *The Aquarian Gospel of Jesus the Christ: The Philosophical and Practical Basis of the Religion of the Aquarian Age of the World.* Marina Del Rey, Calif.: DeVoress, 1864.

Draper, Theodore. *The Rediscovery of Black Nationalism.* New York: Viking, 1969.

Driscoll, Paul A. "Chavis Says He's Converting to Islam." Associated Press, Chicago, February 24, 1997. <http://web.lexis-nexis.com/universe/document?_ansset=GeHauKO-EZYMsSEZYRUUWRA>, accessed November 8, 2000.

Du Bois, W. E. B. "Striving of the Negro People." *Atlantic Monthly* 80 (1897): 194–98.

Dyson, Michael Eric. *Making Malcolm: The Myth and Meaning of Malcolm X.* New York: Oxford, 1995.

Eltman, Frank. "Survey: Blacks Four Times as Likely to Hold Strong Anti-Semitic Views." Associated Press, November 23, 1998. <a410%3aYR% 25a3fm_mg%25a4%25a3to_mg%25a4%25a3&wchp=dGLSIV-ISIAI&-mds=3f781e1d5f22a5c68e5dc1cee0a9f8fe>.

Encyclopedia of World Crime. New York: Paragon House, 1992, 618.

Essien-Udom, E. U. *Black Nationalism.* Chicago: University of Chicago Press, 1961.

Estrada, Richard. "The March That Went Nowhere." *Dallas Morning News*, October 22, 1996.

Evanzz, Karl. *The Judas Factor: The Plot to Kill Malcolm X.* New York: Thurder Month Press, 1992.

Farrakhan, Alvin. Interview by author. University of Islam, Chicago, February 1990.

"Farrakhan Abroad." *Baltimore Sun.* February 18, 1996.

"Farrakhan and the Jewish Rift: How It All Started." *Final Call Online.* <http://www.finalcall.com/perspectives/rift.html>, accessed October 25, 2000.

"Farrakhan Arrives in Tehran for Celebration of Islamic Revolution." *Final Call Newspaper*, February 10, 1996.

"Farrakhan Arrives in Tripoli for Visit." *Chicago Tribune*, January 6, 1997.

"Farrakhan Banned at Bermuda Rally." *Chicago Tribune*, December 20, 1985.

"Farrakhan, Chavis Do the Hustle." *Chicago Tribune*, February 22, 1996.

"Farrakhan Defies Ban on Entering Britain." *Chicago Tribune*, February 7, 1986.
"Farrakhan Detained 11 Hours in London." *Chicago Tribune*, February 8, 1986.
"Farrakhan Fires Up 'Million Man' Anniversary Rally," *U.S. News Story Page*, CNN Interactive, October 16, 1996. <http://www.cnn.com/us/9610/16/mmm.farrakhan/index.html#winnie>, accessed January 11, 1997.
"Farrakhan Fulminations." *Time*, July 2, 1984, 16.
"Farrakhan Lecture Canceled, Nigeria Cops Turn Crowd Away." *Chicago Tribune*, February 10, 1986.
"Farrakhan Meets Castro, Tours Cuban Facilities." Associated Press. September 5, 1996. <http://web.lexis-nexis.com/universe/document? ansset=GeHauKO-EZERMsSEZERUUWRED-AUDCB-AWRAAREDEYCVZCERURARAR URAA&_docnum=11&dateseg=1&_startdoc=1&_fmtstr=FULL&_dltype =CITE&session=433fdd36-ed87-11d4-95d0-a0c581daa77.786719394. 3157305430.54954.%20.0.0&_state=_lastsearchpage%25a4%2funiverse%2 fform%2facademic%2fs_wires.html%25a3AD_FORM%25a4s_wires%25 a3srccat%25a4NEWS%3bWIRES%25a3_source%25a4$srccat%25a3T1% 25a4khallid%20muhammad%25a3T2%25a4nation%20of%20islam%25 a3date%25a4AFT%25a3after%25a410%3aYR%25a3frm_rng%25a4% 25a3to_rng%25a4%25a3&wchp=dGLStSlS1A1&_md5=76c3240ef24ef 3eb39c5796dda98837e>, accessed November 8, 2000.
"Farrakhan Meets the Press." *Final Call Online*, April 13, 1997. <http://www.finalcall.com/national/mlf-mtp5-13-97.html>, accessed August 1997.
"Farrakhan Probed on Libya Visit." *Chicago Tribune*, April 13, 1986.
"Farrakhan's Arrest." *Chicago Tribune*, February 17, 1986.
"Farrakhan Says He'll Defy Reagan, Go to Libya." *Chicago Tribune*, February 6, 1986.
"Farrakhan Says Talks with Castro Wonderful." *Miami Herald*, September 5, 1996. <http://www.herald.com/newslibrary>, accessed March 1997.
"Farrakhan Suggests Suing U.S. over Reports of CIA Drug Links." *Chicago Tribune*, October 15, 1996.
Farrakhan, Louis. Interviews by author. Chicago; Columbus, Ohio; Cincinnati; Accra, Ghana; Daytona Beach; and Indianapolis, 1978, 1982–88, 1992, 1995.
———. "Address to the African American Summit." New Orleans, April 23, 1989.
———. "After the Million Man March—Now What? Guidance and Instructions to the Year 2000." UIC Pavilion, Chicago, February 26, 1996.
———. "Are Black Organizations Really Our Own?" Greater Convention Center, Columbus, Ohio, August 27, 1994.
———. "Believers' Meeting." Chicago, February, 1991.
———. "The Black Agenda." Chicago, July 17, 1988.
———. "Black America to Receive a Visitation from God." Bartle Hall, Kansas City, November 24, 1996.
———. "Black-Jewish Relationship." Northwestern University, Evanston, Ill., May 30, 1988.

201995%25a3to_rng%25a4dec1995%25a3&wchp=dGLStS-lSlAl&_md5=
2568aefd35e06d648f3c7a63cd49be5a>, accessed November 5, 2000.

———. "Minister of Treason." *Boston Globe,* February 15, 1996. <http://web.
lexis-nexis.com/universe/document?_ansset=GeHauKO-EWERMsSEWER
UUARZ-AZUEY-A-WRWREYUEYZVABRURARARURW&docnum=2&
dateseg=1&_startdoc=1&_fmtstr=FULL&_dltype=CITE&_session=65709798-
f7d6-11d4-ab70-8a0c5812aa77.8276310.3158438929.54954.%20.0.0&_state=
_lastsearchpage%25a4%2funiverse%2fform%2facademic%2fs_regional
news.html%25a3AD_FORM%25a4s_regionalnews%25a3T1%25a4louis
%20farrakhan%25a3T2%25a4jeff%20jacoby%25a3R1%25a4V1%25a3S1
%25a4NEWS%3bNEAST%25a3S2%25a4REGNWS%3bALNWS%25
a3srccat%25a4%5bR1%3dV1%2f$S1%5d%5bR1%3dV2%2f$S2%5d%
25a3_source%25a4%5bR1%3dV1%2f$S1%5d%5bR1%3dV2%2f$S2%5d
%25a3date%25a4RNG%25a3after%25a46%3aMO%25a3frm_rng%25a4
FEB%201996%25a3to_rng%25a4feb%201996%25a3&wchp=dGLSz
SlSlzV&_md5=9d5b5734fc24759e327ccc215c6ef556>, accessed November 8,
2000.

James, Frank. "Farrakhan Is Not the One: Black America Has Many Voices and
Many Leaders." *Chicago Tribune,* October 13, 1996.

Jones, O., Jr. "Black Muslims Movement and the American Constitutional System." *Journal of Black Studies* 13 (June 1983): 417–37.

Kamalu, Chukwunyere. *Foundations of African Thought: A Worldview Grounded
in the African Heritage of Religion, Philosophy, Science, and Art.* London:
Karnak, 1990.

Kellogg, Charles Flint. *NAACP, a History of the National Association for the
Advancement of Colored People.* Baltimore: Johns Hopkins University Press,
1967.

Kennedy, David, ed. *Progressivism: The Critical Issues.* Boston: Little, Brown,
1971.

Khan, Robert A. "The Political Ideology of Malcolm X." *Journal of Religious
Thought* 38 (fall/winter 1981–82): 16–33.

Kidd, J. L. "Yes Sir, Mr. Ali." *Christian Century,* October 30, 1985, 1383–85.

Koss, Abu. Interview by author. Brooklyn, New York, October 7, 1991.

Kulungowski, Alex. "Farrakhan and NOI's Chauvanism [*sic*]." <http://www.
stanford.edu/group/thinker/v2/v2n3/kulungowski.html>, accessed January
30, 2001.

Kurtzman, Daniel. "Farrakhan's Critics Applaud Prohibition of Libyan Gift."
Jewish Bulletin. September 6, 1996. Jewish Telegraphic Agency. <http://
www.jewishsf.com/bk960906/uscritic.htm>, accessed January 15, 2000.

Landry, Carole. "Farrakhan's Foreign Contracts Come under Scrutiny at Home."
Agence France Presse. Washington, February 16, 1996. <http://web.lexis-
nexis.com/universe/document?_ansset=GeHauKO-EZERMsSEZERU
UWRA>, accessed November 8, 2000.

Levinsohn, Florence Hamlish. *Looking for Farrakhan.* Chicago: Ivan R. Dee, 1997.

Lincoln, C. Eric. Interview by author. Springfield, Ill., February 1997.

————. *The Black Muslims in America.* Rev. ed. Boston: Beacon, 1973.

Linn, E., and A. Bainette, eds. "Black Muslims Are a Fraud." *Saturday Evening Post,* February 27, 1965, 23–29.

Lomax, Louis. *When the Word Is Given.* New York: World Publishing, 1963.

"Louis in the Sky with Diamonds." *Creative Loafing,* April 27, 1996. <http://www.cln.com/archives/atlanta/newsstand/042796/M_LOUIS.HTM>, accessed November 7, 2000.

Macy, Christy, and Susan Kaplan. *Top Secrets: Documents.* New York: Penguin, 1980.

Madhubuti, Haki R., and Maulana Karenga. *Million Man March: Day of Absence.* Chicago: Third World Press, 1996.

Madison, Joe. "It's 1996. Inhumanity of Slavery Still Exists in Africa." *Philadelphia Tribune,* August 6, 1996.

Magida, Arthur J. *Prophet of Rage: A Life of Louis Farrakhan and His Nation.* New York: Basic Books, 1996.

"Malcolm X." *Nation,* March 8, 1965, 239.

Mamiya, L. H. "From Black Muslim to Bilalian: The Evolution of a Movement." *Journal for the Scientific Study of Religion* 21 (June 1982): 138–52.

Maniam, Hari. "Farrakhan Calls for Muslim 'Superpower.'" *New York Times International News.* February 22, 1996. <http://www3.newstimes.com/archive96/feb2296/ing.htm, accessed November 8, 2000.

Marsh, Clifton E. *From Black Muslims to Muslims: The Transition from Separatism to Islam, 1930–1980.* Metuchen, N.J.: Scarecrow, 1984.

Mathews, T. "Seizing Hostages." *Newsweek,* March 21, 1977, 16–20.

McCloud, Aminah Beverly. *African American Islam.* New York: Routledge, 1995.

McFadden, Claudette X. Interviews by author. Columbus, Ohio; Baltimore; Daytona Beach; Shippensburg, Pa., 1987–94.

————. "The Rhetoric of Louis Farrakhan." Ph.D. diss., Ohio State University, 1987.

"Messenger Departs." *Economist,* March 8, 1975, 69.

"Messenger Passes." *Time,* March 10, 1975, 83.

Million Family March: The National Agenda—Public Policy Issues, Analyses, and Programmatic Plan of Action, 2000–2008. Washington, D.C.: Million Man March, 2000.

"Minister Farrakhan Challenges Black Men: Transcript from Minister Farrakhan's Speech at the Million Man March." *CNN/U.S. News,* byline: Bernard Shaw, October 16, 1995. <http://web.lexis-nexis.com/universe/document?_ansset=GeHauKO-EWYRMsSEWYRUUWRW-EZDE-A-WRAUVREDE ZUYWUWRURARARURAUV&_docnum=61&dateseg=1&_startdoc=51&_

fmtstr=FULL&_dltype=CITE&_session=78c1f948-eb44-11d4-94ac8a0c
5809aa77.50047088.3157056841.54954.%20.0.0&_state=_lastsearchpage
%25a4%2funiverse%2fform%2facademic%2fs_transcript.html%25a3
AD_FORM%25a4s_transcript%25a3T1%25a4million%20man%20march%
25a3T2%25a4farrakhan%25a3srccat%25a4NEWS%3bCNN%25a3_
source%25a4$srccat%25a3date%25a4RNG%25a3after%25a46%3aMO
%25a3frm_rng%25a4oct%201995%25a3to_rng%25a4oct%201995%25
a3&wchp=dGLSzV-lSlzV&_md5=0d130e3e239d4f4b59958eaead9e34bc>.

Mogilner, Alijandra. "Farrakhan Provides Platform to Holocaust Denier." *JDL in America.* <http://www.jdl.org/irving.html>.

Monroe, Sylvester. "The Mirage of Farrakhan." *Time* 146, no. 18 (October 30, 1995): 52. <http://www.time.com/time/magazine/archive/1995/951030/cover. viewpoint.html>, accessed November 9, 2000.

Morgan, Ken. "Slavery in Sudan: A Note to Clarence Page." *Tennessee Tribune* (Nashville), August 12, 1996.

Muhammad, A. "Civil War in Islamic America." *Nation,* June 11, 1977, 721–24.

Muhammad, Abdul Akbar (Larry X). Interviews by author. Atlanta; Daytona Beach; Chicago; Columbus, Ohio; East St. Louis, Ill.; St. Louis, Mo.; Cincinnati; Philadelphia; Bloomsburg, Pa.; Washington, D.C.; Accra, Ghana; Republic of Malta; Tripoli, Libya. 1978, 1980–95.

———. "The Abundance of Good." Final Call Building, Chicago, September 27, 1988.

———. "Brief History of the Nation of Islam." Audiotape of lectures. Chicago: Final Call Publications, 1984.

———. "History of the Nation of Islam." Lecture delivered at the Final Call Building, Chicago, February 16, 1982.

———. "The History of the Nation of Islam." Lecture, St. Louis, Mo., 1990.

———. "Spike Lee: Did He Do the Right Thing?" Mosque Number Seven, New York City, July 16, 1989.

Muhammad, Abdullah (Son of Elijah Muhammad). Interview by author. Chicago, February 1983.

———. Lecture, Million Man March Rally, Freeman Ave. Church, Cincinnati, May 1995.

Muhammad, Abdul Wali. Interviews by author. Chicago; Tripoli, Libya, 1982–86, 1988.

Muhammad, Alim. Lecture, Washington, D.C., 1992.

Muhammad, Barney. Interviews by author. Chicago, 1982–84, 1988, 1996–97.

Muhammad, Benjamin (Benjamin Chavis). Interviews by author. Chicago; Cincinnati; Washington, D.C., 1995–96.

Muhammad, Donnell. Interviews by author. Columbus, Ohio, 1984–95.

Muhammad, Elijah. *The Fall of America.* Chicago: Muhammad Mosque of Islam Number Two, 1973.

———. *How to Eat to Live.* Book 1. Chicago: Muhammad Mosque of Islam Number Two, 1967.

———. *Message to the Blackman in America.* Chicago: Muhammad Mosque of Islam Number Two, 1965.

———. *Our Savior Has Arrived.* Chicago: Muhammad Mosque of Islam Number Two, 1974.

———. *The Supreme Wisdom: Solution to the So-Called Negroes' Problem.* Chicago: University of Islam, 1957.

———. "The Theology of Time." Lecture series, Temple No. 2, Chicago, 1973.

Muhammad, Ishmael. Interview by author. Cincinnati, July 1994.

Muhammad, Jabril (Bernard Cushmeer). *Farrakhan: The Traveler.* Phoenix: PHNX SN, 1985.

———. "Spiritual Instructions for the Laborers." Lecture, Final Call Building, Chicago, May 5, 1985.

Muhammad, John. Interview by author. Chicago, 1982.

Muhammad, Khallid Abdul. Interviews by author. Chicago; Atlanta; New York; Miami; Savannah; Cleveland; Cincinnati; 1984, 1989, 1994–97.

———. "Secret Relationship: Blacks and Jews." Lecture delivered at Kean College, Union, N.J., November 1993.

———. "The Time and What Must Be Done." Vital Data Services, Lincoln Heights, Ohio, April 2, 1994.

Muhammad, Pamela. Interviews by author. Chicago; New York; Malta; Libya, 1987–91.

Muhammad, Rasoul. Interviews by author. Detroit, April 1990; Cincinnati, May 1992.

Muhammad, Toure. *Chronology of Nation of Islam History.* Chicago: Steal Away Creations, 1996.

Muhammad, Tynetta. *The Comer by Night.* Chicago: Honorable Elijah Muhammad Educational Foundation, 1986.

———. "Domestic Life of the Hon. Elijah Muhammad." Lecture, Final Call Building, Chicago, 1984.

———. "Elijah Muhammad: The Sun." Lecture, Final Call Building, Chicago, October 7, 1984.

———. "Unveiling the Number 19: The Encroaching Judgment at the Close of the 20th Century." *Final Call Online,* November 2, 1999. <http://www.finalcall.com/columns/num19/num19-11-2-99.html>, accessed October 25, 2000.

Muhammad, Wahid. Interviews by author. Chicago, 1982–88; New York, 1993.

Muhammad, Wali. Interview by author. Chicago, January 23, 1983.

Muhammad, Wallace D. *As the Light Shineth from the East.* Chicago: WDM, 1980.

———. *Prayer and Al-Islam.* Chicago: Muslim Islamic Foundation, 1982.

————. "Stepping Down and Moving On." *Christianity Today*, October 6, 1978, 45.

Muhammad, Warith Deen. Lecture, Mosque Number Two, Chicago, March 3, 1975.

————. Lecture, University of Cincinnati, February 28, 1995.

Muhammad, Wendell. Interviews by author. Chicago, 1982–84, 1994.

"Muslim Rivalry." *Christianity Today*, February 16, 1973, 53–54.

"Muslim vs. Muslims." *Newsweek*, February 3, 1973, 61.

Muwakkil, Salem. "Chavis Unlikely to Be a Savior for Nation of Islam." *Chicago Sun-Times*, March 4, 1997. <http://web.lexis-nexis.com/universe/document? ansset=GeHauKO-EWYRMsSEWYRUUWRWE-EDAZ-A-AWRARE DEZAVUVCRURARARURA&_docnum=1&dateseg=1&_startdoc=1&_ fmtstr=FULL&_dltype=CITE&_session=78c1f948-eb44-11d4-94ac-8a 0c5809aa77.108476715.3157056841.54954.%20.0.0&_state=_lastsearchpage %25a4%2funiverse%2fform%2facademic%2fs_gennews.html%25a3AD _FORM%25a4s_gennews%25a3T1%25a4benjamin%20chavis%25a3T 2%25a4farrakhan%25a3srccat%25a4NEWS%3bMAJPAP%25a3_source %25a4$srccat%25a3date%25a4RNG%25a3after%25a46%3aMO%25a3 frm_rng%25a4MARCH%204%201997%25a3to_rng%25a4MARCH%204 %20%201997%25a3&wchp=dGLSzV-lSlzV&_md5=9bb450ed6ef196 e22f1b5f941e62a71a>, accessed January 15, 2001.

————. "Face the Nation." *In These Times* 19, no. 25 (October 30, 1995): 15.

"Nation of Islam Press Conference on Petition to U.S. Treasury and Libyan Offer: The Salaam Restaurant—Chicago, Ill., August 27, 1996." *Final Call Online*, August 27, 1996. <http://www.noi.org/press-events/petition.html>, accessed November 6, 2000.

"The Nation of Islam: The Relentless Record of Hate (March 1994–March 1995)." Research report, July 1, 1996. <http://www.adl.org/frames/front_islam.html>, accessed November 6, 2000.

New York Times Index 1974: Book of Record, Vol. 2, Mo to Z, New York: New York Times Company, 1974, 2182.

"OJ, Farrakhan, and the Race Thing." *New Africa*, December 1995, 8–9.

"Original Black Capitalist." *Time*, March 7, 1969, 21.

Partners in Bigotry: The LaRouche Cult and the Nation of Islam. ADL research report. New York: Anti-Defamation League, 1994.

Pasha, Abraham. *Accomplishments of the Muslims*. Chicago: Muhammad Speaks, 1974.

Pement, Eric. "Louis Farrakhan and the Nation of Islam: Part One." *Cornerstone* 26, no. 111 (1997): 11–12.

Perry, Bruce. *Malcolm: The Life of a Man Who Changed Black America*. New York: Station Hill, 1991.

Phillips, Richard. "At Revolutionary Rally, Farrakhan Lauds Iran as Islam's Vanguard." *Chicago Tribune*, February 12, 1996.

Ploski, Harry A., and James Williams. *The Negro Almanac: A Reference Work on the Afro-American.* New York: Bellwether, 1983.

Qadhafi, Mu'ammar. *The Green Book.* Tripoli: Public Establishment for Publishing, 1980.

Rashad, Adib. *Elijah Muhammad and the Ideological Foundation of the Nation of Islam.* Hampton, Va.: U.B. and U.S. Press, 1993.

Rassoull, Abass. *The Theology of Time: The Honorable Elijah Muhammad, the Messenger of Allah.* U.B. and U.S. Press, 1992.

"Religious Split at Back of Killings." *U.S. News and World Report,* February 5, 1973, 83.

"The Rise of the Nation of Islam in London." *Final Call Online.* May 6, 1997. <http://www.finalcall.com/perspectives/noi-london5-6-97.html>.

Ritter, Jim. "Farrakhan Plays Up his Global Ties: Crowds Hear Gadhafi Speech." *Chicago Sun-Times,* February 24, 1997. Online News. <http://web.lexis-nexis.com/universe/document?_ansset=GeHauKO-EZYRMsSEZYRUUBRAW-AUACE-A-WRBREYUADYDDCRURARARURB&_docnum=1&dateseg=1&_startdoc=1&_fmtstr=FULL&_dltype=CITE&_session=33400a30-f07c-11d4be198a0c5822aa77.571754208.3157630532.54954.%20.0.0&_state=_lastsearchpage%25a4%2funiverse%2fform%2facademic%2fs_gennews.html%25a3AD_FORM%25a4s_gennews%25a3T1%25a4farrakhan%20%25a3T2%25a4Jim%20ritter%25a3srccat%25a4NEWS%3bMAJPAP%25a3_source%25a4$srccat%25a3date%25a4AFT%25a3after%25a410%3aYR%25a3frm_rng%25a4%25a3to_rng%25a4%25a3&wchp=dGLStV-lSlAl&_md5=e27cffe62ddbfbe3c8b3afef7c4e8df5>.

Ross, Sonya. "White House Denounces Farrakhan Trip as Thugfest." Associated Press, Washington, D.C., February 26, 1996. <http://web.lexis-nexis.com/universe/document?_ansset=GeHauKO-ESERMsSEZERUUARA>, accessed November 8, 2000.

Sahib, Hatim. "The Nation of Islam." Master's thesis, University of Chicago, 1951.

Salaam, Yusef. "Slavery in Sudan: Controversy vs. Controversy." *New York Amsterdam News,* June 3, 1995.

Saladin, Al. Interviews by author. Chicago; Des Moines, 1982–97.

The Secret Relationship between Blacks and Jews. Chicago: Nation of Islam, 1991.

"Seven 'Executed' in District's Biggest Mass Murder." *Washington Post,* January 19, 1973.

Shabazz, Hakim. *Essays on the Life and Teaching of Master W. Fard Muhammad.* Hampton, Va.: United Brothers and United Sisters Communication Systems, 1990.

Siddique, Kaukab. "Who Is behind Slavery in Sudan?" *New Pittsburgh Courier,* July 31, 1996.

"Slavery in Sudan." *Baltimore Sun,* June 18, 1996.

Sly, Liz. "Nation of Islam Leader Lectured on Racism, Sexism." *Chicago Tribune,* January 29, 1996.

Smith, Jane, and Yvonne Y. Haddad. *The Islamic Understanding of Death and Resurrection.* Albany: State University of New York Press, 1981.

Smolowe, Jill. "Marching Home." *Time,* October 30, 1995, 34–40.

Sniffen, Michael J. "Justice Department Reviewing New Farrakhan Travel." *San Diego Daily Transcript,* October 17, 1996.

Spear, Allan H. *Black Chicago: The Making of a Negro Ghetto, 1890–1920.* Chicago: University of Chicago Press, 1967.

Starr, M. "Jackson Disavows Farrakhan." *Newsweek,* July 9, 1984, 16–17.

Stetler, Daniel. "The Nation of Islam—A History." <http://www.stanford.edu/group/thinker/v2/v2n3/NOIBackground.html>.

Syed, Parveez. "Salman Rushdie Takes on Farrakhan." *Islamic Network,* April 18, 1996. <http://www.isnet.org/archive-milis/archive96/apr96/0335.html>, accessed May 1996.

Thomas, Jerry, and Byron P. White. "Farrakhan Returns to Face New Scrutiny; Trip Tests Unity Built by Million Man March." *Chicago Tribune,* February 25, 1996.

———. "Million Man Group Seeks More Funds; Chavis' Appeal Hits Some as a Shock." *Chicago Tribune,* February 21, 1996.

Turner, Richard Brent. *Islam in the African-American Experience.* Bloomington: Indiana University Press, 1997.

Tuttle, William, Jr. *Race Riot: Chicago in the Red Summer of 1919.* New York: Atheneum, 1970.

"The United Nations of Islam: Solomon, Allah in Person." *United Nations of Islam.* <http://www.qni.com/~unoi/>.

Washington, Joseph R. *Black Sects and Cults.* New York: Doubleday, 1973.

"Washington Siege." *Economist,* March 12, 1977, 43.

Webb, Mohammed Alexander Russell. *Islam in America: A Brief Statement of Mohammedanism and an Outline of the American Islamic Propaganda.* New York: American Islamic Group, 1893.

Weisbrot, Robert. *Father Divine: The Utopian Evangelist of the Depression Era Who Became an American Legend.* Boston: Beacon, 1983.

White, Byron P., and Jerry Thomas. "Farrakhan to Hold Political Convention Event; A Follow Up to Million Man March." *Chicago Tribune,* September 27, 1996.

White, Vibert L. "The Lynene Brotherhood of Senegal and the Nation of Islam in the United States: Religious Fights for Equality." *Journal of Caribbean Studies* 8, no. 3 (winter 1991/spring 1992): 187–95.

———. "Natti Town: The First 150 Years of Black Cincinnati." Exhibit. Cincinnati Historical Society—Arts Consortium, Union Terminal, Cincinnati, 1992–.

————. "Personal Journal of the Nation of Islam: 1982–1992." Unpublished personal notes.

————. "Pullman Porters and Redcaps of Ohio." Exhibit. Cincinnati Historical Society, Union Terminal, Cincinnati, 1989–91.

White, Vibert, and Benny Kraut. "Academic Reader on the Historical Relationship between Blacks and Jews." University of Cincinnati, unpublished class reader, 1989 and 1990.

White, Walter. *Rope and Faggot: A Biography of Judge Lynch.* New York: Alfred A. Knopf, 1929.

Whitehurst, J. E. "Mainstreaming of the Black Muslims." *Christian Century,* February 29, 1980, 225–29.

Williams, D. A., and E. Sciolino. "Rebirth of the Nation." *Newsweek,* July 16, 1984, 80–81.

Woodward, K. L., and N. Davis. "Second Resurrection." *Newsweek,* August 22, 1977, 67.

"World's Islamic People's Leadership Holds First U.S. Conference." *Arab Journal,* February 1997. <http://www.noi.org>, accessed September 1999.

X, Benny. Interviews by author. Chicago, 1983–85.

X, Malcolm. Interview by Alex Haley. In *The Playboy Interview,* edited by G. Barry Golson, 37–53. New York: Wideview Books, 1981.

————. "God's Judgment on America." Lecture. New York City, N.Y., 1963.

X, Malcolm, and Alex Haley. *The Autobiography of Malcolm X.* New York: Ballantine, 1973.

X, Robert. Interviews by author. Chicago, 1983, 1997.

Index

Page numbers in *italic* refer to photographs.

Vibert L. White Jr. is professor of African American studies at the University of Illinois–Springfield. He has lectured extensively on the Nation of Islam and has published articles in the *Journal of Negro History, UCLA Black Law Journal,* the *Chicago Defender,* and the *New York Times.*